ISLAMIC PACIFISM

Global Muslims in the Post-Osama Era

ARSALAN IFTIKHAR

ISBN: 1463553129
ISBN-13: 9781463553128

To God, my loving family
and global peace in our human time.

TABLE OF CONTENTS

ACKNOWLEDGEMENTS

"In the name of God, the Beneficent, the Merciful" is the penultimate prayer that we Muslims around the world utter within our hearts whenever we begin any worldly endeavor in order to acknowledge our appreciation for the infinite loving kindness and immeasurable compassionate grace of the Divine upon all of humanity. Additionally, there are many wonderful people around the world that I would like to personally thank for their endless generosity and steadfast moral support in their undying belief for my book project called *Islamic Pacifism*.

I would first like to thank my chief researcher- Mrs. Taiyyaba Qureshi- who has spent hundreds (if not thousands) of work hours helping me in researching my book manuscript. Throughout the prolonged duration of this book project, in addition to getting married and graduating from law school, she has managed to peerlessly serve as my chief researcher and this book simply would not have been written without all of her hard work and assistance. Similarly, I would also like to personally thank some very special friends including National Public Radio (NPR) host Michel Martin, Tim Sebastian of *The Doha Debates* on BBC World News Television, *New York Times* bestselling author Deepak Chopra, Imam Mohamed Magid (named by TIME Magazine as the 'American Imam' in 2005), author Peter Beinart of *The Daily Beast*, Mrs. Shamina Singh (formerly of the Clinton Administration) and Professor John Esposito of Georgetown University for their loving friendship, invaluable mentorship and unwavering support for *Islamic Pacifism* and my overall life's work trying to bring some peace to our tumultuous world.

Finally- and most importantly- I would like to thank my loving family with all of my heart and soul for graciously putting up with me for the first 33 years of my life and also dealing with me for however many more days I have left here upon God's beautiful earth.

PREFACE

"Every soul shall have the taste of death."

-The Holy Quran (Chapter 29, Verse 57)

During the waning midnight hours of a late Sunday evening on May 1, 2011, United States President Barack Hussein Obama walked into the East Room of the White House to announce to the entire world that Osama bin Laden had finally been killed. Over the last ten years since the attacks of September 11, 2001, although there was not much cause for celebration for our global village over this last decade; the vast majority of our planet was finally able to breathe a sigh of collective relief when President Obama confirmed the death of Osama bin Laden by Navy Seal special forces at a dusty mansion on the outskirts of Abbottabad, Pakistan near the capital city of Islamabad. In addition to the vast majority of Americans who were relieved at the news of his ultimate demise, it is also important to remember that there were also over one billion Muslims around the world who were also breathing a sigh of relief because Osama's ungodly terrorist mischief had finally come to an inglorious end. For Muslims, there had been no one single person in nearly two thousand years of our religion's modern history that has ever destructively misused and ignorantly hijacked our beloved religion of Islam more so than the dastardly terrorist Osama bin Laden himself.

"We must reaffirm that the United States is not and never will be at war with Islam," President Obama told the world during his historic address on May 1, 2011 announcing Osama bin Laden's death. "I have made clear, just as President Bush did shortly after 9/11; that our war is not against Islam....Bin Laden was not a Muslim leader. He was a mass murderer of Muslims. Indeed, Al-Qaeda slaughtered scores of Muslims in many countries including our own. So his demise should be welcomed by all who believe in peace and human dignity." To highlight the fact that Muslims have been the greatest numerical casualties of Al-Qaeda and Osama bin Laden, The Combating Terrorism Center at West Point once released a stunning report which found that Muslims have accounted for a staggering 85 percent of the total number of casualties from Al-Qaeda attacks throughout the world between 2004-2008. Even more astounding was the fact that between 2006 to 2008, the total percentage of Al-Qaeda's victims who were Muslim skyrocketed to an almost-unbelievable 98 percent of the total global casualty figure.

During his famous June 2009 speech to the greater Muslim world at Cairo University, President Obama highlighted the common themes of humanity found within the three major Abrahamic religions. He said that, "The Holy Quran tells us, 'O mankind! We have made you into nations and tribes so that you may know one another... The Talmud tells us: 'The whole of the Torah is for the purpose of promoting peace.'" Finally, he said that, "The Holy Bible tells us, 'Blessed are the peacemakers, for they shall be called sons of God.' ... The people of the world can live together in peace. We know that is God's vision. Now, that must be our work here on Earth."

Now although the death of Osama bin Laden will not be the complete end of extremism around the world, there can be no honest and reasonable observer who could ever deny the fact that this successful mission was most certainly the proverbial 'cutting of the Al-Qaeda snake's head.' Although there are certainly low-level franchisees who will try to continue to create mischievous havoc throughout the world, the killing of Al-Qaeda's symbolic godfather during President Obama's watch cannot be emphasized enough to the general American public. Again, it cannot be underscored enough that Osama bin Laden was not a leader of Muslims; since we Muslims have numerically represented the largest number of casualties of Al-Qaeda's ungodly terrorism. As most Americans rejoiced at the death of Osama bin Laden, it should also be noted again that global Muslims across the planet were also breathing a collective sigh of relief. As millennial Muslims transition ourselves into a post-Osama age of sociopolitical thought of grassroots nonviolent political action in many parts of the Islamic world, our future generations of young girls and boys will be able to sleep peacefully at night because the boogeyman formerly known as Osama bin Laden will thankfully no longer be on this earth to haunt their childlike dreams ever again.

As we have seen from the peaceful 'Arab Spring' nonviolent grassroots pro-democracy protests throughout the Middle East and North Africa, our next generation of young Post-Osama Muslims are beginning to understand that only peaceful nonviolent movements can affect positive sociopolitical change within any corner of the world. Over the last ten years, we have seen that the bankrupt ideology of 'Bin Ladenism' has not helped build one school, educate one girl or build one water purification center to help better any society around the world. Since younger millennial generations of girls and boys of all colors and races around the world are empirically the least racist generation that our world has seen since time immemorial, we can help cultivate this next generation to fully embrace those who are different from themselves and also embrace the concept of 'The Golden Rule' which beats at the heart of all major world religious traditions; including the three major Abrahamic faiths of Christianity, Judaism and Islam. Going back to May 1, 2011 - myself included- there were well over one billion global Muslims around the world who uttered three simple words when we finally heard the official confirmation of Osama bin Laden's death coming from President Barack Obama as he addressed the world from the East Room of the White House that one fine evening. Those three simple words that we global Muslims uttered in collective relief were:

"God is great."

Arsalan Tariq Iftikhar

May 2, 2011

CHAPTER ONE: WE CONDEMN THIS ACT

"If anyone kills a human being...it shall be as though he has killed all of mankind...If anyone saves a life, it shall be as though he has saved the lives of all of mankind..."
-The Holy Quran (Chapter 5, Verse 32)

The attacks of September 11, 2001 came exactly ten days after my twenty-fourth birthday and commemorated the official beginning of my life as a Muslim pacifist. On that saddest of days in my own personal life, as the second airplane (United Airlines Flight 175 en route from Boston to Los Angeles) crashed into the South Tower of the World Trade Center complex at 9:03 am Eastern Standard Time (EST), it soon became abundantly clear that we in the American (and global) Muslim community needed to issue quick, immediate, and categorical condemnations of these horrific terrorist attacks. This heightened sense of collective Muslim responsibility would grow exponentially when we learned that all 19 hijackers were Muslims as well. It has often been truthfully said that they hijacked our Islamic faith along with those airplanes on that fateful day; but there is also an important distinction to make. Although the terrorists had succeeded in taking over the cockpits of those four airplanes, they will ultimately fail in their attempt to hijack our Islamic faith because the vast majority of peace-loving global Muslims are mobilizing together to defeat their miniscule fanatical few in winning the hearts and minds of our future generations to come.

On that fateful September morning in 2001, as a second-year law student at Washington University School of Law in St. Louis, I realized immediately what I needed to do with the remainder of my life. With a fierce sense of urgency and immediately jumping to my trusty laptop, I wasted no time in crafting an editorial condemnation of the 9/11 terrorist attacks on behalf of Muslims worldwide and emailed it to every single major newspaper editorial department around the country. Within the next thirty minutes or so, I had already received confirmation phone calls from the editorial departments at *USA Today*, *Chicago Sun-Times*, *The New York Times* and many more newspapers around the country saying that they would run my editorial piece condemning the 9/11 attacks.[1]

"On behalf of every member of the global Muslim community, I condemn the vicious acts that occurred in Washington and New York," began my *New York Times* editorial condemnation, published only three days later on September 14, 2001. "Nowhere in Islamic doctrine is the killing of innocent civilians condoned.... At this time of numbness, anger and profound sorrow, I, along with the entire American Muslim community, extend my hand in love and peace to our friends, neighbors and children."[2] My other editorial condemnation, which was published the previous day in *USA Today*, reminded everyone that "people of all creeds perished Tuesday....Muslims, as well as Christians, Hindus, Jews and Buddhists, were all victims of this unspeakable tragedy. This act was not consistent with the teachings of Islam nor can it be condoned by any living human soul."[3]

Mohammed Salman Hamdani, a 23-year-old American Muslim 9/11 first-responder paramedic and New York City police cadet, was one of the 2,976 people who tragically died in the September 11 terrorist attacks. Because of his heroism as a first-responder on that day, *The New York Times* posthumously named Mr. Hamdani an 'All-American Jedi' who simply loved his country:

> ***"He wanted to be seen as an all-American kid. He wore No. 79 on the high school football team in Bayside, Queens, where he lived, and liked to be called Sal...He became a research assistant at Rockefeller University and drove an ambulance part time. One Christmas he sang in Handel's "Messiah" in Queens. He saw all the "Star Wars" movies, and it was well known that his new Honda was the one with "Yung Jedi" license plates...***

> *"And yet, some people continued to see him as something he was not. After Mr. Hamdani, 23, disappeared on Sept. 11, ugly rumors circulated: he was a Muslim and worked in a lab; he might have been connected to a terrorist group. Months later the truth came out. Mr. Hamdani's remains had been found near the north tower, and he had gone there to help people he did not know....And then, at last, everyone could see Mr. Hamdani for what he truly was..."*[4]

The United States Congress also honored Mr. Hamdani's legacy when it wrote in section 102(a)(6) of Title I of the USA PATRIOT Act (HR 3126): "Many Arab Americans and Muslim Americans have acted heroically during the attacks on the United States, including Mohammed Salman Hamdani, a 23-year-old New Yorker of Pakistani descent, who is believed to have gone to the World Trade Center to offer rescue assistance and is now missing."[5]

Of course, I was not alone amongst the global Muslim community to immediately condemn and characterize the 9/11 attacks as being completely un-Islamic. From average grassroots citizens to national religious scholars to global political leaders, prominent Muslim voices around the world immediately did their part in publicly condemning the treacherous 9/11 attacks as being completely antithetical to any normative understanding of Islam. For example, Sheikh Mohammed Sayed Tantawi, the former head of Al-Azhar University in Cairo, Egypt (one of Sunni Islam's largest religious educational institutions) told BBC World News shortly after 9/11 that attacking innocent people was "not courageous," but stupid, and would be punished severely by God: "It's not courage in any way to kill an innocent person, or to kill thousands of people, including men, women and children."[6] The BBC also noted that in Iran, all of the audience in Tehran's main soccer stadium "observed an unprecedented minute of silence" in sympathy with the victims of 9/11.[7] Other Muslim religious scholars and political leaders began to follow suit shortly thereafter in their own public condemnations of terrorism. For example, the Grand Mufti of Saudi Arabia, Shaykh Abdul Aziz al-Ashaikh, said in a public statement four days after 9/11: "Hijacking planes, terrorizing innocent people and shedding blood constitute a form of injustice that can not be tolerated by Islam, which views them as gross crimes and sinful acts."[8] For the Muslim world and beyond, the Grand Mufti's words were especially symbolic since fifteen out of the nineteen 9/11 hijackers would turn out to be Saudi Arabian citizens as well.[9]

Two days after 9/11, in a very touching essay entitled "I'm Not the Enemy" for the *Washington Post,* a young American Muslim female journalist named Reshma Memon Yaqub gently captured the restless feeling of over 7 million American Muslims when she wrote that "every time I hear of an act of terrorism, I have two prayers. My first is for the victims and their families."

"My second is: Please don't let it be a Muslim."[10]

From Condemnations to *Fatwas*

In Arabic, the term *fatwa* generally refers to a "religious decree or legal opinion" handed down by a credible Islamic religious scholar. Under Islamic law, the issuing of *fatwas* is exclusively reserved for established Islamic religious scholars with a classical normative education and a record of scholarship within basic Islamic legal sciences. Therefore, it is quite important to understand that mere average citizens on the street (or those living within an oxygen-deprived cave somewhere) may not just simply (or casually) issue *fatwas*; meaning that both Osama bin Laden and Mickey Mouse have about the same amount of Islamic legal authority to issue a *fatwa* (or religious decree). With that being said, the following brief narrative history of some major global initiatives jointly undertaken by prominent Muslim and inter-religious leaders will help to shed some light on some of the major interfaith programs and global dialogues which are helping to bridge the global divide between Muslims and our sisters and brothers of different religious faiths around the world.

The Amman Message (November 2004)

Although ironically launched exactly one day before the July 2005 London train bombings, King Abdullah II bin Al-Hussein of Jordan came up with the much-needed idea for 'The Amman Message' a few months earlier on the 27th night of Ramadan in November 2004.[11] In order to give this global statement more religious authority, King Abdullah of Jordan initially sent the following three-part questionnaire to over twenty-four of the most senior Islamic religious scholars from around the world representing all the major branches and schools of thought within mainstream Islam.

These three main questions that form the central basis of The Amman Message are:

1) *Who is a Muslim?*
2) *Is it permissible to declare someone an apostate (takfir)?*
3) *Who has the right to undertake issuing fatwas (legal rulings)?*

Ultimately, over 200 well-known Islamic scholars from across the globe signed their names onto The Amman Message condemning terrorism, extremism and sectarianism in all of their forms around the world. Signatories to this global declaration included prominent Muslim leaders from over 50 countries including the Grand Mufti of Egypt, former Malaysian deputy prime minister Anwar Ibrahim, George Washington University professor Seyyed Hossain Nasr, the former Minister of Religious Affairs for the Islamic Republic of Pakistan, American Muslim scholar Hamza Yusuf of the Zaytuna Institute and Prince Ghazi bin Muhammad of Jordan.[12]

Stressing the importance of The Amman Message, in a July 2005 column for *Newsweek* magazine, columnist extraordinaire Fareed Zakaria highlighted the importance of the Amman Message: "Now things are changing. The day before the London bombs, a conference of 180 top Muslim sheikhs and imams, brought together under the auspices of Jordan's King Abdullah, issued a statement forbidding that any Muslim be declared *takfir* (an apostate)."[13] Mr. Zakaria went on to further highlight the importance of The Amman Message by stating clearly that: "This is a frontal attack on Al-Qaeda's theological methods...Signed by adherents of all schools of *fiqh* (Islamic jurisprudence), it also allows only qualified Muslim scholars to issue edicts [or *fatwas*]. The Islamic Conference's statement, the first of its kind, is a rare show of unity among the religious establishment against terrorists and their scholarly allies."

In his personal Foreword for The Amman Message, King Abdullah II of Jordan also reiterated that, "Its content is not a collection of empty slogans, political grandstanding, or religious demagoguery. Herein the reader will find no malice, no petty rivalries and no hostility. Its content is a message of unity, mutual respect, and brotherhood."[14] King Abdullah II of Jordan concluded by reminding people around the world that: "And as all True Islam forbids wanton aggression and terrorism, enjoins freedom of religion, peace, justice and good-will to non-Muslims, it is also a message of good news, friendship and hope to the whole world. I pray that [The Amman Message]...will bring us closer to a world where we can be loyal to our religion, live in peace and prosper with all our fellow human beings, and fulfill the purpose for which we all were placed on earth."

The United Nations Alliance of Civilizations (February 2005)

On February 9, 2005, then-Secretary General of the United Nations Kofi Annan announced the official formation of the 'Alliance of Civilizations'. In a press release announcing the formation of the high-level working group, Mr. Annan stated that, "The members [of the Alliance of Civilizations] have been identified through extensive consultations with specialists in the field of inter-civilizational and inter-cultural relations" specifically with the greater Muslim world.[15] Established at the United Nations in 2005 and with the joint co-sponsorship of the governments of Spain and Turkey, the Alliance of Civilizations (AoC) continues to serve as "a bridge builder, catalyst and facilitator to promote respect and understanding across cultures."[16]

In January 2008, at the first Alliance of Civilizations (AoC) Forum held in Madrid, Spain, several notable global initiatives were launched; including Silatech and the Alliance of Civilizations 'Media Fund'. Launched by Her Highness Sheikha Mozah bint Nasser Al Missned of Qatar, the project known as Silatech is a $100-million global youth employment initiative that is being piloted by corporate, governmental, NGO and multi-lateral agencies in at least six Arab countries throughout the Middle East.

Mr. Jorge Sampaio- the former president of Portugal (1996-2006) and United Nations High Representative for the Alliance of Civilizations- once praised Silatech in a November 2008 column when he highlighted that, "This ambitious project, which will tackle unemployment among young Arabs and offer them prospects for the future, has the backing of a global coalition of leading corporations, civil society and philanthropists. This partnership transcends national, cultural and religious divides to help jumpstart job creation in a part of the world where 100 million jobs will be needed over the next 20 years."[17]

Since youth unemployment is a major sociopolitical pandemic issue affecting the greater Muslim and Arab world, the stated objectives of Silatech include: promoting market-based job training; enabling state-of-the-art contact and counseling centers; experimenting with cutting-edge technologies to connect young people with each other and potential employers; providing access to business development services and capital for aspiring young entrepreneurs; and breaking down cultural barriers to risk-taking and entrepreneurship.[18]

To show that it is actually bringing jobs and employment opportunities to the Middle Eastern region, Silatech joined with *Fortune 500* company Cisco Systems to help bring 'youth-led enterprise' to the Muslim and Arab world.[19] Executive Vice President of Cisco Systems Wim Elfrink once said in a statement that, "Cisco will help Silatech scale promising youth-led enterprise... [and help improve] economic and social development projects across the region."[20]

Additionally, the Alliance of Civilizations 'Media Fund' had attracted an initial $10 million commitment and established formal partnerships with major Hollywood production, distribution and talent agencies that seek to "harness the power of mass media to address the urgent need of improving cross-cultural relations and understanding."[21] As former Portuguese president Jorge Sampaio further noted in his November 2008 column: "The film industry plays an important role in shaping perceptions...With the support of three progressive Hollywood companies - including the company behind [George Clooney's] *Syriana* and Al Gore's *An Inconvenient Truth* - a $10-million media fund was created this year to support mainstream movie productions that challenge stereotypes of minorities."

Because of its public diplomacy work in reaching out to the greater Muslim world and beyond, thus far, the Alliance of Civilizations has gained the support of over 89 UN member states, multilateral agencies and international organizations that form the AoC 'Group of Friends' at the United Nations in New York.[22] Some of the 89 nations (or 'friends') of the Alliance of Civilizations include: Australia, every member nation of the European Union (EU) and many more of the 192 Member States of the greater United Nations.

The Danish Cartoon Controversy (September 2005)

On September 30, 2005, a small right-wing conservative newspaper in Denmark called *Jyllands-Posten* (with a circulation of approximately 150,000)[23] published a series of twelve cartoon caricatures of Islam's beloved Prophet Muhammad (peace be upon him). According to BBC World News, one of the most controversial images published by *Jyllands-Posten* depicted the Prophet Muhammad carrying a lit bomb in the shape of a turban on his head decorated with the Islamic creed. The BBC reported that the cartoons depicted the Prophet Muhammad as "angry, dangerous-looking - a stereotypical villain with heavy, dark eyebrows and whiskers."[24] On October 19, 2005, several prominent Ambassadors from over ten Muslim countries requested a meeting with Anders Fogh Rasmussen, the Danish Prime Minister, over the inflammatory cartoons.

Strangely, he refused to meet with them at the time.[25]

Shortly after global protests and violent riots over the Danish cartoons began to erupt around the Muslim world, at a meeting at the Norwegian Embassy on Massachusetts Avenue in Washington DC, the Norwegian Ambassador to the United States personally reminded our small political delegation of American Muslim leaders that *Jyllands-Posten* was nothing more than a right-wing conservative newspaper with a small subscription base and insignificant public support. The Ambassador's message of public diplomacy naturally reinforced the only rational conclusion that any reasonable person could muster. It was clear that the publication of these inflammatory cartoons by *Jyllands-Posten* was purposefully done to incite violence. Unfortunately for the whole world, certain right-wing violent Muslim idiots took their bait; hook, line and bloody sinker.

Shortly after the publication of the cartoons, several Danish and Norwegian embassies in Beirut and Damascus were attacked by angry protestors. In Lebanon, some of these loud protests soon escalated into physical violence between Muslims and Christians- and some protesters threw rocks at a Maronite Catholic church- bringing back memories of the civil war that once gripped the Lebanese capital.[26] In addition, it would not be long before global firestorm episodes like the Danish cartoon controversy would also spread like wildfire around the Internet and global cyberspace shortly thereafter. According to the *Washington Post*, "A posting on one [website]...called for an 'embassy-burning day' to protest the Muhammad cartoons and offered language that supporters could use in a text-messaging campaign urging people to throw Molotov cocktails and storm embassies" in their regions of the world.[27]

As a global Muslim community, our primary religious obligation is to reflect on our own internal shortcomings and then collectively clean our "own house" through non-violent means before we can ever rightfully expect any sort of support for any of our political grievances within the global marketplace of ideas. The reason that the first chapter of this book is entitled 'We Condemn This Act' is to show the collective efforts of the global Muslim community to condemn terrorism and needless violence in all of its forms since the tragedy of September 11, 2001. As such, this analysis is dedicated to giving a comprehensive narrative historical overview of a major cross-section of the global Muslim response to 9/11 and other major geopolitical diplomatic flashpoints involving the Muslim world since that time.

Since some of these major geopolitical flashpoints (like the 2005 Danish Cartoon Controversy) had tragically resulted in different forms of physical violence by some violent fringe members of the global Muslim community; this chapter is also dedicated to highlighting a recurring thesis throughout the remainder of this book:

"All geopolitical issues must only be resolved through public diplomacy and peaceful non-violent means."

As a religious litmus test, it is important to highlight the fact that there is no credible Muslim religious scholar on earth who would ever argue that Islam would ever theologically sanction the preposterous fire-bombing of a Danish embassy in Beirut or the throwing of Molotov cocktails at a Kentucky Fried Chicken (KFC) fast-food restaurant in Karachi, Pakistan.

Jyllands-Posten -the right-wing Danish newspaper who published the cartoons- duplicitously hid behind the fact that they had the 'legal' right to publish the cartoons based on the global doctrines of 'free speech' and 'free press'. However, many veteran journalists, reporters and newspaper editors around the world immediately saw through their disingenuous 'free press' argument. As a civil rights lawyer (and proud First Amendment 'free-speech freak') myself, I freely acknowledge that these silly cartoons had every 'legal' right in the world to be published. However, just because something has the 'legal' right to be published does not automatically mean that they should be deemed worthy of publication if they clearly do not meet any objective journalistic "editorial standards" of most newspapers or global publications.

In explaining why he chose not to publish the inflammatory Danish cartoons, the *Washington Post*'s executive editor, Leonard Downie Jr. said that,

"This newspaper vigorously exercises its freedom of expression every day. In doing so, we have standards for accuracy, fairness and taste that our readers have come to expect from The Post. We decided that publishing these cartoons would violate our [editorial] standards."[28] Echoing the same noble journalistic integrity of his esteemed colleague, the *Washington Post's* editorial page editor, Fred Hiatt, said that he would have also made the same decision: "I would not have chosen to publish them, given that they were designed to provoke and did not, in my opinion, add much to any important debate."[29]

Keeping that in mind, any reasonable human being alive knows that there is no respectable civilized newspaper in the Western world that would ever dare have the audacity to publish a cartoon today depicting a black man being lynched by hooded Klansmen or anything remotely resembling an Anti-Semitic cartoon. As a proud Muslim pacifist, I fully agree with that overall philosophy and condemn any media outlet in the world that would ever publish any gratuitously racist and xenophobic cartoons against any religion or race of people; with absolutely zero exceptions. Just to be quite clear again, this categorical condemnation of any racism, xenophobia or religious intolerance within the global press most certainly includes any and all Arab/Muslim newspapers around the world that routinely publish deplorable Anti-Semitic cartoons on their pages on a regular basis.

To these newspapers and publications, I would simply ask how they can ever claim to have any moral authority to be angered about anti-Muslim cartoons in Danish newspapers when they shamefully carry the same sort of xenophobic and Anti-Semitic nonsense on a regular basis. This is simply yet another reason that we as a global community (of all religious traditions) have a collective moral responsibility to make certain that every single form of racism, xenophobia and religious bigotry in the world is completely and utterly eradicated from this day onwards.

A few weeks after the global firestorm controversy over the Danish cartoons began to die down; *The Guardian* newspaper in the United Kingdom unmasked the hypocrisy of the Danish newspaper when it reported the following: "*Jyllands-Posten*, the Danish newspaper that first published the cartoons of the prophet Muhammad that have caused a storm of protest throughout the Islamic world, refused to run drawings lampooning Jesus Christ."[30] According to *The Guardian* newspaper story, in April 2003, Danish illustrator Christoffer Zieler submitted a series of cartoons dealing with the resurrection of Jesus Christ to *Jyllands-Posten* for publication. The British newspaper story further reported that Mr. Zieler had received an email response back from the paper's Sunday editor, Jens Kaiser, which stated that, "I don't think *Jyllands-Posten*'s readers will enjoy the drawings. As a matter of fact, I think that they will provoke an outcry. Therefore, I will not use them."[31]

The duplicitous (and sinister) hypocrisy of the right-wing Danish newspaper's 'free press' argument should now be completely obvious (and utterly mind-boggling) to any reasonable observer within any corner of the world today.

Pope Benedict XVI's Speech at Regensburg University (September 2006)

On a different political side of the global interfaith velvet rope, another major post-9/11 public diplomacy challenge involved Pope Benedict XVI and the Vatican Ambassador to the United States; His Excellency Archbishop Pietro Sambi. In September 2006, Pope Benedict XVI (born Joseph Alois Ratzinger) gave a high-profile (and controversial) speech about Islam at the University of Regensburg in Germany, in which he quoted the 15th century Byzantine emperor Manuel II Paleologos as saying: "Show me just what Muhammad brought that was new and there you will find things only evil and inhuman, such as his command to spread by the sword the faith he preached."[32]

Shortly thereafter, political protests against Pope Benedict XVI's Regensburg speech were held around the world in the streets of Pakistan, Turkey, India and the Gaza Strip. Because of the global firestorm created by the speech, two churches in the West Bank were attacked with firebombs in what was believed to be a direct response to the Regensburg speech.[33] In the Somali capital of Mogadishu, several media reports stated that the fatal shooting of an Italian nun may have also been connected to strong criticism of the Pope's speech by a radical Somali religious cleric.[34]

Back here in Washington DC- as we all continued to see the global fallout from the Pope's speech at Regensburg- many prominent interfaith leaders quickly mobilized together to convene public diplomacy talks between Vatican officials and Muslim community leaders. Led by Reverend Dr. Clark Lobenstine of the Interfaith Conference of Metropolitan Washington, I was part of a small delegation of some prominent American Muslim leaders who personally met with the Vatican Ambassador to the United States, His Excellency Archbishop Pietro Sambi, shortly after the controversy began in September 2006. As we met at the Vatican Embassy on Massachusetts Avenue, the overall goals for our interfaith meeting and public diplomacy delegation with the Vatican Ambassador were two-fold: 1) To condemn the global violence by Muslims in response to the Pope's speech and 2) To speak further about ways to continue to improve the ecumenical legacy and peaceful interfaith dialogue which has been occurring between the Catholic Church and the Muslim world for decades.

We highlighted the fact that (the late) Pope John Paul II was beloved by many people around the Muslim world because of his ecumenical interfaith work which included becoming the first pope ever to visit both a synagogue and mosque during his papal tenure. In addition to making history during his 1986 visit to a Rome synagogue, Pope John Paul II was also the first pope ever to set foot inside of a mosque in Damascus, Syria. During his May 6, 1991 visit to the Umayyad Mosque in Damascus, the pontiff told his Muslim audience that he was mindful of past centuries of conflict in the Middle East between Christians and Muslims and that he truly hoped that all global religions would now "find new ways, at the start of the third millennium, to present their respective creeds as partners and not as adversaries."

"For all the times that Muslims and Christians have offended one another, we need to seek forgiveness from the Almighty and to offer each other forgiveness," Pope John Paul II also stated during his address to Muslim leaders, which included the Grand Mufti of Syria. "May the house of Christians and Muslims turn to one another in experience of brotherhood and friendship so God the Almighty may bless us with peace," he concluded during his landmark mosque visit in May 1991.[35]

Getting back to our small private meeting at the Vatican Embassy in September 2006, our delegation implored the Vatican Ambassador to ensure that Pope Benedict XVI's recent Regensburg controversy would be used only to improve Catholic-Muslim dialogue and global interfaith relations around the world. At the end of our private meeting at the Vatican Embassy, one of the Catholic priests in attendance placed his hand gently on my shoulder and smilingly said to me:

"We should send you to Rome to be the Pope's friend."

At the global level, after several further political rounds of 'non-apology' apologies from the Vatican, Pope Benedict XVI issued his final official apology on the Regensburg speech from the balcony of his residence at Castel Gandolfo outside Rome on September 17, 2006.

"I am deeply sorry for the reactions in some countries to a few passages of my address at the University of Regensburg, which were considered offensive to the sensibility of Muslims," Pope Benedict XVI told Catholic pilgrims during the Angelus blessing that day.[36] He continued to say: "These in fact were a quotation from a medieval text, which do not in any way express my personal thought...I hope this serves to appease hearts and to clarify the true meaning of my address, which in its totality was and is an invitation to frank and sincere dialogue, with mutual respect."[37]

As this incident clearly illustrates, it is only through peaceful global interfaith dialogue that we can help further advance our collective human conversation.

A Common Word Between Us and You (September 2006)

As a token of Muslim goodwill after Pope Benedict XVI's speech at Regensburg University- exactly one month to the day after the Pope's speech- a group of over 135 Islamic religious scholars from diverse schools of thought (both Sunni and Shia) around the world collectively issued an open letter to Pope Benedict XVI calling for "mutual understanding" between Christianity and Islam. This open letter called "A Common Word Between Us and You" simply states that Muslims and Christians have the religious (and moral) obligation to show mutual respect and seek common ground based on the shared Abrahamic 'Golden Rule' commandments of "Love Thy God" and "Love Thy Neighbor."

The response to the Common Word initiative was overwhelmingly positive throughout the world. Karen Hughes- former Under Secretary of State for Public Diplomacy and Public Affairs under the George W. Bush administration from 2005 to 2007- applauded the sentiments of the 'Common Word' message when she wrote that: "As the open letter from 138 Muslim scholars notes, 'our common future is at stake' and we must 'sincerely make every effort to make peace and come together in harmony.'"[38] Even conservative author Dinesh D'Souza noted that initiatives like Common Word clearly showed that "America should ally with traditional Muslims to defeat the radical Muslims."[39]

During a February 2009 interview with *Islamica* magazine- to which I have served as contributing editor for many years- the head of the Anglican Church in England, Archbishop of Canterbury Dr. Rowan Williams spoke extensively about the Common Word message and his on-the-record views about the future of Christian-Muslim global relations in our post-9/11 world:

"[The Common Word message] is particularly important in underlining the need for respect towards minorities in contexts where either Islam or Christianity is the majority presence." he said, adding that "the letter rightly makes it clear that these are scriptural foundations equally for Jews, Christians and for Muslims, and are the basis for justice and peace in the world."[40] Archbishop Williams further summed up the overall sentiment of the Common Word message when he told *Islamica* magazine that, "The letter's understanding of the unity of God provides an opportunity for Christians and Muslims to explore together their distinctive understandings and the ways in which these mold and shape our lives. The call to respect, peace and goodwill should now be taken up by Christians and Muslims at all levels and in all countries and I shall endeavor, in this country and internationally, to do my part in working for the righteousness which this letter proclaims as our common goal."[41]

The Doha Debates on BBC World News Television (March 2008)

It should come as little surprise to any knowledgeable global observer that the basic concept of 'freedom of speech' is virtually non-existent within the Muslim (and Arab) world today because of well-founded fears of governmental, despotic or monarchic censorship and political retribution. Whether it is the unjust arrest and imprisonment of pro-democracy activists like Professor Saad Eddin Ibrahim by former Egyptian President Muhammad Hosni Mubarak or the complete national shut-down of Pakistan's largest satellite news television network (GEO Television) by a former two-star soft dictator named General Pervez Musharraf; there has never truly been a global 'free-speech zone' debating forum within the Islamic world where high-caliber intellectual debates on the burning geopolitical questions of today can take place in a fair-and-free public arena within the global marketplace of ideas.

Until now; welcome to the wonderful world of *The Doha Debates* on BBC World News Television. Originally created in 2004, *The Doha Debates* is an

Oxford Union-style debate television program broadcast eight times a year to over 300 million people worldwide and has become the highest-rated weekend television program on BBC World News Television.[42] With a staggering international television broadcast transmission to over 200 countries every month, *The Doha Debates* stage has been shared with the likes of 1984 Nobel Peace Prize winner Archbishop Desmond Tutu, former Israeli prime minister Shimon Peres, 2005 Nobel Peace Prize winner Dr. Mohamed El-Baradei of the International Atomic Energy Agency (IAEA) and former United States president Bill Clinton. At the helm of the television show, legendary former BBC World News HARDTalk program host Tim Sebastian has been the chairman and host of *The Doha Debates* since its inception in 2004. *The Doha Debates* are sponsored by the Qatar Foundation for Education, Science and Community Development.

When asked how he came up with the idea for *The Doha Debates*, Tim Sebastian once told National Public Radio (NPR) in April 2009 that, "I came up with the idea of town hall debates, thinking that if they [the Muslim world] really want to talk about controversial issues in a region where nobody talks about anything except under very strict censorship, then let's give it a try.... We gave it a try. We started in 2004, and the rest is history. We have aired some very, very controversial issues."[43]

On the issue of government interference or potential censorship, Mr. Sebastian reiterated that there is absolutely "no discussion of any kind with the government about topics, about what is said during the course of the debate or, interestingly enough, who is invited" to serve as debaters on the globally-televised show.

"We want to be controversial," he emphasized during the interview with NPR host Michel Martin. "We want to be provocative. We want to talk about areas which don't get much of an airing in that particular region. And we bear in mind that we appear on an international news channel [BBC World News Television]. So we want to make news, as well."[44]

Each televised debate focuses on one single controversial issue or 'motion'; with two debaters 'for' and two debaters 'against' each *Doha Debates* house motion. After each debater has outlined his or her own arguments in an opening statement, each debater is then questioned (and cross-examined) by host Tim Sebastian for several minutes. After that initial round of on-stage questioning, the debate is then opened up to the general television studio audience. At the end of each debate, the entire 350-person television studio audience votes electronically on the house motion and decide which team wins each debate. In several of these televised debates on BBC World News Television, the predominantly-Muslim audiences have voted for radical, unexpected and controversial house debate motions. For example, clear majorities in the past have stated that "Muslims are failing to combat extremism" and that Palestinians "risk becoming their own worst enemy." A student at Texas A&M-Qatar once said that *The Doha Debates* had taught her things of great importance: "I have learned not to judge, but to think with maturity and logic, and not to accept things straight away; instead I require proof and evidence."[45]

So when I was selected to participate as one of the four global debaters on the March 2008 televised episode of *The Doha Debates* on BBC World News Television, it was truly one of the greatest honors of my professional life. Our debate motion for that evening's BBC World News television broadcast was: ***"This House believes that Muslims are failing to combat extremism."***[46] My debate partner (Ed Husain, author of *The Islamist* and senior fellow at the Council on Foreign Relations) and I were the two debaters "for" the motion. On the other side of our debate, Egyptian televangelist Moez Masoud and Daisy Khan from the American Society for Muslim Advancement were debating "against" the motion.

Ed Husain, co-founder of the Quilliam Foundation (a UK-based counter-extremism think tank) and who currently serves as Senior Fellow for the Council on Foreign Relations, opened our debate that evening by highlighting the following during his opening statement "for" the motion; restating our debate position that we as Muslims, thus far, have *not* done enough to combat extremism. "It worries me today when I sit here in Qatar that is home to a leading scholar [Yusuf Al-Qaradawi] who, without any reservations, gives endorsement for suicide bombings, killing of innocent people in the Arab-Israeli conflict. It's that double standard that we apply, it's that disregard for innocent human life that worries me deeply."[47] He concluded his opening statement that evening in March 2008 by saying that, "I sit here today and implore on you to make sure that at the end of this debate, you vote for the right side and you vote and you be honest with ourselves and say out loud, 'That is enough of burying our heads in the sand and it's high time that we admitted the nature of the problem and that we Muslims thus far have not done enough to combat extremism.'"

The first debater 'against' the motion that evening was my dear friend Daisy Khan of the American Society for Muslim Advancement (and who is also the wife of Imam Feisal Abdul Rauf; the founder of the Park51 project in lower Manhattan which came to be sinisterly referred to as the 'Ground Zero Mosque' during the 2010 midterm congressional elections here in the United States). "I am rejecting this motion," Daisy began during her opening statement, "because I am part of the combat team that is working against extremism, and soon you will see a tidal wave of visionary Muslim thought and activism mounting on the horizon, which will change the face and focus of Muslim life worldwide." Daisy concluded her opening statement 'against' the motion by highlighting the work that all of us on-stage were doing on a daily basis and asking the audience to "not forget the tireless effort of ordinary combatants like myself and others here in this room, who are fighting extremism without ever raising a sword, using a stick, a stone, a bullet or a bomb... This peaceful tactic, led by visionary men and women leaders, is forming the tidal wave; the wave that will push away all remnants of extremism once and for all."

Then it was my turn to give my opening statement for the March 2008 episode of *The Doha Debates* on BBC World News Television. "Islam is a religion that strives for the good of all people and a religion that can only be defended in ways that are ethical... The ends do not justify the means in our religion... It is a religious, spiritual and moral obligation for us Muslims to self-reflect and speak out against injustice wherever it occurs and most importantly, regardless of whoever the perpetrator is... We must clean our own house first before we can expect others to have any sort of sympathy for our causes." I concluded my opening statements for the house debate motion that evening by reminding the audience that "two wrongs do not make a right.... Islam does not teach us that... And the great American civil rights leader, Dr. Martin Luther King Jr. once said that, 'We will have to repent in this generation, not only for the actions and words of bad people, but also for the appalling silence of good people.' As someone who has dedicated his life to Islamic work, I honestly believe that my Muslim brothers and sisters around the world need to change this appalling silence and help make our community better for all."

The fourth (and final) debater 'against' the motion that evening was young Egyptian televangelist Moez Masoud. During his opening statement, Moez said that, "I believe the truth or the reality of the matter is that

Muslims are not failing to combat extremism... I believe there certainly is a *perception* that Muslims are failing to combat extremism. I fully agree with that, and one of the things that I want to do tonight is make that clear distinction between the currently existing perception and between the reality." As someone who has extensively studied classical normative traditional Islam, Moez Masoud continued by saying that, "I also want to talk about how the orthodox and authoritative understanding of Islam is the majority, and I also want to show that it's not very silent. I would disagree with my colleagues here regarding the silence of that majority. I believe that radical Islam does exist, but I also believe it's a minority, that's why I'm on this side, but I believe that it has the microphone and so it has an amplified voice."

After all four of us debaters had now finished our opening statements and went through cross-examination; *Doha Debates* host Tim Sebastian then opened the floor to field questions from the 350-person television studio audience. The first question came from a young man who asked whether the West had helped the Muslim world in combating extremism. My debate partner Ed Husain began to answer this question by saying: "This is part of the mentality that constantly shifts the blame to the 'Other'...This is our problem...It was in the 18th century that the roots of this problem started in earnest [within Saudi Arabia] when one man decided that with him and his tribe they will oust everyone else who opposes him...So for me, its about becoming more tolerant *within* the Muslim tradition and then extending that tolerance outside, so let's put our house in order first before we constantly blame the other." After he completed his portion of the response, I continued our answer by offering the ethical argument on moral equivocation by stating that in Islam that "two wrongs do not make a right...If I come to you and I slap you in the face, that gives you no right to go and slap Ed in the face...As Muslims, we have a religious obligation in Islam to not only help our oppressed brothers but also call-out our brothers when they are being the oppressors."

One of the next audience questions was on the controversial issue of suicide bombings. Our fellow debater Moez Masoud offered a brilliantly simple interpretation of the mainstream traditional orthodox Islamic perspective on suicide bombings: "The orthodox Islamic standpoint is anti-suicide...The orthodox standpoint is 'anti-' the killing of civilians...And the orthodox standpoint is anti-suicide for the purpose of killing civilians."

During a subsequent question from an Iraqi female audience member on Sunni/Shia sectarian violence, our fellow debater Daisy Khan addressed that issue by highlighting the fact that we Muslims "do not have a central authority in Islam...There is no Pope to speak for us, so each person has to take responsibility for their own affairs...This issue is not Shia and Sunni...This issue is a political power play" within Iraq. During a later question by an audience member on combating extremism, Daisy Khan outlined a several-part plan to help us combat extremism within our respective communities. She stated that we first need to cultivate a new generation of young community leaders, those people who will instill hope and inspire others around them. She also reiterated the need for women's empowerment within many parts of the Muslim world today. "You have to empower women," Daisy said. "They are the glue that hold the community together...and women have the most to gain by combating extremism. Wives, mothers and sisters do not have to weep any more in silence because they have lost their husbands, sons and brothers."

After Daisy finished her answer, I also highlighted some positive trends that Muslim women themselves have undertaken within the Islamic world to help female empowerment within their respective societies at the grassroots level. "For example, [we must not forget] the case of Saudi women objecting to the proposal to bar women from praying in the central portion of the grand mosque in Mecca...or when Muslim scholars issued an official *fatwa* against female genital mutilation [FGM] in light of Islamic teachings or when grassroots women used Quranic teachings to amend the discriminatory rape laws" in Pakistan as just some of the other concrete examples of increased female empowerment in the Muslim world discussed during our memorable evening on *The Doha Debates* on BBC World News.

Towards the end of the television program, my debate partner Ed Husain reminded our 350-person studio audience that "our Prophet once said to us to 'beware of extremism in your faith'....and in the Quran, Allah talks about this religion being the carrier of this faith and the prophet being a mercy to the world...So the onus is on us to sort out our houses...and unless we do that, we will continue to be the laughing stock of the world." In one of her final closing statements that evening, Daisy Khan again emphasized that the Quran "teaches us that a condition of a people does not change unless you change yourself" and that in order to combat extremism, we must all begin with changing ourselves, our families and our local communities. During his final closing statements that evening, Moez Masoud highlighted his perspective on the 'moral equivalency' argument against extremism.

"I agree with Arsalan on this whole 'ends justify the means' argument...It is completely un-Islamic and it needs to be fully rejected" by Muslims everywhere. When asked about how he personally helps combat extremism as a prominent Egyptian television personality every day, he said that he gets "rid of self-righteousness masquerading itself as spirituality." He continued by saying that no matter how unjustly Muslims are being treated anywhere in the world, the true ethics of Islam revolves around patiently persevering during times of duress and not in succumbing to the politics of rage. One of my closing arguments during that March 2008 episode of *The Doha Debates* revolved around the "imperative for us as self-reflective and sincere Muslims who want to see the advancement of Islam... to not only have the moral clarity to point out the flaws of foreign policy initiatives around the world, but also to have the equal moral clarity to look at the flaws within ourselves" as global millennial Muslims.

At the end of the evening, the 350-person television studio audience voted 70.4% in favor of our house motion. Far more important than our debate team actually winning *The Doha Debates* was the fact that four prominent Muslim public intellectuals who are all trying to better the global Muslim community in our own unique ways were able to freely debate this controversial issue at the heart of the Islamic world today.

Shortly upon my return home to Washington DC, I visited the studios (and my second home) of National Public Radio for a March 2008 interview with NPR host Michel Martin of *Tell Me More* on the importance of *The Doha Debates* within the greater Muslim world. As a regular weekly commentator for the *Barbershop* segment of her NPR show, Michel Martin wanted her listeners nationwide to learn about our debating experience in Doha as a part of her weekly 'Faith Matters' segment on religious and spiritual issues affecting our world today.

"As Muslim public intellectuals, we are trying to raise the level of intellectual honesty" within the global Muslim marketplace of ideas.[48] Channeling my inner-Obama, I highlighted to her NPR listeners the fact that Muslim public intellectuals around the world are trying "to give people an 'audacity of hope'... to let [young] Muslims [around the world] know that there is hope out there for a better life,...that you do not need to resort to the politics of rage in order to have a good and fruitful life. "For example, when Saudi Arabia does not allow a woman to drive.... That is the most absurd thing to any Muslim sensibility all around the world.... It is a cultural and tribal tradition, but unfortunately, it has been associated with Muslim[s]." In explaining the obvious importance of global free-speech debating forums like *The Doha Debates*, chairman and host Tim Sebastian once told National Public Radio that, "Free speech isn't going to be popular with everybody...[T]he Middle East is a rough neighborhood...Free speech is at a premium because there isn't any of it. We are a little island in a sea of censorship, which is restrictive, which stunts the growth, the normal, natural growth of free societies."[49]

During an exclusive interview for this book, my dear friend Tim Sebastian told me that there are several reasons that *The Doha Debates* continues to be increasingly important for the sociopolitical growth of the greater Muslim world today. "One reason is that they provide some good role models - courageous, outspoken panelists, who are not afraid to mention unpleasant truths. The fact is that not everything in the Muslim world is perfect - but what it lacks most of all is the culture of self-criticism that is essential if real problems are to be addressed. I hope that *The Doha Debates* persuades people that it's beneficial to question everything. Only then can they move beyond the tired and unsuccessful doctrines that have created so much damage around the world."[50]

The Mecca and Madrid Declarations (July 2008)

Five times a day, from Azerbaijan to Zimbabwe, every Muslim in the world points their prayer rug in the cardinal direction of the *Ka'aba* (literally translated in Arabic as the "Cube") in Mecca, Saudi Arabia. Regardless of whether your skin is white, black, brown, green or purple; if you are a Muslim in any corner of the world, you are one of the living shareholders of the Islamic custodial holy city of Mecca. Because of the significance of Islam's holiest city, the initial Mecca Declaration of 2006 was important in adopting an official platform to help end the sectarian violence between Sunni Muslims and Shia Muslims within Iraq. A joint initiative of the Organization of the Islamic Conference (OIC) and the International Islamic Fiqh Academy, the Mecca Declaration "categorically forbids sectarian-motivated violence as counter to Islam, while also condemning violence [generally] in the name of Islam."[51] The 2006 Mecca Declaration was subsequently followed up with other global interfaith initiatives; including a June 2008 International Islamic Conference for Dialogue sponsored by King Abdullah Al-Saud of Saudi Arabia.

The 500 Muslim scholars from both the Sunni and Shia schools of thought in attendance from across the world agreed that cross-cultural dialogue "is one of the most significant ways in which Muslims can address the world; and through which Muslims can achieve a number of objectives."[52] Among these objectives are the important international legal obligation of addressing human rights violations anywhere in the world and developing positive working relationships with people of all other cultures and faiths.[53]

The July 2008 Madrid Declaration was created during the culmination of a major global interfaith summit from July 16-18, 2008 at the Royal El Prado Palace in Madrid, Spain[54] under the dual patronage of King Abdullah of Saudi Arabia and King Juan Carlos of Spain. The Madrid Declaration affirms ten guiding principles. The first principle of the 2008 Madrid Declaration is: "Unity of mankind at its origins is one; and equality among human beings irrespective of their colors, ethnic backgrounds and cultures."[55] The Madrid Declaration also called upon the UN General Assembly to support the overall outcome reached by the global summit and asked the Secretary General to take this seriously by "holding a special [UN] session on dialogue".

This global call was taken seriously by the United Nations and a special session of the UN General Assembly was convened on this specific issue on November 12-13, 2008, primarily because of The Madrid Declaration.[56] Prominent world leaders, including then-U.S. President George W. Bush, former British Prime Minister Gordon Brown and other high-ranking officials and heads-of-state attended the UN high-level meeting in New York. As our *Islamica* magazine noted about the historic meeting at the United Nations: "Where initiatives like *A Common Word* are only as far-reaching as the constituents of those religious leaders present…the participants of the UN General Assembly held political weight and therefore greater power to affect more immediate change" around the world.[57]

The U.S.-Muslim Engagement Project (September 2008)

Former United States Secretary of State Madeleine Albright (1997-2001) is one of over 30 leadership group members for the U.S.-Muslim Engagement

Project.[58] Convened jointly by two American organizations- Search for Common Ground and the Consensus Building Institute- the primary goal of the U.S.-Muslim Engagement Project is to "create a coherent, broad-based and bipartisan set of strategies to improve relations between the U.S. and the Muslim world." During an April 2009 private dinner reception announcing their group's final policy study entitled *Changing Course: A New Direction for U.S. Relations with the Muslim World* (at the exclusive Metropolitan Club in Washington, D.C.), former U.S. Secretary of State Madeleine Albright briefed a small group of dinner attendees on the state of U.S.-Muslim relations within the current presidential framework of the administration of President Barack Obama.

"When I became Secretary of State, we did not have Muslims employed in the State Department," Secretary Albright began to tell us that evening during her dinner remarks. "I went back to my notes, when I was writing my book... And I had various notes which read 'Learn more about Islam'," she continued. In light of President Barack Obama's April 2009 speech to the Turkish Parliament in Ankara and his political appointments of George Mitchell and (the late) Richard Holbrooke as his special envoys to the greater Muslim world (to Israel-Palestine and Afghanistan-Pakistan, respectively); former Secretary Albright graded President Obama an "A+" thus far in terms of his overall engagement with the Muslim world. She concluded her remarks to our private group that evening by emphasizing the fact that this work "cannot be done without the people in this room." She then laughed and finished her speech to us by saying, "So, I do think we have our work cut out for us."

We do indeed, Madame Secretary.

Most everyone in the Muslim and Arab world remembers her slightly infamous May 1996 CBS News television interview with Lesley Stahl of *60 Minutes* on the effects of Iraq sanctions on the innocent children of that Arab Muslim nation; in which Stahl asked Albright- then the U.S. Permanent Representative to the United Nations- point blank: "We have heard that half-a-million children have died [from the Iraq sanctions]....I mean, that's more children than died in Hiroshima. And, you know, is the price worth it?" At the time, Madeleine Albright calmly replied to Lesley Stahl's question by saying on-camera: "I think this is a very hard choice, but the price — we think the price is worth it..."[59]

Needless to say, Mrs. Albright's *60 Minutes* calm assertion that U.S. policy objectives were worth the sacrifice of half-a-million Iraqi Muslim children has been much quoted in the Muslim world since that time. To her credit though, Secretary Madeleine Albright has come a long way since that *60 Minutes* interview many years ago. For instance, during a question-and-answer segment following her keynote address at the April 2008 Samuel Dash Conference on Human Rights at Georgetown University Law Center, I asked her on-microphone in front of the packed auditorium crowd whether or not she "still stands by those statements" that she made on *60 Minutes*.

She directly responded to me by saying, "Thank you. Well, I'll begin by answering the question about the Iraqi children. I've answered this question many times and it's always interesting that what I say doesn't seem to penetrate on this...I was interviewed [by *60 Minutes]* and I said something genuinely stupid... .I have said it was stupid..."[60]

"Obviously, I regret any loss of life," continued Mrs. Albright. "I have said this so many times...I know that if you Google me...that I'm there as a war criminal," she joked in her direct response to my question. "I can explain," she further added. "It was a stupid statement...And I regret having made it and I've said it so many times that I would appreciate it if you would actually put that in somewhere," she smiled as she finished her answer.

Well, Madame Secretary, consider it done.

Getting back to her more recent involvement with the U.S.-Muslim Engagement Project, their 153-page policy study issued in September 2008 entitled *Changing Course: A New Direction for U.S. Relations with the Muslim World* highlights four major goals for this global initiative:

1) *Resolving conflicts through diplomacy;*
2) *Improving governance in Muslim countries;*
3) *Promoting broad-based economic development in Muslim countries and regions; and*
4) *Building mutual respect and understanding.*[61]

According to their exhaustive report, more than 75 percent of the American public is worried that the U.S. is on the 'wrong track' in its relations with the Muslim world.[62] Their report concluded by also stating that there is a convergence of "values and interests" among the vast majority of Muslims and Americans that provides a "starting point for relationships based on mutual confidence and respect."[63] They further highlighted some of these other major global interfaith and outreach initiatives since September 11 between the greater global Muslim community and our sisters and brothers of all other races and religions around the world.

What Would Muhammad Do? (WWMD?)

Since all Muslims know that the true religion and moral ethics of Islam at its core emphasizes the 'Golden Rule' tenets of peace, compassion and forgiveness, there is absolutely no religious (or moral) justification for any illegal criminal violence or wanton civilian murder in response to stupid Danish cartoons, French police brutality or silly Dutch movies about the Quran. For us Muslims, the next time that there is a silly cartoon or inflammatory movie anywhere in the world, we should all collectively just ask ourselves one very simple question:

"What Would Muhammad Do?"(WWMD?)

By actually contemplating and reflecting on the peaceful prophetic traditions of Islam's final prophet (may peace be upon him), we can collectively have a better understanding of how our global Muslim community should respond to geopolitical flashpoints by using only non-violent peaceful means and simply asking ourselves these four simple aforementioned words each and every time there is a global crisis dealing with the Muslim world:

"What Would Muhammad Do?"

For example, if our Prophet Muhammad were alive today, would he ever support the senseless firebombing of any embassy anywhere around the world because of a bunch of silly cartoons?

Of course not.

If our Prophet Muhammad were alive today, would he ever applaud suicide bombings killing innocent civilians under any circumstances?

Of course not.

To clearly illustrate this point, we should all be reminded of a well-known Islamic parable within the biography of the Prophet Muhammad which told of his daily interactions with an overtly hostile female neighbor who would violently curse him and then literally dump her daily garbage onto him each day from her perch-top window every time he would ever walk by her house on his way to the mosque on any given day. One day, the Prophet noticed that the woman was not present to throw garbage outside of her window. In the spirit of true Islamic kindness, he actually went out of his way to inquire about her well-being and then proceeded to visit his unfriendly neighbor at her bedside within her own home when he had found out that she had fallen sick.

This genteel act of prophetic kindness towards unfriendly (and even overtly hostile) neighbors is the Muslim *'Ubuntu'* standard that we should all strive for within our collective lives - not threats of violence aimed at the silliness of some sophomoric cartoons aimed at inciting a provocative violent response around the world.[64] Of course, anyone in the world who wants to peacefully protest a bunch of stupid and silly cartoons has the legal right to do so under international law in a legal non-violent manner. More than a right, it's a civic responsibility as members of the global community.

Again, we as a millennial global Muslim community have a higher religious and ethical standard to ensure that we peacefully protest any of these global issues using only lawful, Islamic and non-violent methods to address these geopolitical grievances. By continuously asking ourselves *"What Would Muhammad Do?"* our global Muslim community can collectively help reclaim the peaceful message of 21st century millennial Islam from the razor-sharp claws of our dinosaur extremists within our own collective midst around the world by only responding to international events through only nonviolent means. As we continue down our human experiment with our co-religionist sisters and brothers of all faiths, we can continue to send our classical religious scholars, public intellectuals and sociopolitical leaders to meet with our Abrahamic (or non-Abrahamic) counterparts to help facilitate a more peaceful coexistence for all human beings; regardless of any race, religion or socioeconomic status in every corner of our globe today.

Notwithstanding the endless global Muslim condemnations of terrorism which continue to this very day, our world has also seen some of the major birth pangs of Islamophobia; a sinister new form of global neo-racism and xenophobia against Muslims and Islam around the world. This myopic right-wing xenophobic worldview of Islamophobia revolves around Samuel Huntington's ancient 'clash of civilizations' orientalist mantra.[65] Its 'midwives' (or minions) have contributed to the birthing of this new form of neo-racism, religious bigotry and anti-Muslim sentiment which continues to spread like a raging wildfire around the world to this very day. With that being said, because of the overall treacherous magnitude of his terrorist wingspan during his lifetime and because of his one infamously immortalized terrorist event within human history which sadly hijacked Islam in a notorious manner never seen since time immemorial; for these reasons, I place the late Osama bin Laden at the top of my global list of the "midwives" of Islamophobia.

CHAPTER TWO: THE MIDWIVES OF ISLAMOPHOBIA

"Here is America struck by God Almighty in one of its vital organs, so that its greatest buildings are destroyed."[1]

-Osama bin Laden

October 7, 2001

"We should invade their countries, kill their leaders and convert them to Christianity."[2]

-Ann Coulter

September 13, 2001

Again, it should be made quite clear to the rest of the world that I absolutely despise Osama bin Laden and his hateful extremist ideology that he espoused during his life with every single ounce of my 100% Muslim being. As such, it then becomes our collective Islamic religious and moral imperative as the modern-day millennial Muslim *ummah* (global community) to continue categorically condemning the ungodly terrorist acts and irreligious rhetoric coming from the likes of Al-Qaeda Inc. who continue to self-righteously (and casually) proclaim all of their inhumane murderous actions to somehow bizarrely be in the 'name of Islam'. On the flip side of the Islamophobia coin, there has also been overwhelming empirical evidence over the years that infamous right-wing neoconservative high-profile professional anti-Muslim provocateurs such as Ann Coulter and Reverend Pat Robertson- among many others- have also successfully played roles as professional hate-mongers in the meteoric growth of Islamophobia within the global media during the last decade. Even so, there can simply be no honest analysis of the global phenomenon of Islamophobia without accepting the tragic empirical fact that the birth of modern Islamophobia can be traced directly to the dastardly Osama bin Laden himself. Empirically speaking, Osama bin Laden had been the primary instigator and principal cause of modern Islamophobia by generating more universal animosity and mistrust of Muslims today around the world than any other single human being in recent memory.

Having said all of that, whether we are dealing with ungodly criminal terrorists like OBL or rhetorical professional hate-mongers like the infamous Ann Coulter; we first need to re-introduce the concepts of tolerance and humanity back into our current global human conversation by understanding that the demonization of the 'Other' has been at the heart of all xenophobia and racism in existence within modern history. We must remember, since time immemorial, there have always been agents of intolerance who have wreaked ungodly havoc upon our earth to further their own short-sighted political agendas. Within the relatively short span of our human historical record, the shared religious and spiritual transcendental concepts of tolerance and humanity have always been the first (and greatest) casualties of any conflict or war. From the Nine (9) Crusades to the immeasurable tragedy of the Holocaust to the ethnic cleansing in Bosnia to the Rwandan genocide in the mid-1990s to the current human misery inside Darfur; most every major violent conflict within modern human history has at some point thrived upon the demonization of the 'Other'.

In fact, genocide and war have practically required that demonization as a prerequisite.

A Brief Overview of Demonization

The universal phenomenon of 'demonization' is generally understood to mean the characterization of individuals, groups, and/or political bodies as evil or subhuman for the purposes of justifying and making plausible an attack; whether in the form of character assassination, legal action, circumscribing of civil liberties, or even military warfare. The overall purpose is to justify oppressive actions against the demonized individual or group, ranging from ostracism to genocide; as in the case of the 1992-95 ethnic cleansing of Bosnian Muslims at the sinister hands of the ruthless Slobodan Milosevic. Given that the subjects of historical demonization have traditionally been portrayed as 'evil' and/or 'sub-human' beyond any rational dispute; any method of attack (whether violent or rhetorical) is then considered to be legitimate in their eyes.

Within our own checkered American history, a noteworthy historical example of demonization can clearly be found in the attitudes and practices of white Southerners towards African-Americans, especially in the one hundred years between the end of the Civil War and the passage of the 1964 Civil Rights Act. Our own American version of demonization was epitomized during that time with the widespread practice of lynching and stereotypically subhuman depictions of African-Americans within the U.S. media and greater American popular culture. Other examples abound, from the portrayals of German-Americans during World War I and Japanese-American internment during World War II to depictions of Native Americans in Hollywood films. Also, misogynistic and homophobic 'hate crimes' would also clearly fall into this category as well; hence the expansion of civil rights laws within our American legal system.

One of the intended purposes of demonizing any group of people is to divert attention from the actual validity of their arguments by discrediting them personally with baseless *ad hominem* attacks. Labeling your adversaries as jihadists, evangelical nutjobs, fascists, communists or some other 'despised' category of individuals is particularly effective not only in undermining individuals with controversial political views; but more importantly, in alienating them from further garnering general public support. As in other chapters of our own American civil rights historical narrative, it was from this tragic historical legacy of minority 'demonization' that the birth of Islamophobia was allowed to come to complete fruition on September 11, 2001 and has continued to metastasize in the years thereafter to this very day.

Just as all Germans were painted as "bloodthirsty Huns" and Japanese-Americans as "the enemy race" after World Wars I and II, respectively; there is a small vocal right-wing minority within global media and American political elite circles today which has sinisterly used the tragedy of 9/11 to smear, caricaturize and demonize Islam and Muslims in order to further their myopic (and asinine) "clash of civilizations" theory and their own respective right-wing political agendas.

9/11 and the Birth of Islamophobia

First of all, it should be noted that the term "Islamophobia" was official coined over fourteen years ago in 1997 by the Runnymede Trust- the leading independent multiculturalism think tank in the United Kingdom- within a report entitled *Islamophobia: A Challenge for Us All*, released in November 1997 by then-British Home Secretary (and future British Foreign Secretary), Mr. Jack Straw.[3] Although by no means a total compilation (or comprehensive record) of Islamophobic statements made since September 11, 2001, this cross-sectional sampling of high-profile global public statements made below against Islam and Muslims provides a revealing three-dimensional analysis into the growth of Islamophobia in America today. From Ann Coulter publicly stating that we should "kill their [Muslim] leaders and convert them to Christianity" to Reverend Pat Robertson of *The 700 Club* once bizarrely telling the Associated Press that neither American Muslims nor Hindus should be allowed to serve as federal judges in the United States; these professional fear-mongers have nurtured, facilitated and expanded the growth of Islamophobia from its effective birth on September 11, 2001. Thus, in many ways, they are also responsible for the exponential growth of Islamophobia today along with Osama bin Laden and Al-Qaeda Inc.

Osama bin Laden (1957-2011)

Since Osama bin Laden's terrorist actions on September 11 made him the proverbial father of Islamophobia, a brief overview of his own ridiculous public statements demonstrate how far away he sinisterly lurked from the true global mainstream fold of Islam. For example, on October 17, 2001, Osama bin Laden remarked in one of his first public appearances after the 9/11 attacks: ***"Here is America struck by God Almighty in one of its vital organs, so that its greatest buildings are destroyed."***[4] To give the casual observer an accurate nutshell, the overall 'mission statement' for Al-Qaeda would probably sound something like this on-the-record March 1997 OBL interview with CNN: ***"For this and other acts of aggression and injustice, we have declared jihad against the US, because in our religion it is our duty to make jihad."***[5]

Whenever he has been publicly challenged (by both Muslims and non-Muslims alike) on his un-Islamic suicide attacks which murder innocent civilians and other non-combatants; OBL usually resorted to his predictable moral equivocation, as in this comment from a 1996 interview with *Nida'ul Islam* magazine: ***"As for their accusations of terrorizing the innocent, the children, and the women, these are in the category of 'accusing others with their own affliction in order to fool the masses.'"***[6]

To the contrary, the overwhelming majority of global Muslims alive today are fully aware of the fact that Islam categorically forbids suicide and does not *ever* teach us to wantonly and unjustly murder any human being; regardless of any race, religion or political persuasion. Even so, in a February 1998 public statement, Osama bin Laden further stated that, *"We...call on every Muslim who believes in God and wishes to be rewarded to comply with God's order to kill the Americans and plunder their money."*[7]

"In our religion, it is not permissible for any non-Muslim to stay in our country," he also once self-righteously proclaimed[8] during the previously aforementioned March 1997 CNN interview. The sheer lunacy of his absurd statements can be gleaned from the simple historical fact (taught in any Islam 101 university course) that priests, rabbis and monks of all different religions were present (and prospered) during the early historical societies of the Prophet Muhammad and the first four *Khulifa-e-Rashidoon* ('Rightly Guided') post-prophetic Muslim caliphates ***"There is no more important duty than pushing the American enemy out of the holy land. ... The presence of the USA Crusader military forces on land, sea and air of the states of the Islamic Gulf is the greatest danger threatening the largest oil reserve in the world..."***

Alas, so the truth finally comes out. It was always about the oil and global politics, Osama.

Like many of the wars and conflicts around the world today, this unholy quest of global terrorism by OBL is simply (and in his own words above) stated to protect "the largest oil reserve in the world". As such, you do not then have to be a rocket scientist to clearly see that he haphazardly guises his political agendas loosely within the rubric of (ir)religious rhetoric by duplicitously telling the rest of the world that somehow ***"hostility toward America is a religious duty"*** as he did during a December 1998 interview[9] with TIME Magazine. Even though Osama bin Laden was the millionaire mouthpiece of Al-Qaeda during his infamous lifetime, there are still many global analysts around the world who would overwhelmingly agree that Dr. Ayman al-Zawahiri was the actual brains behind their terrorist operational franchise known as Al-Qaeda Inc.

Dr. Ayman Muhammad Rubbaie al-Zawahiri

"While bin Laden putters about in his premature forced retirement, making the odd cameo appearance, Ayman al-Zawahiri has taken control of al-Qaeda," once wrote Georgetown University professor and former CIA scholar-in-residence Bruce Hoffman in a September 2007 column for the *Washington Post*.[10] He noted that while OBL had been relatively off-the-radar in terms of video and audio messages since 2005, Ayman Al-Zawahiri "has issued about 30 statements on a range of subjects – pontifications on Iraq, Palestine, Kashmir and Pakistan, alongside al-Qaeda's bread-and-butter condemnations of the United States, Britain, Israel, the West and its various other enemies."

Professor Hoffman further noted that although he may lack Osama bin Laden's "charisma," it is actually Ayman Al-Zawahiri who was the superior geopolitical strategic 'brain' of their operation. In fact, it was Al-Zawahiri who, more than a decade ago, first defined al-Qaeda's geopolitical strategy in terms of 'far' and 'near' enemies within the global public record. According to him, the United States is the 'far enemy' whose defeat, he argued, was an essential prerequisite to the elimination of the 'near enemy' – the corrupt and authoritarian 'anti-Islamic regimes' in the Middle East, Central Asia, South Asia and Southeast Asia that could not remain in power without American and Western political and financial support.[11]

In December 2001, Ayman Al-Zawahiri published his treatise entitled *Knights Under the Prophet's Banner* for the London-based Arabic-language *Asharq al-Awsat* newspaper. Within this 'treatise', Al-Zawahiri painted a picture of Islam under siege by a predatory, Western-dominated world in which ***"there is no solution without jihad."*** Furthermore, Al-Zawahiri argued in his treatise for: "(1) The need to inflict maximum casualties on the opponent, no matter how much time and effort such operations take, for this is the language understood by the West" and "(2) The need to concentrate on martyrdom operations as the most successful way to inflict damage and the least costly in casualties to the *mujahiddin* [those who engage in *jihad*]."[12]

For these and many reasons, although not as prominently in the limelight as Osama bin Laden was during his lifetime; in many ways, Dr. Ayman al-Zawahiri is actually a lot scarier than Osama himself.

The (In)Famous Ann Coulter

On our own American side of the Islamophobia debate, there is probably no better person more deserving of being the proverbial 'poster child' for this neo-racist phenomenon of Islamophobia within the United States after 9/11 than our own resident American right-wing professional provocateur, Ann Coulter. Although she was already a well-known polemicist commentator, since 9/11, she has brilliantly (and deviously) taken the self-promotional professional provocateur phenomenon to new xenophobic heights within our American political discourse and media landscape. Coulter has mastered the art of shameless self-promotion by verbalizing outlandishly racist and jingoistic political platforms as being part and parcel of our American social fabric.

For example, a mere two days after 9/11, in an internet column for *National Review Online*, Coulter astoundingly suggested that we ***"should invade their countries, kill their leaders and convert them to Christianity."***[13] When later given a chance to clarify her remarks on FOX News Channel's *Hannity and Colmes* show, this is how her television interview that evening would eventually transpire:

ALAN COLMES (co-host): "Would you like to convert these people [Muslims] all to Christianity?

ANN COULTER: The ones that we haven't killed, yes.

ALAN COLMES: So no one should be Muslim. They should all be Christian?

ANN COULTER: That would be a good start, yes."[14]

Amid the national (and bipartisan) uproar over her Islamophobic tirade, even the conservative *National Review* magazine wisely decided to sever its employment relationship with her shortly thereafter. Commenting on the controversy, *National Review Online* editor Jonah Goldberg wrote that, "Well, she told the *Washington Post* yesterday that she loves [the controversy], because she's gotten lots of great publicity. That pretty much sums Ann up."[15]

Unfortunately, even with *National Review* dumping her sophomoric column, it would not be long before Islamophobia and Ann Coulter would soon be fighting over throw pillows as racist bedfellows yet again. In a subsequent October 2001 column on another right-wing Internet website, Miss Coulter further suggested that **there should be a *"mass deportation"* of Muslims from America**.[16] Furthermore, in September 2002, Coulter remarked on Islamophobic statements made at an annual meeting of the Southern Baptist Conference (SBC) by remarking that, ***"To say that Muhammad was a demon-possessed pedophile is not an attack...It's a fact."***[17] In April 2004, our American 'queen of intolerance' would soon take her xenophobic crown into the legal arena of racial profiling. In one of her nationally syndicated columns, she brilliantly decided that this was her opportunity to offer marketing slogans to airlines in regards to the racial profiling of its American Muslim and Arab passengers. Our *jingoiste extraordinaire* proudly pitched these as possible post-9/11 airline ***"slogans the airlines could use"*** within her syndicated column:

"Now Frisking All Arabs – Twice!"

"More Civil-Rights Lawsuits Brought by Arabs Than Any Other Airline!"

"The Friendly Skies – Unless You're an Arab..."

"You Are Now Free to Move About the Cabin – Not So Fast, Mohammed!"[18]

Her next Islamophobic swipe regarding racial profiling occurred in November 2006 when she wrote that racially ***"profiling Muslims is more like profiling the [Ku Klux] Klan."***[19] Moving onwards, in response to the 2005-06 international hullabaloo over the Danish cartoon controversy depicting the Prophet Muhammad as a terrorist (with a bomb-laden turban on his head), Coulter suggested in her February 8, 2006 nationally syndicated column that **Islam is *"a car-burning cult"*** and wrote that **Muslims have *"a predilection for violence."***[20] Even better, in front of hundreds of adoring fans at the 2006 Conservative Political Action Conference (CPAC), Ann Coulter told everyone that our post-9/11 American motto should be**: *"Raghead talks tough... Raghead faces consequences."***[21]

Bloggers from both sides of the political aisle called her comments "a bigot eruption," "beyond the pale," and even added that Ann Coulter was now everyone's favorite "Muslim-hater."[22] Even fellow conservative commentator

Michelle Malkin responded by saying that she wanted young conservatives-including Muslims who attended CPAC- to know that "not everyone uses that kind of epithet."[23]

Reverend Pat Robertson of *The 700 Club*

"These people are crazed fanatics, and I want to say it now: I believe it's motivated by demonic power; it is satanic...and the goal of Islam, ladies and gentlemen, whether you like it or not, is world domination...And, by the way, Islam is not a religion of peace."[24]

These are the infamous March 2006 words of the American televangelist Reverend Pat Robertson, founder and host of *The 700 Club* (the flagship news show of the Christian Broadcasting Network [CBN]). According to the media watchdog group Media Matters for America, the Christian Broadcasting Network (CBN) program subsequently removed Robertson's aforementioned inflammatory comments from its website "out of concerns they could be misinterpreted if taken out of context."[25] However, when a religion is called "satanic", motivated "by demonic power" and "not a religion of peace," it is quite hard to imagine how these blatantly bigoted and false statements could ever be taken out of context by any human being; even by a fifth-grade child.

But then again, it will become quite apparent that there are countless reasons why former 2008 Republican presidential candidate and United States Senator John McCain (R-AZ) would once rightfully refer to 'professional reverends' like Pat Robertson and (the late) Jerry Falwell as being some of our major American "agents of intolerance."[26] For example, in September 2002, when discussing Islam on FOX News Channel's *Hannity and Colmes* show, Reverend Pat Robertson said that, ***"[Prophet Muhammad] was an absolute wild-eyed fanatic. He was a robber and a brigand. And to say that these terrorists distort Islam, they're carrying out Islam."***[27] In addition, according to the Associated Press (AP), during a 2002 broadcast of *The 700 Club* program, Pat Robertson declared that Islam ***"is not a peaceful religion that wants to coexist. They want to coexist until they can control, dominate and then, if need be, destroy."***[28]

A September 2002 public statement by People For the American Way (PFAW) further highlighted Reverend Robertson's continued Islamophobia within the public record. According to their report, the infamous televangelist portrayed Muslims as both evil and treacherous yet again:

> *Muslims "in America particularly are trying to put on a smiley face so that they'll make people think, 'Well, we're just like you are.' I don't want to have a religious bigotry [sic], but this political correctness has gone out of control because these people at their core are the enemies of the United States, the enemies of freedom, and they're sworn enemies of Israel, and they will–are trying to destroy us… I'm talking about hundreds of millions of them."*[29]

Even more astonishing was a May 4, 2005 national television interview where Reverend Robertson told ABC News' *This Week with George Stephanopoulos* that **he did not believe that either American Hindus or American Muslims should be allowed to serve as either federal judges or become members of the President's cabinet**:

> *GEORGE STEPHANOPOULOS: "[I]n your book The New World Order you wrote, 'How dare you maintain that those who believe in the Judeo-Christian values are better qualified to govern America than Hindus or Muslims.' My simple answer is, 'yes, they are.'" Does that mean no Hindu and Muslim judges?"*
>
> *PAT ROBERTSON :"Right now, I think people who feel that there should be a jihad against America, read what the Islamic people say. They divide the world into two spheres, Dar al Islam Dar al Harb. The Dar al Islam are those who've submitted to Islam, Dar al Harb are those who are in the land of war and they have said in the Koran there's a war against all the infidels. So do you want somebody like that sitting as a judge? I wouldn't."*[30]

Of course, Reverend Pat Robertson's Islamophobia did not end there. For example, on his July 14, 2005 broadcast of *The 700 Club*, Reverend Robertson told his entire television audience: ***"Ladies and gentlemen, Islam, at least at its core, teaches violence."***[31] True to form, in April 2006, the fine reverend wasted little time in telling us (yet again) how he really feels about Islam and Muslims. This time, Reverend Robertson decided that it would be both prudent and wise to equate the religion of Islam with Nazism and Adolf Hitler. Notwithstanding the primary fact that Nazism was started by an uber-racist German Christian genocidal maniac named Adolf Hitler who killed over 6 million innocent Jews in the horrific human tragedy of the Holocaust; Robertson felt it not only prudent to equate Islam with Nazism, but again used this latest opportunity to take another bellicose religious potshot swipe at all Muslims worldwide. In April 2006, our resident televangelist stated on-the-record: ***"And, ladies and gentlemen, if we had listened to what Adolf Hitler said in* Mein Kampf*, the West might have been prepared, and World War II would have been averted. We are not listening to what these guys say. We are not listening to what not only the radical Muslims but Islam in general, we're not listening to what it says."***[32]

Needless to say, more nonsensical Islamophobic statements followed soon thereafter. In the April 28, 2006 broadcast from his usual bully pulpit, he again reiterated his racist mantra by stating that, "***Who ever heard of such a bloody, bloody, brutal type of religion? But that's what it is...It is not a religion of peace."***[33]

The fine reverend would yet again continue his Islamophobia the very next month. In May 2006, *The 700 Club* host said ***"Islam is essentially a Christian heresy."***[34] In the same televised broadcast, he additionally perpetuated certain Jewish stereotypes, stating that, "When you think of Jewish people, you think of successful businessmen" who are "very wise in finance and who are prosperous." Pat Robertson would later add that it shocks people to find out "there's poverty in Israel," **because *"Jewish people"* are *"very thrifty"* and *"extraordinarily good business people."***[35] Clearly, it is hard not to call out someone like Reverend Pat Robertson for their Islamophobia when they provide so much hilarious late-night talk show material on a seemingly regular basis.

(The Late) Reverend Jerry Falwell

As mentioned earlier, in a February 2000 speech in Virginia, former 2008 Republican presidential candidate and U.S. Senator John McCain (R-AZ) once referred to both Reverend Jerry Falwell and Revered Pat Robertson as "agents of intolerance."[36] Even though the senior senator from Arizona would eventually predictably back-pedal and sheepishly distance himself politically from his own 'agents of intolerance' statement from February 2000, the late Reverend Jerry Falwell's own on-the-record public statements after 9/11 will clearly show his agency for intolerance for Muslims and Islam during the span of his lifetime. In one of his most infamous (and widely-televised) Islamophobic remarks to date, during a notorious CBS News *60 Minutes* interview on October 6, 2002, Reverend Jerry Falwell told CBS News correspondent Bob Simon the following about the Prophet Muhammad on that nationally-televised episode of *60 Minutes*: ***"Jesus set the example for love, as did Moses...I think Muhammad set an opposite example...I think Mohammed was a terrorist. I read enough of the history of his life, written by both Muslims and non-Muslims, that he was a violent man, a man of war."***[37]

Amid international condemnations from people of all religious traditions, the Reverend Falwell simply issued a half-hearted tepid "apology" a few days later saying: "I sincerely apologize that certain statements of mine made during an interview for CBS's *60 Minutes* were hurtful to the feelings of many Muslims. I intended no disrespect to any sincere, law-abiding Muslim."[38] Of course, the blatantly obvious omission within Falwell's "apology" was the fact that he did not renounce his "Muhammad was a terrorist" statement. Seeing his unwillingness to admit his own mistakes, some of the most scathing condemnations of Reverend Jerry Falwell's Islamophobia came from some of his own high-profile Christian sisters and brothers here in America. For example, the executive board of the National Council of Churches (NCC)- representing over 50 million Christians in the United States- voted unanimously to "condemn and repudiate" Jerry Falwell's statements on *60 Minutes*. In the unanimous NCC resolution, the leaders of U.S. Protestant, Orthodox and Anglican denominations also called on then-President George W. Bush to repudiate and condemn Falwell's remarks.

"Falwell's 'hateful and destructive' statements...are NOT those of the majority of Christians in this country nor in the rest of the world," said the governing body of the NCC.[39]. ***"His statements about Islam and the***

Prophet Muhammad are not only factually untrue and offensive, but are dangerous to the national security of every nation where Christians and Muslims are seeking a peaceful relationship."The NCC board further concluded that Jerry Falwell's words were "not Christian and shockingly uninformed."

Reverend Franklin Graham (former spiritual adviser to President George W. Bush)

In addition to being the son of legendary American evangelist Reverend Billy Graham, when a person is also the former 'spiritual adviser' to President George W. Bush, that person (or his public words) simply cannot be ignored by the general populace. Islam is ***"a very wicked and evil religion...not of the same god... [and] I don't believe this is this wonderful, peaceful religion,"*** once said Reverend Franklin Graham during a November 2001 broadcast of *NBC Nightly News* with Tom Brokaw. At the time, even Mr. Brokaw stated that Graham's statements were very harsh and most Americans chalked Reverend Graham's statements up to being a verbal gaffe. However, when Graham was again publicly given the opportunity to apologize and retract his ridiculous statements- not only did he not apologize- but he felt the compulsive audacity to repeat his inflammatory Islamophobic remarks yet again. In 2002, Kim Lawton of PBS *Religion & Ethics NewsWeekly* asked the good reverend again during an interview if the God of Islam is the same monotheistic Abrahamic God of Christians and Jews.

(Hint: The answer is yes.)

Franklin Graham simply replied, "No, it's not."[40] He continued by saying that, "After 9/11, there were a lot of things being said about how the God of Islam and the God of the Christian faith were one and the same, but that's simply not true."[41] Unfortunately, many people on the American 'Evangelical Right' were also very quick to jump on the Franklin Graham bandwagon of Islamophobia. Chuck Colson, founder of Prison Fellowship Ministries (and a former convicted felon of Watergate criminal infamy), responded to Franklin Graham's comments by adding that, ***"I agree that Islam is a religion, which, if taken seriously, promotes violence."***[42]

On the June 22, 2005 evening television broadcast of CNN *Anderson Cooper 360*, Reverend Franklin Graham continued his Islamophobia by boorishly claiming that the only way that Muslims could attain salvation was through dying in a holy war. Notwithstanding the very simple fact that Graham is completely ignorant about the elementary fact that Muslims worship the same monotheistic Abrahamic God of Christians and Jews; his blatant hatred for anything related to Islam is evident in his continued regurgitation of xenophobic right-wing talking points about Islam and Muslims.

"In Islam, there is a lot that I have serious questions about, but the god that I worship doesn't require me to strap a bomb on myself and go blow up innocent people to prove to God that I love him and that is the way I can have salvation," Franklin Graham said to CNN's Anderson Cooper during that June 2005 television interview. When rightfully challenged by Anderson Cooper about the fact that neither the Quran nor Islam justifies the murdering of innocent civilians, Franklin Graham further showed his blatant ignorance of Islam by self-righteously asserting that, ***"Well, no, in Islam, the only way that you can have salvation – be assured of your salvation – is to die in what they would call, what the clerics would call a holy war."*** With the younger Graham's continued unwillingness and stubborn inability to see the sheer lunacy of his own Islamophobia, some much-needed context and explanation was offered by his father, the elder (and more respected) Reverend Billy Graham. Finally contradicting his own son's infamous remarks about Islam once and for all- in an August 2006 cover story with Jon Meacham of *Newsweek* magazine- the patriarch Reverend Billy Graham responded to the publicly controversy created by his son when he said:

"I would not say Islam is wicked and evil ... I have a lot of friends who are Islamic. There are many wonderful people among them. I have a great love for them.... I'm sure there are many things that [my son Franklin] and I are not in total agreement about."[43] When it comes to Islamophobia and his seething hatred for anything related to Islam and Muslims, the younger Reverend Franklin Graham might want to take some advice from his older (and seemingly wiser) father on this issue about which the younger Graham clearly knows nothing.

United States Congressman (now U.S. Senator) Saxby Chambliss (R-GA)

Even more baffling than the fact that an elected Member of Congress would ever be stupid enough to promote Islamophobia within the American public record is the astounding fact that he was then effectively rewarded for his xenophobia and religious bigotry by then being promoted by the electorate of his state to represent them in the hallowed halls of the United States Senate. During a November

19, 2001, meeting with emergency responders in Valdosta, Georgia, the Associated Press reported that then-Republican Congressman Saxby Chambliss from the 8th congressional district of Georgia once remarked that they should ***"turn the sheriff loose and arrest every Muslim that crosses the state line."***[44] Even more frightening than the sheer lunacy of his ridiculous statements was the fact that Saxby Chambliss was also then-chairman of the House Judiciary Subcommittee on Crime, Terrorism and Homeland Security at the time he made these blatantly racist (and patently stupid) remarks in 2001.

In a letter to then-Speaker of the House Rep. Dennis Hastert (R-IL), the American-Arab Anti-Discrimination Committee (ADC) accurately summed up the global implications of Chambliss' racist remarks. ADC's letter to Hastert stated that, "Having the chair of this crucial House Subcommittee making remarks of this kind sends the worst possible message to the Arab-American and Muslim communities in the United States, to the Arab and Muslim worlds, and to society in general about the level of intolerance and anti-Muslim bigotry that is considered acceptable in the U.S. Congress."[45]

"We feel that the important work of this Subcommittee may well be undermined by the taint of Rep. Chambliss' outrageously bigoted remarks," concluded ADC's letter to former House Speaker Dennis Hastert. Strangely enough, instead of voting him out of office, on November 5, 2002, the people of the great state of Georgia instead decided to elevate and elect Saxby Chambliss to become their next United States senator.

United States Congressman John Cooksey (R-LA)

Although it should come as little surprise to most tolerant Americans, the xenophobic right-wing anti-Muslim political rhetoric from elected government officials after 9/11 did not simply end with Senator Saxby Chambliss and actually continues to grow unchallenged in certain political circles to this very day. Six days after 9/11, in a radio interview on September 17, 2001, when asked about the concept of 'racial profiling', then-Republican congressman John Cooksey from Louisiana brilliantly admitted that, ***"If I see someone that comes in that has a diaper on his head and a fan belt wrapped around the diaper on his head, that guy needs to be pulled over."***[46]

Actor Wil Wheaton, best known for his roles in *Stand by Me* and *Star Trek: The Next Generation*, summed up many Americans sentiments perfectly when he wrote in a public letter to the congressman: "Holy crap! A United States Representative actually said that."[47]

"These remarks are not the remarks of someone who is worthy of a position in our government," continued Mr. Wheaton. "Your remarks, sir, are ignorant, disgusting, and racist. I expect much more from a member of Congress... We Americans turn to you, our elected leaders, to provide leadership and guidance, especially during times such as these, when our democracy is threatened, and our population is frightened and confused... I suggest that you take some time to read about the mass internment of Japanese-Americans during the aftermath of the attack on Pearl Harbor, as those who are not familiar with history are condemned to repeat it."

Former United States Attorney General John Ashcroft

Even former Attorney General John Ashcroft was not above taking a religious potshot at Islam while still an official member of the George W. Bush administration. According to a November 2001 interview with syndicated conservative columnist Cal Thomas published on the Internet website Crosswalk.com, Attorney General John Ashcroft was quoted as saying, ***"Islam is a religion in which God requires you to send your son to die for him...Christianity is a faith in which God sends his son to die for you."***[48] Knowing that people were probably not going to believe him, the right-wing columnist Cal Thomas again reiterated that, "I'm going to repeat it. John Ashcroft said, 'Islam is a religion in which God requires you to send your son to die for him. Christianity is a faith in which God sends his son to die for you.'" Instead of condemning such hateful, ignorant and untrue words, Thomas went even further by asking for "prayers" for Ashcroft for making these ignorant remarks.

"If you are not already doing so, pray for this good man and for the president [George W. Bush] and the many others in government here in Washington who seek to follow the will of God ... the real God, who has sent His Son to die for all," wrote Cal Thomas; who is also (frighteningly) the most widely syndicated columnist in all of America. You know that the spirit of Islamophobia is alive and well when one of their leading columnists is read in over 540 newspapers around the country each and every day.[49]

Former U.S. Deputy Undersecretary of Defense William "Jerry" Boykin

In 2003, according to the *Los Angeles Times*, President George W. Bush decided to appoint as deputy undersecretary of defense an American army general who saw the war on terrorism as a clash between Judeo-Christian values and "Satan". This high-level American army official who once compared "Satan" to Islam was former U.S. Deputy Undersecretary of Defense for Intelligence, Lieutenant General William "Jerry" Boykin. In June 2003, then-General Boykin, the newly appointed deputy undersecretary for intelligence in the Defense Department was once seen in a video (in full U.S. Army military fatigues with medals a-blazin') in his official Army uniform telling a Christian church group in Oregon that "they" hated the United States ***"because we're a Christian nation, because our foundation and our roots are Judeo-Christian...and the enemy is a guy named Satan."***[50] Discussing his own battle against a Muslim warlord in Somalia, General Boykin once told an audience on video: ***"I knew my God was bigger than his. I knew that my God was a real God and his was an idol."***

"We in the army of God, in the house of God, kingdom of God have been raised for such a time as this," General Boykin continued to say on the same video in his official U.S. Army uniform. In addition, on at least one occasion, in Sandy, Oregon, in June 2003, Boykin said of President Bush: ***"He's in the White House because God put him there"***[51] Although there was no public condemnation or rebuke by the Bush Administration, the diplomatic repercussions of General Boykin's inflammatory remarks were felt around the world. Notwithstanding the deafening silence from the Bush administration on Islamophobic remarks made by two of their own high-ranking Administration officials (Ashcroft and Boykin), the *Los Angeles Times* reported that one high-ranking State Department official once told visiting Arab leaders that the Bush Administration should have fired Boykin at the first opportunity because he "helps Osama bin Laden's recruitment efforts."[52]

"Everybody in the Middle East pays attention to the news now. They're all hooked up to satellite television and car radios," said Harold Pachios, an attorney who served on the State Department's Advisory Commission for Public Diplomacy. "If you took a poll in the United States, you might get 1% who know who General Boykin is and what he said. If you took a poll anywhere in the Islamic world, a majority would know," Pachios added.

"And they would believe that he was speaking for the U.S. government."[53]

Glenn Beck

On the November 14, 2006 broadcast of his CNN Headline News program, television host Glenn Beck interviewed Congressman-elect Keith Ellison (D-MN), who had just made history by becoming the first American Muslim ever elected to the halls of Congress only one week earlier on November 7, 2006. True to form, Glenn Beck wasted no time at all and asked Congressman Ellison if he could "have five minutes here where we're just politically-incorrect and I play the cards up on the table." After Keith Ellison agreed to this strange request, Glenn Beck proceeded to state that, "I have been nervous about this interview with you, because what I feel like saying is: 'Sir, prove to me that you are not working with our enemies.'" He graciously added that, "I'm not accusing you of being an enemy...but that's the way I feel, and I think a lot of Americans will feel that way."

Only two months earlier, in September 2006, the watchdog group *Media Matters for America* noted that Beck previously warned that if "Muslims and Arabs" don't "act now" by "step[ping] to the plate" to condemn terrorism, they will be "looking through a razor wire fence at the West." A month before that statement, in August of the same year, Mr. Beck declared that "Muslims who have sat on your frickin' hands the whole time" rather than "lining up to shoot the bad Muslims in the head"[54] will face dire consequences.

Please tell us how you really feel, Glenn.

Hate Crimes After 9/11: The Murder of Balbir Singh Sodhi

Although protected by the First Amendment, the concept of 'hate speech' is a broad phenomenon that should also be understood to have unintended consequences and often presents serious tangible harms to individual victims and greater society at large. Even though racist and xenophobic statements may be legally protected exercises in free speech, we must also remember that they do not occur within a sociological vacuum. In his book *Opposing Hate Speech*, Southern Methodist University professor Dr. Anthony Cortese outlined how "societies have used hate speech to stereotype a group as 'stupid, dangerous or impure' - and later deployed that stereotype to justify atrocities" such as slavery, genocide or hate crimes against targeted minority groups. Within the context of anti-Muslim sentiment and Islamophobic rhetoric after 9/11- to highlight the sheer tragic irony and stupid human ignorance of bias-motivated 'hate crimes' within America- the first actual tragic victim of a post-9/11 'hate crime' murder in the United States was neither a Muslim nor an Arab.

Four days after 9/11- Mr. Balbir Singh Sodhi- a 49-year-old Indian Sikh-American businessman was brutally shot several times and killed instantly by Frank Roque in a Mesa, Arizona gas station.[55] According to BBC World News, the county attorney stated that Mr. Sodhi was killed "for no other apparent reason than that he was dark-skinned and wore a turban."[56] Several media outlets also reported that as Frank Roque was being taken away by police in handcuffs, he kept shouting over and over: ***"I stand for America all the way...I am a patriot!"***[57]

Two other tragic hate-crime murders took place around America on the same day as the Sodhi murder. Mr. Adel Karas, a 48-year old Egyptian Orthodox Coptic Christian and father of three, was viciously murdered outside of his suburban Los Angeles import shop.[58] In Texas, both the FBI and local police investigated the murder of Mr. Waqar Hasan, a Pakistani store owner who was found shot to death outside of his grocery store in suburban Dallas.[59] Similarly, it seemed as though hardly a day would pass before American Muslim mosques, schools and community centers would also soon become the next bulls-eye target for a severe hate-crimes backlash from our own American friends and neighbors who we have lived peacefully with our entire lives.

One day after 9/11- in the early morning hours of September 12, 2001- at least six (6) bullets shattered several windows of the Islamic Center of Irving in suburban Dallas, Texas.[60] According to the Associated Press story about the hate crime, the drive-by shooting caused several thousands of dollars in damage.[61] In Columbus, Ohio, members of the Islamic Center in Columbus arrived to their mosque one day to find holes drilled into floors, water pipes pulled from the walls and ceilings severely destroyed from water damage by vandals who broke into the mosque.[62] Similarly, on September 12, 2001, a 29-year old man named Eric Richley of Middleburg Heights, Ohio, decided to drive his white Ford Mustang into the front glass doors of the Grand Mosque at the Islamic Center of Greater Cleveland.[63] Although luckily unoccupied at the time, the mosque was severely damaged to the tune of nearly $100,000.

Mr. Richley subsequently pled guilty to his hate crime and was sentenced to five years in prison.[64]

The Federal Bureau of Investigations (FBI) Hate Crimes Unit regularly monitors and collects data on crimes motivated by bias or hate. In analyzing the FBI's 2002 annual report on the subject of hate crimes against Muslims alone, the *San Francisco Chronicle* noted that the "most dramatic change" in the 2002 official FBI report was the "more than 1,600 percent increase in reported hate crimes against Muslims – a jump from 28 hate incidents in 2000 to 481 [in 2001]."[65] Although this is only a brief societal snapshot of some major high-profile hate crimes against the American Muslim, Arab and South Asian communities after 9/11, when we begin to see entrenched societal intolerance and institutional racism slowly enter into our national 'public opinion' circles, we should all be even more concerned for the overall well-being and advancement of our American pluralistic society.

Islamophobia and Public Opinion

In simple terms, within any nation or society around the world, the most sociologically devastating impact of any form of global neo-racism (like Islamophobia and/or Anti-Semitism) will many times occur within our own respective spheres of global 'public opinion'.

When average citizens of a nation collectively believe that their neighbors are somehow inherently more "dangerous" or "evil" simply based on demographic features (like religion or skin color), that is when our respective societies have historically devolved into bias-motivated criminal actions against houses of worship like the burning of black churches, spray-painting of swastikas on synagogues, or drive-by shootings at mosques. Regardless of whether it is Anti-Semitism, Islamophobia or any other form of racial and religious intolerance in existence today, it becomes the shared moral imperative of our civilized humanity worldwide to ensure that every single legal and constitutional protection applies to all minorities; regardless of their religion, color, gender or sexual orientation anywhere around the globe.

To show the practical impact of Islamophobia on the general American public, a September 2004 Pew Forum on Religion and Public Life Poll once found that:

- **Almost 4 in 10 Americans have an unfavorable view of Islam**, about the same number that has a favorable view.

-A plurality of Americans **(46 percent) believes that Islam is more likely than other religions to encourage violence** among its believers.[66]

Similarly, a March 2005 ABC News Poll found that over one-third of Americans (34 percent) believe that mainstream Islam encourages violence. During the same ABC News poll, forty-three (43) percent of Americans think Islam does not teach respect for the beliefs of non-Muslims. Among Americans who feel they "understand the religion of Islam,'" nearly fifty-nine percent (59%) of Americans call it "peaceful" and 46 percent think it teaches respect for the beliefs of others.[67] Again, in terms of general public animosity towards the religion of Islam itself, a April 2006 CBS News poll produced similar findings: ***nearly forty (40) percent of Americans believed that Islam encourages violence more than other religions***.[68] It should naturally come as little surprise to anyone that this general distaste for the religion of Islam would soon correlate directly towards devastating public opinion polls focused on how we as Americans view citizens of American Muslim, Arab and South Asian descent within our country since 9/11.

For instance, a December 2004 public opinion poll commissioned by Cornell University found that ***about 44 percent of Americans said that they believe that "some curtailment of civil liberties is necessary for Muslim-Americans."*** Similarly, over 26 percent of Americans in the same poll stated that they believe that American mosques should be closely monitored by U.S. law enforcement agencies; and over 29 percent of Americans agreed that undercover law enforcement agents should infiltrate Muslim civic and volunteer organizations in order to keep tabs on their activities and fund-raising.[69] Nearly the same overall public sentiments were captured in a March 2006 *Washington Post*/ABC News poll which found that over 46 percent of Americans said that they personally held "unfavorable views" about Islam and Muslims.[70] In that same poll, about one-fourth of the respondents admitted to feelings of prejudice: 27 percent said that they held "prejudiced feelings" towards Muslims, whereas 25 percent of Americans polled said that they have prejudiced feelings against Arabs.[71]

The sheer mind-boggling hysteria of post-9/11 America came to light[72] when a July 2005 USA TODAY/CNN/Gallup poll found that nearly 53 percent of Americans were in favor of "requiring all Arabs, including those who are U.S. citizens, to undergo special, more intensive security checks before boarding airplanes." In the same July 2005 poll, the most shocking finding was that over **46 percent of Americans favored "requiring Arabs, including those who are U.S. citizens, to carry a special ID."**[73]

Even right before President Barack Obama's June 2009 first major address to the Muslim world from Cairo University, a CNN/Opinion Research Corporation national survey released two days before President Obama's June 2009 Cairo address **found that 46 percent of Americans admit to having an unfavorable opinion of Muslim countries**. According to a CNN news story on this public opinion poll: "That's up 5 percentage points from 2002, when 41 percent indicated that they had an unfavorable view" of Muslims.[74] Additionally, the same June 2009 poll also suggested that over six 6 out of 10 Americans think that the Muslim world considers itself at war with the United States. "The feeling seems to be mutual," once noted CNN senior political analyst Bill Schneider, interpreting the June 2009 poll results. "We distrust Muslims. They distrust Americans. Views of Americans have not changed very much over the past seven years. There are some indications that Muslims' views of Americans have improved a bit since Barack Obama took office, but they are still not positive."

Barack Hussein Obama: Islamophobia and the 2008 U.S. Presidential Election

"Again, let it be known to the world that Barack Obama is not (and has never been) a Muslim,"[75] I once wrote in a November 2008 column for CNN immediately after his election. A mere ten days after America had proudly celebrated the election of Barack Obama as the 44th President of the United States of America; even though we had achieved a major societal milestone by electing our first African-American president in history, the political road to the White House had still been paved with nothing but xenophobic innuendo and whisper campaigns galore involving Islam and Muslims. Throughout the near-entirety of the 2008 presidential election campaign cycle, so toxic were the innuendoes that when certain nasty (and xenophobic) right-wing elements of the

Republican party tried to paint Barack Obama as some of 'Crypto-Muslim Manchurian Candidate'; we Americans did not see then-candidate Obama go within twelve feet of an American mosque entrance even once during the entirety of his 2008 presidential political campaign[76].

Even more shocking was the fact that this pandering to anti-Muslim sentiment was not even limited to the Republican Party. For example, the 'Muslim' insinuation against President Obama became so toxic and radioactive within our American society that in June 2008, two American Muslim women in Michigan were removed from a photo opportunity at an Obama rally in Detroit[77] by Obama's own Democratic campaign volunteers simply because the two women wore the *hijab* (headscarf). Ironically enough, it took the bipartisan gravitas of a former Republican Secretary of State to finally put the Obama "crypto-Muslim" rumors to rest (at least temporarily, for these toxic rumors persist to this very day).[78]

During a October 2008 interview with NBC News' David Gregory on *Meet the Press*- in one political fell swoop- former Secretary of State Colin Powell bravely challenged the xenophobic undertones of his own Republican Party by highlighting the ultimate sacrifice of an American Muslim soldier from New Jersey who died in Iraq for his country, our United States of America. "I'm also troubled by...what members of the [Republican] party say," former United States Secretary of State Colin Powell said. "And it is permitted to be said such things as, 'Well, you know that Mr. Obama is a Muslim'...Well, the correct answer is...He is not a Muslim, he's a Christian...He's always been a Christian."[79] Secretary Powell continued: "But the really right answer is... What if he is? Is there something wrong with being a Muslim in this country? The answer's no, that's not America. Is there something wrong with some seven-year-old Muslim-American kid believing that he or she could be president?"[80]

Echoing the same noble sentiments of Secretary Colin Powell's grand political gesture on *Meet the Press*, regardless of whether it is Islamophobia, Anti-Semitism or any other form of racial or religious intolerance in existence today; it again becomes our collective moral ethical imperative as members of the human race to work towards eradicating all forms of intolerance in existence; whether it is Anti-Semitism, Islamophobia or any other form of xenophobia today.

The Great Anti-Mosque Movement of 2010

By now, most Americans are probably aware of the heated national protests against the high-profile Islamic community center called 'Park51' that was planned to be built a few blocks from ground zero in lower Manhattan. Although opponents of the proposed center sinisterly named it the 'Ground Zero Mosque' and even though the story captured international headlines throughout the midterm election cycle of 2010; many people are still unaware that these anti-Muslim political campaigns are continuing to spread throughout our country as a new wave of Islamophobia hits our American shores. The national debate over the Park51 Islamic center had become so ridiculously absurd that a proposed advertisement objecting to the mosque depicted a plane flying toward the World Trade Center's towers as they burned on the left- with an image rendering of the Park51 center on the right- and was set to run in New York city buses around Manhattan.

Following suit, some right-wing activists in Murfreesboro, Tennessee, similarly denounced plans for a large Muslim center proposed near a residential subdivision and hundreds of angry protesters had subsequently turned out for a protest march and county meeting on the matter. A few months earlier- members of a tea party group in Temecula, California- actually took barking dogs and anti-Muslim picket signs to Friday prayers at a neighborhood mosque that was seeking to build a new worship center on a vacant lot nearby. In Wisconsin, a few Christian ministers in Sheboygan decided to lead a noisy fight against a Muslim group that sought permission to open a mosque in a former health-food store bought by a local Muslim doctor. Even in Bridgeport, Connecticut, certain American Muslim community leaders had to eventually ask local police and elected officials for enhanced security so that they could worship in peace after an angry mob protested outside a mosque. According to reports, about a dozen members of a Texas-based group self-righteously calling itself 'Operation Save America' confronted peaceful worshippers at the Masjid An-Noor mosque in Bridgeport and yelled what mosque members described as "hate-filled slogans" against Muslims.

For those who argue that American mosques are somehow inherently breeding grounds for extremism, a two-year joint study by Duke University's Sanford School of Public Policy and the University of North Carolina concluded that American "mosques are actually a deterrent to the spread of militant Islam and terrorism." The professors in the joint study further highlighted that many mosque leaders had put significant effort into countering extremism by building youth programs, sponsoring anti-violence forums and scrutinizing teachers and texts.

Even so, let us get back to the 'Ground Zero Mosque' dispute for a moment.

Certain vocal right-wing national critics of the project – an infamous political coalition that included Sarah Palin, Newt Gingrich and members of the tea party movement – had assailed it as an unnecessary provocation. Sarah Palin had brilliantly asked people to *"refudiate"* (sic) the mosque project on Twitter and some protesters- including the aforementioned televangelist Pat Robertson- had pledged to organize legal efforts to actually block its construction. On the other side of the debate, many brave supporters of the mosque project- including New York's Mayor Michael Bloomberg- were true champions of religious tolerance during those heated times. During an emotionally stirring August 2010 press conference on the Park51 center, Mayor Bloomberg bravely said: "Whatever you may think of the proposed mosque and community center, lost in the heat of the debate has been a basic question – should government attempt to deny private citizens the right to build a house of worship on private property based on their particular religion?

"That may happen in other countries, but we should never allow it to happen here. This nation was founded on the principle that the government must never choose between religions, or favor one over another. There is no neighborhood in this city that is off-limits to God's love and mercy," said Mayor Bloomberg. First of all, the lower Manhattan building in question (which was an old Burlington Coat Factory clothing store) already included a prayer space for Muslims. This would have been the building which would be torn down in order to build a larger $100 million community center for New Yorkers of all religions; where there will be bookstores, restaurants, basketball courts, art galleries and yes, even a Muslim prayer room.

As former MSNBC host Keith Olbermann once sarcastically said: "What a cauldron of terrorism that would be... Terrorist chefs and terrorist point guards."

Another unsung hero in the whole Park51 debate was *Newsweek* editor and CNN host Fareed Zakaria. Without any personal obligation whatsoever, Mr. Zakaria decided to return an award and $10,000 honorarium to the Anti-Defamation League after the civil rights group's bizarre opposition to the Manhattan mosque project. In an August 6, 2010 *Newsweek* column that he wrote on the matter called, "Build the Ground Zero Mosque," Mr. Zakaria stated that, "If there is going to be a reformist movement in Islam, it is going to emerge from places like the proposed institute. We should be encouraging groups like the one behind this project, not demonizing them. Were this mosque being built in a foreign city, chances are that the U.S. government would be funding it." Finally, as author and journalist Jeffrey Goldberg of *The Atlantic* magazine rightfully noted on the Park51 matter: "Americans who seek the marginalization of Muslims in this country are unwittingly doing the work of Islamist extremists. ...We must do everything possible to avoid giving them propaganda victories in their attempt to create a cosmic war between Judeo-Christian civilization and Muslim civilization. ...The fight is not between the West and Islam."

My dear friend Daisy Khan- who was one of the co-founders of the proposed Park51 Islamic community center in lower Manhattan and wife of Imam Feisal Abdul Rauf- told me during an exclusive interview for this book about their joint mission and vision for the proposed $100 million Park51 community center. During our exclusive interview, Daisy told me that the mission of the community center was two-fold:

"1) To increase interfaith collaboration between all faith communities to prove that pluralism is at the heart of the Islamic faith; and

2) To show that American Muslims are leading this effort because there is a perception that Muslims tend not to be progressive or tolerant."

"The community center is there to amplify the voice of moderation," Daisy Khan told me further about the Park51 project during her interview for this book. She also stated that their greater vision was to use it as a "counter-momentum used to counteract the acts of the extremists". When asked about the rabid anti-mosque campaigns targeting their project, she highlighted that "the historical trajectory of minority religions in America has been the same" and this type of societal marginalization was "fought by American Jews and Catholics before us". She continued to say that "there will always be a group of people within America that will always want to keep the fear of the 'Other' alive." To her, there is a small group of committed xenophobes "trying to keep the fear of Islam and Muslims alive" in America thinking that it will somehow "gain them some sort of political capital" by using the Park51 project as a "political wedge issue during the 2010 midterm election cycle against the Obama administration" and beyond, according to Daisy.[81]

Thomas Jefferson once said, "The most sacred of the duties of a government is to do equal and impartial justice to all of its citizens." However, unless we successfully tackle this upsurge of anti-Muslim rhetoric from New York to California, from Tennessee to Connecticut and other places across our great land, it saddens me to think that the infamous lunatic terrorist known as Osama bin Laden was in a cave somewhere in central Asia for over ten years laughing at us – and perhaps even mockingly referring to our beloved country as the United States of Islamophobia.

Millenial McCarthyism: The Congressional Hearings of Peter King (March 2011)

Based on the political grandstanding over the Park51 center in Lower Manhattan by prominent right-wing conservative politicians during the 2010 midterm congressional elections, it has become abundantly clear that Islam and Muslims will continue to be a political 'wedge issue' aimed at dividing our nation on religious and ethnic lines for the foreseeable future. Political candidates who run on 'anti-Muslim platforms' find the effectiveness of demonizing American Muslims as a successful wedge issue; solidifying their political base and activating xenophobic nativist fears under the banner of fighting against the anti-liberal euphemism of 'political correctness'.

In March 2011, Congressman Peter King (R-NY) provided a new form of political legitimacy for this societal bias as he basically sanctioned the religious profiling of American Muslims based on the pernicious stereotypes that followers of Islam are uniquely more vulnerable to violent extremism. As the incoming chair of the House Committee on Homeland Security, Mr. King (who I have debated on MSNBC before) decided to hold a high-profile congressional hearing on "The Extent of Radicalization in the American Muslim Community and that Community's Response". Reminiscent of the shadow cast by the McCarthy witch-hunts of the 1950s, these high-profile congressional hearings now signaled the acceptability of Congress to investigate the protected First Amendment religious beliefs, practices and activities of a minority demographic group in America simply because of their faith affiliation.

In the past, Congressman Peter King has made numerous factually inaccurate and blatantly prejudicial assertions against Muslims in the last several years alone. Mr. King once went on-camera to say that "we have too many mosques in this country" and that "80-85% of American mosques" are led by extremists. Because of King's past statements on American Muslims, it became quite clear that the focus of these congressional hearings would clearly violate the spirit and core beliefs of our constitution; the presumption of innocence, the promise of fairness and equity afforded to all people, irrespective of one's race, nationality or religious belief. In the lead-up to the most high-profile congressional hearings of 2011, the spectacle of a Congressional hearing specifically targeting a religious minority like American Muslims had already generated serious concerns amongst political leaders, editorial boards and prominent media commentators around the country.

"Rep. King's intent seems clear: To cast suspicion upon all Muslim Americans and to stoke the fires of anti-Muslim prejudice and Islamophobia," wrote Congressman Michael (D-CA) in a February 2011 opinion editorial for the *San Francisco Chronicle*. Calling the congressional hearings a "sinister" ploy by Peter King, Congressman Honda (who also spent several years of his early childhood in a Japanese-American internment camp during World War II) continued to state that, "By framing his hearings as an investigation of the American Muslim community, the implication is that we should be suspicious of our Muslim neighbors, co-workers or classmates solely on the basis of their religion. This should be deeply troubling to Americans of all races and religions. An investigation specifically targeting a single religion implies, erroneously, a dangerous disloyalty, with one broad sweep of the discriminatory brush."[82]

Rabbi Marc Schneier, the president of the Foundation for Ethnic Understanding, was among some 500 people at a March 2011 rally in Times Square that was called to protest Mr. King's hearings. "To single out Muslim-Americans as the source of homegrown terrorism," he said, "and not examine all forms of violence motivated by extremist belief — that, my friends, is an injustice." Similarly, even national security experts like Richard Clarke- who was a well-known counter-terrorism 'czar' for both Presidents Bill Clinton and George W. Bush- once told the *Los Angeles Times* that, "To the extent that these hearings make

American Muslims feel that they are the object of fear-mongering, it will only serve Al Qaeda's ends."[83]

In a brilliant column for *The Washington Post* entitled "Peter King's Modern-Day Witch Hunt", my dear friend and Pulitzer Prize-winning columnist Eugene Robinson wrote that, "If [Rep.] King is looking for threats to our freedoms and values, a mirror would be the place to start."[84] Similarly, the editorial board at the *Philadelphia Inquirer* called the congressional hearings "Un-American" and columnist Bob Herbert of *The New York Times* wrote that, "To focus an investigative spotlight on an entire religious or ethnic community is a violation of everything America is supposed to stand for...But that does not seem to concern Mr. King" at all.[85]

The only law enforcement official to testify at the Peter King hearings was Los Angeles County Sheriff Lee Baca. Mr. Baca testified in opposition to King's premise- citing figures demonstrating that radical, extremist acts of crime are committed by non-Muslims as well- and that "7 of the past 10 known terrorist plots involving al-Qaeda have been foiled in part by information provided by Muslim Americans" themselves. Sheriff Baca also stated that his officers have "good, productive relationships with Muslim leaders" and citizens. To highlight this point further, a February 2011 joint report from Duke University and the University of North Carolina examined terrorism investigations since 9/11 and found that American Muslims provided useful tips that "helped arrest 48 of 120 Muslims suspected of plotting attacks" in the United States. Furthermore, the joint report also showed a drop in attempted or actual terrorist activity by American Muslims - 47 perpetrators and suspects in 2009 went down to 20 in 2010.

"This does not mean that there is no threat, but, when measured against ordinary violent crime, it is slight," once wrote Richard Cohen of *The Washington Post*. "In fact, the threat from non-Muslims is much greater, encompassing not only your run-of-the-mill murderers but about 20 domestic terrorist plots, including one in which a plane was flown into an IRS building" in Austin, Texas. Mr. Cohen continued to say that, "[Peter] King is setting a dangerous precedent. The government has no business examining any peaceful religious group because a handful of adherents have broken the law. If it did, it would be past time to look into the Roman Catholic Church, which clearly was - or maybe still is - concealing the sex crimes of priests and others."[86]

The Obama administration also echoed these same sentiments to the American Muslim community a few days before the King hearings were scheduled to begin on Capitol Hill. "The most effective voices against Al Qaeda's warped worldview and interpretation of Islam are other Muslims," deputy national security adviser Denis McDonough told a diverse interfaith audience at the All Dulles Area Muslim Society (ADAMS) in suburban Virginia the week prior to the Peter King hearings. Mr. McDonough perfectly summed up the nearly unanimous opposition to the 2011 Peter King congressional hearings on American Muslims perfectly when he simply said:

"In the United States of America, we don't practice guilt by association."[87]

From Islamophobia to the 'Golden Rule'

In a 1964 handwritten letter to his assistants back in Harlem, Malcolm X once conveyed his changed attitudes on performing his first *Hajj* pilgrimage and seeing people of all races from every corner of the globe congregate in the Islamic holy city of Mecca. Within that now-famous letter back to his family and friends back in New York, Brother Malcolm marveled at the colorless camaraderie which was clearly apparent and did not mince his words when he wrote that: "They were of all colors, from blue-eyed blondes to black-skinned Africans... We were all displaying a spirit of unity and brotherhood...I have never before seen sincere and true brotherhood practiced by all colors together, irrespective of their color."[88]

By shedding his own past militantly racist persona, Malcolm X thus began the immediate transformation into his post-racial (and truly final) persona- El-Hajj Malik El-Shabazz- during that life-altering 1964 Hajj trip to Mecca. Similarly, with neo-racist global beasts like Islamophobia and Anti-Semitism (and every other form of racial, religious or sectarian intolerance today) still hungrily on the prowl from the streets of Paris, Cleveland, Islamabad and Nairobi; it has now become of paramount importance to successfully destroy these racist cancers before they successfully destroy us all. For only when we jointly address and eliminate every outward manifestation of neo-racism in the world today can we truly continue towards our less-taken path of greater human enlightenment together.

Regardless of religious tradition, every single major religion in the world within the specter of human history has the essence of 'The Golden Rule' beating at the essential core of their respective hearts. Within Islam, the essence of the 'Golden Rule' is personified from the final sermon of the Prophet Muhammad when he told all believers that we as Muslims must always remember:

"Hurt no one so that no one may hurt you."[89]

Although concededly an impossibly daunting human undertaking, if we fail together in eradicating every form of racial and religious intolerance in existence today (including Islamophobia and Anti-Semitism, with absolutely zero exceptions); our entire human race will all one day probably be left scratching our heads pondering these famously haunting words of German Pastor Martin Niemöller:

> *"At first, they came for the communists and I did not speak out because I was not a communist... Then they came out for the socialists and I did not speak out because I was not a socialist... Then they came for the trade unionists and I did not speak out because I was not a trade unionist... Then they came for the Jews and I did not speak out because I was not a Jew... Then they came for me and there was no one left to speak out for me."*[90]

CHAPTER THREE: THE GHOSTS OF JOHN ASHCROFT PAST

"They who can give up essential liberty to obtain a little temporary safety, deserve neither liberty nor safety..."[1]

- Benjamin Franklin

In the first minutes, hours, days, weeks and months immediately following the September 11, 2001 terrorist attacks, then-United States Attorney General John Ashcroft (of the George W. Bush presidential administration) used his brand-spanking new expansive legal authorities (specifically under Section 412 of the now infamous USA PATRIOT Act)[2] to summarily 'round-up' and imprison over 1,200 Muslim, Arab and South Asian males[3] around the United States during that time period alone. The most disconcerting fact about these massive dragnets (or 'round-ups') was the fact that the Ashcroft Justice Department had initially refused to disclose the detainees' identities, give them access to lawyers or allow them to have any contact with their own families.

In addition to this indiscriminate immigrant legal dragnet affecting millions of people within America, several post-9/11 high-profile legal cases further stigmatized the American Muslim community within the court of global public opinion. In many of these high-profile legal cases, virtually all of the people involved were vilified mercilessly within the American media (and the greater court of public opinion) before ever having the constitutional privilege of actually appearing before a court of law. Thus, not surprisingly at all for many American Muslims, Arabs and South Asians after September 11, there was virtually no semblance of the 'presumption of innocence' legal concept within our own American justice system. To the contrary, millions of American Muslims, Arabs and South Asians still feel today that they are somehow 'guilty until proven innocent' within our own American legal system simply because of their religion, race and/or immigration status.

In addition to a holistic legal overview analysis of some major post-9/11 legal dragnets of the George W. Bush administration (led by former United States Attorney General John Ashcroft), this chapter shall also analyze certain major high-profile post-9/11 legal cases which made headlines around America and the rest of the greater world. The first high-profile legal case analyzed in this chapter will be that of U.S. Army Captain James Yee, who spent over seventy-six (76) days in solitary confinement, being labeled a 'spy' in many media circles—despite the fact that he was never convicted of any criminal offense. The second major case analyzed herein involves American attorney Brandon Mayfield, who was once falsely linked by the FBI to the infamous 3/11 Madrid train bombings of March 11, 2004. The third and fourth high-profile legal cases analyzed in this chapter will revolve around the Transportation Security Administration's (TSA) 'No-Fly' suspected terrorist 'watch-lists' and involve the high-profile cases of Swiss professor Dr. Tariq Ramadan (named in 2004 as one of *TIME* Magazine's Top 100 Innovators of the 21st Century)[4] and Yusuf Islam (the world-famous pop music artist formerly known as Cat Stevens). Each one of these post-9/11 legal cases provides a different insight into the ethno-religious profiling and egregious constitutional violations of civil liberties and legal rights that have been experienced by thousands of American Muslims, Arabs and South Asians since the tragic attacks of September 11, 2001.

Under American immigration law, the legal term 'absconder' is generally defined as an "alien who, though subject to... [deportation], has failed to surrender for removal or to otherwise comply with the order."[5] According to a January 2002 official memorandum sent to federal immigration and law enforcement officials, the Deputy Attorney General of the United States estimated that there were approximately 314,000 absconders[6] (or deportable illegal aliens) living in the United States at the time.[7] Out of these 314,000 total absconders living in the United States, only about 6,000 of them[8] (less than 2 percent of the total) originated from either Muslim and/or Arab countries. Nonetheless, although over ninety (90) percent of absconders in the United States are from Latin American countries, after September 11, 2001, the Justice Department began selectively targeting absconders mainly from predominantly Muslim and Arab countries. However, this selective legal targeting of Muslims and Arabs yielded almost no criminal convictions whatsoever. By the end of May 2002, the Justice Department admitted that out of 314,000 absconders, only 585 had been located. More embarrassingly; <u>not a single terrorist</u> had been apprehended in that mass roundup during that time period.[9]

Although there is no doubt that all Americans were affected by the tragic attacks of September 11, 2001, there can also be little empirical debate about the fact that young Muslim and Arab males (mainly between the ages of 18 and 40) have been the most disparately impacted demographic group of the legal dragnets which were conducted by the Justice Department in our ongoing (and seemingly perpetual) 'War on Terror' since 9/11. In addition to the law enforcement dragnets conducted by the Justice Department since 9/11, there have also been major pieces of congressional legislation (which have since become law) that have stirred great public debate within all American political circles on how to best balance our rightful national security interests while still safeguarding the civil liberties guaranteed to every American by our beloved constitution.

The Secret Roundup: "Calling All Brown Men..."

Glenn A. Fine, then-Inspector General for the U.S. Department of Justice (and former 10th round draft pick of the San Antonio Spurs in the 1979 NBA Draft),[10] once officially reported that <u>at least</u> 1,200 men from predominantly Muslim and Arab countries were detained by law enforcement officials nationwide within the first two (2) months alone after September 11, 2001.[11] Surprisingly, the Inspector General also ultimately conceded within this official report that a senior officer in the Office of Public Affairs stopped reporting the total number of detainees after 1,200 because the **"statistics became too confusing."**[12] In August 2002, Human Rights Watch (HRW) released a 95-page report entitled *Presumption of Guilt* which documented cases of prolonged detention without any charge, denial of access to bond release, interference with detainees' rights to legal counsel and unduly harsh conditions of confinement for the over 1,200 detainees of Muslim, Arab and/or South Asian descents.[13] Human Rights Watch's findings were later confirmed by Inspector General Fine's report, which also identified a pattern of "physical and verbal abuse" by correctional staff at the Metropolitan Detention Center (MDC) in Brooklyn, New York.[14]

In terms of demographics, the post-September 11 detainees comprised citizens from more than twenty (20) countries. The largest number of detainees- 254 (or 33 percent) -were from Pakistan, more than double the number of any other country.[15]The second largest number (111) was from Egypt and there were also substantial numbers of detainees from Jordan, Turkey, Yemen and India.[16]The overall ages of the detainees varied, but by far the greatest number, 479 (or 63 percent), were between the ages of 26 and 40.[17]

The overall fruits of these legally-suspect and egregiously over-reaching legal dragnets was nicely summed up by American constitutional law expert and Georgetown University Law Center Professor David Cole who said that, "Thousands were detained in this blind search for terrorists without any real evidence of terrorism, and ultimately without netting virtually any terrorists of any kind."[18]

The 'List of 5,000', NSEERS ('Special Registration') and US-VISIT Programs

On November 9, 2001, Attorney General John Ashcroft directed the FBI and other federal law enforcement officials to seek out and interview at least 5,000 men between the ages of 18 and 33 who had legally entered into the United States on non-immigrant visas in the past two years before 2001 and who came from specific countries linked by the government to 'terrorism'.[19] This 'List of 5,000' individuals was comprised solely on the basis of national origin; for even the Justice Department acknowledged at the time that it had no basis for believing that any of these men had any knowledge relevant to any criminal terrorism investigation.[20] Subsequently, the FBI and other law enforcement officials then began arbitrarily visiting American mosques, Islamic schools and community centers to conduct 'interviews' with these 5,000 Muslim and Arab men (all of whom were again lawfully present within the United States). According to the American Civil Liberties Union (ACLU), although these were allegedly 'voluntary' interviews, the ACLU noted at the time that "the interviews were highly coercive and few [people] felt free to refuse."[21]

In March 2002, the Justice Department announced another round of national interviews. During this new round of interviews, they were targeting an additional 3,000 Arab, Muslim and South Asian men who again were legally residing in the U.S. as students, businessmen or visitors.[22] This time, however, even many American law enforcement officials expressed concern over the mistrust that these legal fishing expeditions were causing within their respective immigrant communities around the United States. Most Americans know that the legal concept of 'community policing' has always been a hallmark of American law enforcement; which is usually exemplified by local community members reporting crimes within their respective communities to their local law enforcement officials. Many key law enforcement officials on the ground anticipated major problems that the implementation of these new federal legal policies specifically targeting immigrant populations would create on their own local communities and their overall chilling effect on 'community policing' as a whole within their local respective jurisdictions in major American cities around our country. For example, in response to post-9/11 federal law enforcement initiatives implemented by the Ashcroft Justice Department, Denver Chief of Police Gerald Whitman once said that, "Communication is big...and an underpinning of that is trust...If a victim thinks that they're going to be a suspect in an immigration violation, they're not going to call us, and that's just going to separate us even further."[23]

In June 2002, Attorney General John Ashcroft instituted the **N**ational **S**ecurity **E**ntry **E**xit **R**egistration **S**ystem, more commonly referred to as **NSEERS**.[24] One of the most ambiguous and publicly debated aspects of NSEERS was known as 'Special Registration'. Special Registration required all male nationals over the age of 14 from twenty-five (25) different countries to report to the federal government to be registered and fingerprinted or face immediate deportation. With the sole exception of North Korea, every single one of the twenty-five (25) countries[25] on the Special Registration bulletin was either a Muslim or Arab nation.[26] The ACLU denounced the Special Registration plan as "a thinly veiled effort to trigger massive and discriminatory deportations of certain immigrants."[27]

Not long thereafter, in December 2002, nearly 700 men and boys from Iran, Iraq, Libya, Sudan and Syria were arrested in Southern California by federal immigration authorities after they had voluntarily complied with the NSEERS 'call-in' program. Some of these nearly 700 people were college students who were only 'guilty' of not attending enough classes (or credit hours) for a given semester at their local university. Other people caught up in the massive arrests were just simply awaiting the outcome of their valid green card applications.

In response, several high-profile national American civil rights organizations led by the Center for Constitutional Rights (CCR) and several Muslim and Arab-American organizations filed a class action lawsuit against Attorney General John Ashcroft on behalf of the hundreds of men and boys who had been unfairly arrested in Southern California in violation of their Fourth and Fifth Amendments rights.[28]

In that one year alone, the Special Registration program registered 83,310 foreign nationals. Out of these 83,310 people, the NSEERS program placed 13,740 (nearly 20 percent of those registered) into immediate deportation proceedings. Ironically enough, out of these 13,740 total deportations, a grand total of zero of these individuals was ever convicted of a terrorism crime.[29] In January 2004, the Department of Homeland Security (DHS) officially suspended a portion of the Special Registration (NSEERS) program and subsequently launched the 'U.S. Visitor and Immigrant Status Indicator Technology' or US-VISIT program.[30] Many American advocacy groups, communities and individuals who had roundly criticized Special Registration (NSEERS) for its blatantly prejudicial overall design and shoddy legal implementation foresaw similar potential problems with the implementation of the US-VISIT program as well.

"Contrary to assertions by the Homeland Security Department, the US-VISIT program is an addition to—not a substitute for—the notorious Special Registration (NSEERS) program that singled out Arab and Muslim men because of their national origin and that continues to subject them to special and confusing requirements," said Timothy Edgar, former legislative counsel for the American Civil Liberties Union (ACLU)[31] in January 2004. "Only one part of the special registration program—the part that requires re-registration at local immigration offices—was suspended last year. But, Arab and Muslim men are still subject to different requirements than other visitors,"[32] said Mr. Edgar, who would eventually go onto become a civil liberties protection officer at the Office of the Director of National Intelligence (DNI)[33] in Washington DC.

The USA PATRIOT Act of 2001 (H.R. 3162)

The editors of *Esquire* magazine once wrote that, "If there is one thing that always comes out of a terrible tragedy, it is really dumb legislation."[34] On

October 25, 2001, a mere 45 days after the attacks of September 11, 2001, Congress passed with virtually no debate, House Resolution 3162 entitled the, "**U**niting and **S**trengthening **A**merica by **P**roviding **A**ppropriate **T**ools **R**equired to **I**ntercept and **O**bstruct **T**errorism Act"[35], which has come to be ominously (and infamously) known around the world simply as **USA PATRIOT**. The text of USA PATRIOT- at over 340 pages long- amended over fifty (50) current federal statutes and was passed in the Senate by an astonishing vote of 98-1; with the lone (and brave) dissenting vote being then-Democratic Senator Russell Feingold of Wisconsin.[36] At the time of the October 2001 Senate vote on USA PATRIOT, even staunchly and faithfully liberal United States Senators like (the late) Ted Kennedy and (the late) Paul Wellstone ultimately voted in favor the controversial piece of congressional legislation.[37]

Many provisions of USA PATRIOT opened up a new chapter in our American debate on the application of constitutionally-suspect laws during a time of war. Although not all entire 340 pages of USA PATRIOT were considered to be legally controversial, there were major sections of the federal law which tremendously concerned those Americans who value the democratic concepts of due process, free speech and other fundamentally-protected rights guaranteed to every one of us by our beloved United States Constitution. For example, Sections 411 and 802 of USA PATRIOT broadly expanded the official definition of "domestic terrorism", so that university or college student groups who engage in certain types of legal and peaceful protests could very well find themselves labeled as 'domestic terrorists'.

For example, the Sheriff of Hennepin County, Minnesota once declared that the student groups 'Anti-Racist Action', 'Students Against War' and 'Arise' were potential "domestic terrorist" threats[38] based on newly granted powers to him under USA PATRIOT. Similarly, under Sections 215 and 505 of USA PATRIOT, law enforcement officials were given broad access to any type of record—sales, library, financial, medical, etc.—without having to show <u>any</u> probable cause of a criminal act. Furthermore, USA PATRIOT also forbids the holders of this information, such as university librarians and college registrars, from disclosing that they have even provided any such records of their students and/or patrons to federal law enforcement officials.

For example, a University of Illinois survey of American public libraries once found that at least 545 libraries had been asked for patron records by federal law enforcement officials in the one year following 9/11 alone. Furthermore, according to the American Association of Collegiate Registrars and Admissions Officers, approximately 200 colleges and universities around the country had turned over student records and information to the FBI, INS and other law enforcement agencies[39] since the inception of the USA PATRIOT Act. Furthermore, the 'sneak-and-peak' provision of USA PATRIOT (Section 213) allowed law enforcement agencies to conduct secret searches of anyone's home or apartment without a warrant or even notification to the home owner in question. This meant that investigators can potentially enter anyone's place of residence, take pictures, download computer files and seize items without informing them of the search until days, weeks or even months later.[40]

In the first three years alone since its initial inception in October 2001, the debate over privacy and constitutional issues raised by USA PATRIOT had motivated more than 4 American states and over 357 major cities (representing over 55 million Americans in 44 states)[41] to pass official resolutions publicly condemning portions of USA PATRIOT as being unconstitutional within their respective local, city and/or state legislatures. In addition to resolutions passed in more than 200 smaller cities, the list of successful anti-USA PATRIOT Act resolutions included those passed in large American metropolitan cities like New York[42], Los Angeles, Chicago, Detroit, St. Louis and Philadelphia.[43] Additionally, the states of Hawaii, Alaska, Maine and Vermont had passed statewide resolutions condemning portions of USA PATRIOT as being unconstitutional and infringing on the individual civil rights of Americans.

Privacy and civil rights advocates, both Democratic and Republican, have also called for greater congressional oversight on extensions or additions to USA PATRIOT over the years. In addition to state and local governments, several bipartisan national American organizations had also adopted similar pro-civil liberties resolutions condemning USA PATRIOT. Among these major American organizations included the National League of Cities (NLC), American Conservative Union (ACU), the American Library Association (ALA), the Japanese American Citizens League (JACL), National Association for the Advancement of Colored People (NAACP), the Organization of Chinese Americans (OCA) and Veterans for Peace.[44]

Even traditionally conservative voices like former Republican Speaker of the House Newt Gingrich had publicly voiced criticism of USA PATRIOT at the time. Douglas Dow, professor of government at the University of Texas once perfectly summarized the national American grassroots movement in opposition to USA PATRIOT when he once said that, "It is necessary for us to secure our values in those institutions closest to home and to rely on ourselves and our local officers, rather than waiting for the courts or Congress to defend minorities from racial targeting, or protect the privacy of our personal records."[45]

The Case of U.S. Army Chaplain James 'Yusuf' Yee

Former United States Army Captain (and Muslim chaplain) James Yee was born in Springfield, New Jersey in 1968 to Chinese-American parents and graduated as a commissioned Army officer from West Point Academy in 1990. In 1991, Captain James Yee converted to Islam and adopted the name 'Yusuf', which is the Arabic version of the name 'Joseph'[46]. Captain James Yee left active military service in 1993, joining the United States Army Reserves so that he could go to Syria to learn Islam and Arabic to prepare to become one of the U.S. Army's first Muslim chaplains.[47] It was during this visit to Damascus that he ultimately met and married his wife, Huda.[48] When he returned home to the United States, Captain James Yee then became a Muslim army chaplain with the 29th Signal Battalion at Fort Lewis, Washington and was actually stationed there during the tragic terrorist attacks of September 11, 2001.

In November 2002, Captain James Yee was then re-assigned to become an army chaplain at Guantanamo Bay, Cuba; where would he minister to Muslim detainees and would teach his Army superiors about Islam and pertinent issues relating to the 660 detainees that were once held at Camp X-Ray in Guantanamo Bay.[49] During their time stationed there, Captain Yee and other Muslim workers used a vacant office in the prison compound for their daily prayers and meals.

On September 10, 2003, Captain James Yee arrived at the Jacksonville (FL) Naval Air Station on leave for a one-week vacation. According to published reports, investigators at Guantanamo Bay had "tipped off" customs agents at the airport that Captain Yee was possibly carrying classified materials. A customs agent would later testify at a future Article 32 military investigation hearing[50] that he had been "tipped" off to stop Captain Yee and that he then subsequently confiscated "suspicious" documents from him.[51] At the time, federal agents said that the Army captain was found in possession of sketches of the military prison at Guantanamo Bay and lists naming U.S. interrogators and imprisoned Taliban/

Al-Qaeda fighters jailed within Guantanamo Bay.[52] After being searched and found in possession of these classified documents, Captain James Yee was then arrested.

Thus, began Captain James Yee's seventy-six (76) day imprisonment;[53] the vast majority of which would be shockingly spent in solitary confinement without him ever being convicted of any crime. During his confinement hearing on September 12, 2003, a Navy prosecutor argued that Yee should be held under maximum-security conditions since he was a "flight risk". This determination was made despite the fact that Captain Yee was a commissioned U.S. Army officer (and West Point graduate) with no history of ever fleeing a subpoena. According to official records, on September 16, 2003, Captain James Yee was subjected to sensory-deprivation treatment and subsequently driven to Charleston, South Carolina. Shackled, blindfolded and deafened by ear covers, he was then transported to the Navy brig and given the same treatment used on Camp X-Ray prisoners being flown to Guantanamo Bay.

Court papers from the initial confinement hearing reported that Captain Yee was being charged with espionage, spying, aiding the enemy, mutiny or sedition, and disobeying an order. At the time, some media reports were already speculating that Captain Yee could face the death penalty, if convicted.[54] Surprisingly, details of Captain Yee's arrest appeared in the American media before he was ever charged with a crime within any court of law. Subsequently, a September 20, 2003 *Washington Times* newspaper article[55] would proudly proclaim that **"Islamic Chaplain is charged as spy"** and proceeded to lay out details about the unsubstantiated charges against Captain Yee. Such media reports before any actual legal charges were levied against Captain Yee led many Americans to believe that there had been obvious leaks by government officials to certain American media outlets.[56]

Captain James Yee was then finally brought to trial on October 10, 2003. Despite the severity of the initial accusations originally levied against Captain Yee, he was actually only indicted on two much lesser charges; counts of 'failing to obey orders'.[57] The Department of Defense's Southern Command (which oversees Guantanamo Bay) reported that Captain Yee was charged with "taking classified material to his home and wrongfully transporting classified material without the proper security containers or covers."[58] Air Force Master Sergeant Jose Ruiz, a spokesman for the Southern Command, reported that the Army "had sufficient evidence that [Captain Yee] violated the procedures in place for classified material given what he had in his possession."[59] After his trial, Captain Yee's security status would be reduced to a lower security clearance.[60]

Despite being a commissioned U.S. Army officer and without ever being convicted of any criminal act, Captain James Yee was still imprisoned under maximum security conditions in 23-hour solitary confinement for an astonishing grand total of seventy-six (76) calendar days.[61] According to his army-appointed civilian lawyer, American military law expert Eugene Fidell, Captain Yee was let out of solitary confinement for only one (1) hour a day for exercise which he had to perform wearing leg-iron shackles and handcuffs.[62] Additionally, lower-ranked military personnel at the Navy brig in Charleston refused to recognize Captain Yee's status as a commissioned officer, refused to salute him and required him to identify himself as an E-1; the lowest enlisted military rank.[63]

His attorney Eugene Fidell also reported that brig personnel were "needlessly interfering with his daily prayers and religious practices" by refusing to provide him with a prayer rug, a liturgical calendar or telling him the time of day or direction of Mecca.[64] "They let him languish in solitary confinement for 76 days. That's outrageous. When he saw his legal counsel, he was in leg irons," said John Fugh, a retired Army judge advocate general in a May 2004 *USA TODAY* newspaper article about Captain James Yee's ordeal.

"We don't treat commissioned officers that way," former Major General John Fugh once told USA TODAY. "I don't care what they did."[65]

Captain James Yusuf Yee was finally released from prison on November 25, 2003 after two and a half months of total confinement. Instead of issuing an official apology for unjustly imprisoning a commissioned U.S. Army officer for over seventy-six (76) days in solitary confinement; the Army would now somehow find it prudent to absurdly charge Captain Yee with 'adultery' and 'storing pornography' on a government-issued computer.[66] According to media reports, the alleged 'adultery' was said to have occurred with Navy Lt. Karyn Wallace[67] between July and September 2003 and the 'pornography' was alleged to have been stored on his government-issued computer at Guantanamo Bay.

Captain Yee would now be scheduled to face an Article 32 hearing; the military legal equivalent of a grand jury or preliminary hearing.[68] Meanwhile, a U.S. Southern Command spokesman said the military would graciously "allow" Captain Yee to return as a chaplain to the base at Fort Benning, Georgia;

noting that he would not be allowed to have further contact with any prisoners at Guantanamo Bay.[69] The Article 32 hearing on the new charges against Captain James Yee was postponed a total of six (6) times before finally being cancelled altogether.[70] The first postponement occurred on December 2, 2003 when the hearing was postponed after military officials realized they had "mishandled classified information".

These Army officials seemed to have committed the same "mishandling" of classified information which had initially been one of the initial charges in Captain Yee's litany of 'treasonous' charges. Apparently, officials accidentally released pages from Yee's diary to his defense attorneys. The prosecution even admitted that it was uncertain if Captain Yee had even actually possessed any 'classified materials' when he left Guantanamo Bay in September 2002.[71] Nonetheless, there would be four more subsequent court postponements for Captain James Yee until March 19, 2004.

Finally, on March 19, 2004, all criminal charges against Captain James Yee, including failure to obey orders and the mishandling of classified information, were completely dropped. However, the Army still would not admit Captain Yee's innocence despite the fact that they had just dropped every single criminal charge against him. At the time, General Geoffrey Miller's reasoning for dismissing all criminal charges was not because Captain James Yee was innocent, but was (conveniently) due to the fact that "national security concerns...would arise from the release of the evidence."[72]

Even though Captain James Yee had been completely exonerated of any criminal misconduct and had now been transferred to a new posting at Fort Meade, Maryland;[73] his personal ordeal was unfortunately far from over. Although not a criminal offense within our American legal system, 'adultery' is actually punishable under the Uniform Code of Military Justice (UCMJ); which is the legal standard for American soldiers within our United States Armed Forces. At a non-criminal administrative hearing on March 22, 2004, Captain Yee was given a reprimand for the adultery and pornography charges.[74] Although he was never convicted of any crime and would now be a free man, Captain James Yee and his civilian attorney, Eugene Fidell, nonetheless reiterated his complete innocence and even appealed this military reprimand for the alleged 'adultery' and 'pornography' ridiculous charges.

On April 14, 2004, General James T. Hill, head of the Southern Command at the time, granted Captain James Yee's appeal, dropping all of these remaining reprimands from Captain Yee's official record.[75] General Hill stated that he granted Captain Yee's appeal because of the "extensive media attention given.... [to] Chaplain Yee's personal misconduct...While I believe that Chaplain Yee's misconduct was wrong," General Hill once said, "I do not believe, given the extreme notoriety of his case in the news media, that further stigmatizing Chaplain Yee would serve a just and fair purpose."[76]

Cleared of all criminal and military charges against him, Captain James Yee finally returned to being a U.S. Muslim Army chaplain at his home base of Fort Lewis, Washington in early May 2004. He was, however, placed under a strict 'gag order' not to wear his uniform in public when making public comments about his case and was told that he should be careful when speaking publicly so as to not to undermine military "loyalty, discipline or unit morale."[77] Throughout Captain Yee's case, numerous high-profile American critics of the Army, including several members of Congress and former military prosecutors and judges, had been demanding further examination of his case. Pointing to media leaks, lack of evidence, unjust confinement and unusual courtroom procedures, critics of the Army often felt that Captain James Yee was treated unfairly and was being targeted simply because of his faith as an American Muslim.

Most observers found it odd that despite the severity of the initial 'espionage' charges for which Captain Yee was first arrested- charges again for which he could have been given the death penalty- Captain James Yee ultimately received only a simple reprimand for 'adultery'.

Eventually, even that reprimand was ultimately dropped.

Retired Coast Guard Judge Kevin Barry would be one of the first military officials to speak out publicly against the legal injustices against Captain James Yee. Judge Kevin Barry once said about the James Yee case that, "This is a case that's so obviously wrong that [even] people who don't know military law are, if not outraged, then very concerned about what happened." Speaking further about the dismissal of charges against Captain Yee, Judge Barry reiterated again, "There apparently was no evidence. If they had the goods, they would have prosecuted."[78] Certain patterns also emerge when Captain Yee's case is compared with other terrorism-related cases, noted Bob Barr, a former Republican congressman from Georgia. Former Congressman Barr once noted that, "What we're seeing in Guantanamo, and perhaps in this case [of Captain James Yee], is what happens when you've removed any judicial oversight over what the government is doing."[79]

Mr. Eugene Fidell- Captain James Yee's civilian attorney and one of the nation's leading military law experts in America- has always consistently (and courageously) spoken out against major discrepancies in the James Yee case and has often called upon the Army to apologize for their numerous mistakes. Mr. Fidell once said about the lack of evidence against his client: "When you see a gulf between the shrill charges and this ant-hill of evidence...you have to wonder." He also further noted that the prosecutors never showed the defense any evidence of the classified materials Captain Yee was suspected of carrying. "The government has never produced the evidence that it believes was classified," said Mr. Fidell.

"So I am somewhat at a loss...We were playing Hamlet without Hamlet here."[80]

In finally realizing the blatant injustice committed against Captain James 'Yusuf' Yee, four United States Congressmen officially called for a formal investigation into the Army's unjust treatment of Chaplain James Yee. Representatives Michael Honda (D-CA), House Armed Services Committee Ranking Member Rep. Ike Skelton (D-MO), House Armed Services Total Force Subcommittee Ranking Member Rep. Vic Snyder (D-AR) and Armed Services Committee member Rep. Adam Smith (D-WA); who also happened to be Captain Yee's own personal congressman, once wrote a May 2004 letter to Joseph Schmitz, then-Inspector General of the Department of Defense, demanding an immediate investigation into the criminal probe and court martial hearings against Captain Yee. The following are excerpts from the joint congressional letter to the Department of Defense from the four (4) congressmen:

> ***"We write to formally request that your office investigate the U.S. Army's criminal probe and court martial of Army Chaplain, Captain James Yee. The Army's decision to drop all charges against Captain Yee raises important questions about the strength and legitimacy of initial***

> ***assertions by Army officials that Captain Yee had engaged in espionage and treasonous conduct at Guantanamo Bay, Cuba..."***[81]
>
> ***"Press reports alleged that while confined, Captain Yee, a commissioned officer of the United States Army, was not afforded the military courtesies commiserate with his rank and that he was unduly targeted because of his religious affiliation with Islam. Given the unusual facts of this case, it is critical to determine whether Captain Yee was appropriately investigated, arrested and charged for criminal conduct by the U.S. Army..."***[82]

Additionally, on the Senate side of Congress, both Senators Carl Levin (D-MI) and the late Edward Kennedy (D-MA) separately demanded that then-Secretary of Defense Donald Rumsfeld begin an official investigation into the Captain James Yee legal debacle as well.[83] In response to this official request by these prominent Congressmen and Senators, the Inspector General of the Defense Department agreed in August 2004 to investigate the case. At the time, Defense Department Assistant Inspector General John Crane said that the investigation would be launched in the Fall of 2004 and could not be started sooner because of "other ongoing and urgent matters."[84]

Eugene Fidell commented that the Inspector General's investigation was long overdue. He had hoped that the probe would eventually lead to an official apology, something that Captain Yee had been demanding for months. Mr. Fidell rightfully noted that congressional intercession should not be required for the Army to finally apologize to Captain James Yee for its blatant mistakes and the undue hardships imposed upon him and his family. "The more tooth-pulling involved, it seems to me...the less the apology," once said Mr. Fidell regarding the official government investigation.[85]

Understandably, these trials and tribulations had a profound impact on Captain James Yee and the rest of his family. In August 2004, Captain James 'Yusuf' Yee tendered his official resignation to his Army superiors, asking to be discharged effective January 7, 2005. A portion of Captain Yee's letter at the time cited several reasons for leaving the Army. Some relevant excerpts from his letter are as follows:

> ***"In 2003, I was unfairly accused of grave offenses under the Uniform Code of Military Justice and unjustifiably placed in solitary confinement for 76 days. Those unfounded allegations – which were leaked to the media – irreparably injured my personal and professional reputation and destroyed my prospects for a career in the United States Army..."***[86]

> ***"The only formal punishment I received (on matters having nothing to do with national security) was overturned, but at the same time official statements again unfairly tarnished my reputation..."***

"Because of the gag order," continued Captain James Yee in his resignation letter, "My ability to defend myself against this pattern of unfairness has been impeded by official correspondence, the clear purpose of which is to chill the exercise of my right to free speech." Furthermore, he also wrote that he had waited for months for a government apology, "but none has been forthcoming. I have been unable even to obtain my personal effects from Guantanamo Bay, despite repeated requests. In the circumstances, I have no alternative but to tender my resignation."[87] After his harrowing legal ordeal and honorably completing his tenure with the United States Army, Captain James 'Yusuf' Yee was once again finally a free man and said that he hoped to one day complete his master's degree in international relations and returned with his family to their home state of Washington.

The Case of Brandon Mayfield and the 3/11 Madrid Train Bombings

On March 11, 2004, over ten (10) different bombs exploded on four (4) commuter trains in Madrid, Spain. According to media reports, the official death toll exceeded 190 people (with at least 1,800 people being injured) in the now-infamous 3/11 Madrid train bombings.[88] A partial fingerprint found shortly thereafter on a bag containing detonators was matched by FBI analysts and the Justice Department subsequently proclaimed the match to be a "100% identification"[89] of American lawyer Brandon Mayfield;[90] who was then arrested and jailed as a 'material witness' in the 3/11 Madrid bombings.[91]

Two weeks later, as the American lawyer Brandon Mayfield languished in prison, Spanish federal law enforcement authorities confirmed their previous suspicions that the fingerprint did not actually belong to Mr. Mayfield. After over two weeks in jail and hundreds of media stories already labeling him a potential 'terrorist', he was finally released with a rare official apology from the FBI; who claimed that errors in fingerprint analysis were the sole cause for the catastrophic legal mistake of arresting American attorney Brandon Mayfield for the 3/11 Madrid train bombings.[92] After his harrowing ordeal, Brandon Mayfield once spoke quite candidly about his arrest:

"I am a Muslim, an American, and an ex-officer of the U.S. military. I believe I was singled out and discriminated against... [for simply being] a Muslim."[93]

Before the beginning of this ordeal, Mr. Brandon Mayfield was a 40-year old licensed American attorney who lived with his wife Mona and their three children in a suburb of Portland, Oregon. After graduating from high school, he joined active duty in the United States Army and also spent time serving in the U.S. Army Reserves.[94] After an honorable discharge from the Army, he served in the ROTC and was eventually commissioned as a Second Lieutenant. Mr. Mayfield then returned to active duty service as an Air Defense Artillery Officer and was later honorably discharged due to a shoulder injury.[95] After completing law school and passing the Oregon State Bar Examination, Brandon Mayfield began to work as a family lawyer in Oregon.[96] Mr. Mayfield eventually became a Muslim in the late 1980s after he had married his wife Mona Mayfield, an Egyptian-American. Thus, he also became a regular attendee of Friday prayers at a local mosque in their Portland suburb of Beaverton, Oregon.[97]

According to the affidavit issued by FBI Special Agent Richard K. Werder requesting Mr. Brandon Mayfield's arrest after the 3/11 Madrid bombings, the Spanish National Police (SNP) sent the FBI several digital photographic images of fingerprints found during the investigation of the Madrid train bombings. Latent Finger Print (LFP) #17, found on a plastic bag containing detonators believed to be used in the Madrid bombings, was then run through the Automated Fingerprint Identification System (AFIS)[98] here in the United States.

According to the AFIS results, Brandon Mayfield was one of more than twelve (12) possible persons who eventually emerged as a "potential match" for Latent Finger Print #17.[99] After being identified at fifteen points and after a confirming second opinion, American fingerprint analysis experts determined that LFP #17 was indeed "a 100% identification"[100] of Brandon Mayfield. Two senior American law enforcement officials once told the Associated Press (AP) that Mr. Mayfield and his home had already been under FBI surveillance for several weeks prior to his arrest; due mainly to the fingerprint analysis[101] results of LFP #17.

FBI Agent Richard Werder's affidavit also stated that surveillance agents observed Mr. Mayfield drive to his regular mosque on several occasions beginning on March 21, 2004. This did not go unnoticed by the Mayfield family, who felt that their house had been previously searched. Upon seeing the surveillance agents, even nearby neighbors of the Mayfield's also questioned the surveillance officers about why they were in their residential neighborhood in their Portland suburb[102] at the time.

One would hope that before arresting and linking an American citizen (and licensed attorney-at-law) for links to a major international terrorist attack, the FBI would have investigated all other potential leads and again fully scientifically verified the fingerprint 'match' before rushing to judgment and informing the media of a 'terrorist' arrest. However, despite the fact that Spanish law enforcement officials continued to remain doubtful about the fingerprint match to Brandon Mayfield; nonetheless, the American Muslim lawyer from Oregon was quickly arrested anyway. On March 20, 2004, the FBI analyzed the partial fingerprint sent from Spain and concluded that it did indeed belong to Brandon Mayfield. At the time, notwithstanding the fact that a Scotland Yard fingerprint expert found any claim of a fingerprint match to be "horrendous,"[103] part of the other evidence used to detain Mr. Mayfield for over two weeks were "miscellaneous Spanish documents" that the FBI had found inside of his home.

The absurdity of the Justice Department's case was quickly revealed when *The New York Times* reported that these miscellaneous "Spanish documents" were later identified as nothing more than his children's Spanish homework.[104] Unfortunately, since the story had already been leaked to the media and many major American news outlets were now already carrying the breaking story of the "American connection"[105] to the Madrid bombings; the damage to Mr. Mayfield and the American Muslim community had already been done yet again.

Less than a month later, Spanish forensic experts officially informed the FBI of their doubts on the fingerprint match and the two groups met in Madrid on April 21, 2004. The affidavit of FBI Agent Werder had this recollection of that meeting with Spanish officials: "Before the meeting, SNP [Spanish National Police] personnel indicated that their examination of LFP#17 was preliminary and that a final determination had not been rendered. The SNP also indicated that they had not gone into the level three characteristics [...] utilized by the FBI when making their initial comparison. At the conclusion of the meeting it was believed that the SNP felt satisfied with the FBI Laboratory's identification of LFP #17..."

However, Spanish forensic experts and law enforcement officials at the joint meeting had quite a different take on the same exact meeting with their FBI counterparts. According to Spanish law enforcement officials on the case, it seemed that the Spanish officials had little success in convincing their FBI counterparts of their 'mistake' and commented on the FBI's unwillingness to accept this major mistake regarding Latent Finger Print #17.

"The Spanish officers told them with all the affection in the world that it wasn't him [Brandon Mayfield]," said one Spanish police official during a June 2004 interview for *The New York Times*. "We never wanted to simply come out and say the F.B.I. made a mistake. We tried to be diplomatic, not to make them look bad."[106] Furthermore, the head of the Spanish National Police (SNP) fingerprint unit, Pedro Lledo, noted that in the Brandon Mayfield case, the FBI "had a justification for everything...But I just couldn't see it."[107] A commissioner of the SNP's science division, Carlos Corrales further stated quite clearly that, "It seemed as though they had something against him and they wanted to involve us."[108]

The Werder FBI affidavit did also concededly highlight the fact that Mr. Mayfield had no record of international travel or any border crossing.[109] Even further, Mr. Mayfield's American passport had been expired for almost an entire year before the 3/11 Madrid attacks and he had never filed for its renewal; thus making it virtually impossible for an American lawyer named Brandon Mayfield to even travel internationally to Madrid, Spain. Although some federal officials claimed that Brandon Mayfield may have traveled under a false or fictitious name, even FBI Agent Richard Werder ultimately conceded within his official affidavit that no known aliases for Brandon Mayfield could ever be found[110] by the FBI or any other American federal law enforcement agencies.

In his affidavit, Agent Werder nonetheless requested Brandon Mayfield's arrest because "based upon the likelihood of false travel documents in existence, and the serious nature of the potential charges, Mayfield may attempt to flee the country if served with a subpoena to appear before the federal grand jury..."[111] This claim was made notwithstanding the fact that Agent Werder had admitted himself that Mr. Mayfield had never used any aliases nor had ever left the United States since his American passport was expired. Nonetheless, Agent Werder asked for Mr. Mayfield's arrest and went even further by requesting that the Court issue a 'seal' on the affidavit, thereby making further unavailable to the public any of the 'evidence' (like his children's spooky Spanish homework) allegedly linking Brandon Mayfield to the tragic 3/11 Madrid terrorist attacks.

On May 24, 2004, after noisy public outrage and scathing criticism from dozens of newspaper editorial boards around America, the FBI finally issued an official (and extremely rare) one-page public apology to Mr. Mayfield after his complete exoneration. In its one-page press release apology, the FBI blamed their monumental error simply on the "substandard image quality"[112] of the fingerprints involved in identifying Mr. Mayfield. The vast majority of the FBI's press release dealt with the technical and scientific fingerprint methodological analyses used in the case. Only in the last line of the press release does it clearly state:

"The FBI apologizes to Mr. Mayfield and his family for the hardships that this matter has caused."[113]

Like many Americans, *The New York Times* believed that this 'apology' was insufficient and proclaimed that "The Justice Department and the Federal Bureau of Investigation ought to hang their heads in shame" over the case of Brandon Mayfield.[114] Mr. Mayfield summed up his own ordeal in a written statement at the time stating that, "The government's handling of this case has been prejudicial and discriminatory in the extreme. Upon initially being arrested, I was informed by the arresting officers that the media was close behind. Within minutes of my arrest, the allegations of my involvement in the Madrid bombing were being disseminated through the media. Notwithstanding the judge's gag order, the government put out its theory and its facts while we were prevented from saying anything."

"The whole thing was unbelievable," said William Mayfield, Brandon's father.[115] "It was [simply] a witch hunt."

The *Washington Post* further reiterated these sentiments by stating that "an apology is not enough"[116] and roundly criticized the Justice Department for their unjust treatment of Mr. Mayfield and their continued misuse of the Material Witness Statute.[117] Many legal critics of the Justice Department's tactics and procedures in the Mayfield case (and other post-9/11 cases) repeatedly point to the Justice Department's continuing misuse of the 'Material Witness Statute',[118] which allows the government to arrest and hold 'material witnesses' who have information essential to a case but are considered to be a "flight risk"[119].

Under the current American federal statute, these 'material witnesses'- many of whom are never charged or convicted of any crime- can be held secretly and indefinitely, without any access to legal counsel. The Material Witness Statute has become an unfortunate legal technique (and loophole) that has been used after September 11, 2001 to detain many 'terrorism suspects' for long periods of time without any knowledge of the charges against them or any access to their lawyers. As in the case of Brandon Mayfield, when a person is summarily detained pursuant to the Material Witness Statute, the media often paints these people as 'terrorists' based solely on selective government leaks and not on any public (or 'unsealed') evidence from the case itself. As in the case of Mr. Mayfield, the government conveniently 'sealed' all of the evidence and then duplicitously leaked to the media selective tidbits of choice information which helped form negative public opinion about Brandon Mayfield.

Traditionally and legally speaking, in order to successfully obtain a 'material witness' warrant, a prosecutor is usually required to prove that a witness is likely to flee (or be a 'flight risk') when summoned to court[120] for the subpoena in question. In this case, Brandon Mayfield was a licensed Oregon attorney and there was simply no evidence (or reason to believe) that an officer of the court like Mr. Mayfield would ever not respond to a subpoena (let alone 'flee') had he ever been served with that subpoena. Again, as mentioned before, there was virtually no 'flight risk' involved because Mr. Mayfield's passport again had been expired and even the FBI had admitted that he had never left the country before the 3/11 Madrid bombings in Spain.[121]

Many American legal experts and critics have spoken out repeatedly in the past against the Justice Department's misuse of the Material Witness Statute after 9/11 to round up Muslims and Arabs who have never been charged with any criminal act. For instance, the former second-in-command in President Bill Clinton's Justice Department said that former Attorney General John Ashcroft was converting the Material Witness

Statute into a 'preventive detention policy' without any congressional approval whatsoever. "After all, if they can pick people up like this, anyone can be picked up like this," once said Professor Michael Greenberger, who now served as director for the Center for Health and Homeland Security at the University of Maryland School of Law. "I am fearful that this is a long line of dramatic detentions, and we will find as time goes on that the evidence just peels away,"[122] Professor Greenberger further stated about our government's continued legal misuse of the Material Witness Statute.

The Material Witness Statute was issued a severe legal blow on May 1, 2004, when a federal judge called the imprisonment of material witnesses in government terrorism probes to be "unconstitutional."[123] United States District Judge Shira Scheindlin once wrote that "imprisoning a material witness for a grand jury investigation raises a serious constitutional question under the Fourth Amendment," which prohibits unreasonable searches and seizures.[124] Judge Scheindlin further cogently stated that, "Since 1789, no Congress has [ever] granted the government the authority to imprison an innocent person in order to guarantee that he will testify before a grand jury conducting a criminal investigation."[125]

On August 26, 2004, Mr. Brandon Mayfield hired one of the nation's most well-known plaintiff attorneys to represent him in a major civil lawsuit against the Department of Justice.[126] Celebrity lawyer Gerry Spence said that he had decided to help Brandon Mayfield sue the government because "it's an important case to Mr. Mayfield, and it's an important case to all Americans."[127] In his civil lawsuit against the Department of Justice, Brandon Mayfield claimed that the federal government targeted him solely because of his Muslim faith and violated his Fourth Amendment rights by searching his home and office; seizing his family's belongings and unjustly incarcerating him for over two weeks.[128]

"It's called the Muslim factor," said celebrity lawyer Gerry Spence about the Mayfield case. "It's profiling. It even affects what you see on a fingerprint, which is supposed to be science."[129] After such a catastrophic legal blunder by the Department of Justice and the FBI, the case of Brandon Mayfield serves to remind all Americans about our nation's legal and constitutional hallmarks of due process, evidentiary analysis and every American's right to be presumed innocent until proven guilty in a court of law.

Kent Mayfield, Brandon's brother, accurately summed up the frustrations of many Americans when he once said that Brandon Mayfield's only crime was that "he is of the Muslim faith and … not super happy with the Bush administration…"[130]

"So if that's a crime, well, you can burn half of us."

In late 2006, the United States government agreed to settle the civil lawsuit filed by Brandon Mayfield outside of court for a total of $2 million dollars.[131]

The 'No-Fly' List: Flying While Muslim

The Transportation Security Administration (TSA) was created by the Aviation and Transportation Security Act of 2001 and is charged with overseeing the security of all modes of interstate transportation.[132] Much of the TSA's current system for preventing terrorist access to airplanes relies on airline 'watch-lists' compiled from a variety of government sources and databases. There are at least two different types of watch-lists that are currently maintained: 1) A 'No-Fly' list of terrorist suspects, and a 2) 'Selectee' list targeting people who must be subjected to rigorous secondary screening before they are ever allowed to fly on an airplane.[133] Since the inception of these watch-lists, the TSA has refused to supply sufficient details on whom or why someone is on either the No-Fly or Selectee watch-lists.

However, according to TSA documents obtained through an April 2004 Freedom of Information Act (FOIA) lawsuit filed on behalf of six ethnically-diverse plaintiffs by the American Civil Liberties Union (ACLU);[134] the list of targeted people has been growing daily in response to requests from the intelligence community, Department of Homeland Security (DHS) and other federal agencies around the United States. In their April 2004 FOIA lawsuit, the ACLU was asking the federal court to declare that the No-Fly list violates airline passengers' constitutional rights of freedom from unreasonable search and seizure and also violates due process under the Fourth and Fifth Amendments.[135] The ACLU was also asking the TSA to develop satisfactory procedures that would allow innocent people to fly without being treated as potential terrorists and without being subjected to humiliation and unnecessary delays.

Reverend John Shaw was one of the six plaintiffs in the 2004 ACLU FOIA lawsuit and one of the many names of Americans who were on the No-Fly list. "I am joining the ACLU lawsuit because I have been repeatedly interrogated, delayed, and have experienced enhanced screening procedures and detention since 2002," said Reverend Shaw. "I have also tried without success to have my name removed from the list,"[136] once said the 74-year-old Presbyterian minister from Sammamish, Washington.

The Case of Professor Dr. Tariq Ramadan

Dr. Tariq Ramadan is a Swiss Muslim academic who was once named in 2004 as one of *TIME* Magazine's "100 Innovators of the 21st Century".[137] Because of his extensive and prolific academic record, Dr. Tariq Ramadan was appointed to the Henry R. Luce Professorship of Religion, Conflict, and Peace Building[138] for the Fall 2004 semester at the Joan B. Kroc Institute for International Peace Studies at the University of Notre Dame in South Bend, Indiana.[139] Dr. Ramadan's visa application for admittance to the United States was initially accepted for his Notre Dame professorship and he subsequently received his family's visa from the U.S. State Department. After initially receiving this visa, Dr. Ramadan then began preparing to move his family and young children from Geneva, Switzerland to South Bend, Indiana and was scheduled to begin teaching his classes at Notre Dame in late August 2004.

However, just days before Dr. Tariq Ramadan was set to travel, his American visa was summarily revoked without any explanation at the behest of the Department of Homeland Security (DHS)[140] in Washington DC. It would later turn out that Dr. Tariq Ramadan's visa was revoked pursuant to Section 411 of the USA PATRIOT Act, which bars entry to foreigners who have used a "position of prominence . . . to endorse or espouse terrorist activity."[141] Although government officials had provided little evidence or any explanation concerning Dr. Ramadan's visa revocation, some noted academics and scholars said that they suspected the government's decision to bar Dr. Ramadan could have been influenced by certain right-wing American political forces that have waged a campaign against Muslim scholars and intellectuals whose views on Islam and the Middle East conflict with their own myopic right-wing worldviews.[142]

Middle East expert Graham Fuller, a senior Rand Corporation analyst and former Vice Chair of the National Intelligence Counsel, once told the *Chicago Tribune* in August 2004 on the Tariq Ramadan case that there are "organizations [who] want to block people who can speak articulately and present the Muslim dilemma in a way that might be understandable and sympathetic to Americans."

Mr. Fuller further told the *Chicago Tribune* that, "They succeed by presenting this as a 'security' matter. There is no way homeland security would initiate this on its own."

"They want to say all Muslims are a monolithic threat," said Professor John Esposito of Georgetown University, who once described Dr. Ramadan as "an established academic . . . with a strong record."[143] Professor Scott Appleby, director of the Joan B. Kroc Institute for International Peace Studies at the University of Notre Dame, challenged Dr. Ramadan's critics to provide any credible evidence of any 'terrorist' links.

"If...anyone else has solid evidence that Tariq Ramadan has connections with [terrorists]—whatever that might mean—I would like to see it," Professor Scott Appleby once said about the matter. "Otherwise, unsubstantiated charges intended to defame a Muslim intellectual is troublingly reminiscent of some of the darkest moments in U.S history."[144] Further commenting on the arbitrary denial of an American visa to Dr. Tariq Ramadan and his appointment to Notre Dame, Professor Scott Appleby further stated that despite numerous requests to DHS and federal government officials, the University of Notre Dame has been given, "no substantial evidence of any of the various things that have been said about him."[145]

Professor Appleby went even further to state that the University of Notre Dame "stand[s] behind Tariq fully, and are proud of the appointment, and believe and continue to believe it's the proper appointment."[146]

The Case of Yusuf Islam (the artist formerly known as Cat Stevens)

"It started with a simple spelling error..."[147]

-- TIME Magazine, September 25 2004

On September 21, 2004, United Airlines Flight 919 was en route from London Heathrow (LHR) to Washington-Dulles (IAD) International Airport here in suburban Virginia; when American government officials soon realized that the world-renowned singer and global pop-star Cat Stevens (now known as Yusuf Islam) was aboard that United Airlines flight.[148] After learning of Mr. Islam's presence on the flight, the plane was then diverted over 600 miles to Bangor International Airport in Maine where federal authorities questioned Mr. Islam at 3:00pm Eastern Standard Time on that day.[149] After the lengthy initial interview between American government officials and Cat Stevens, the American officials summarily ordered his deportation stating that he was on a "security watch list because of suspicions that he was associated with potential terrorists."[150] As one of the most prominent national American Muslim civil rights lawyers in the United States, I was quoted on-camera the very next night on CNN *Anderson Cooper 360* during that evening's televised broadcast when I said during a press conference that "Mr. Islam has always categorically denied the fact that he has ever knowingly given any money or support to any terrorist group...If, in fact, these allegations were true by the government, then why wasn't Mr. Islam arrested?"[151] Alas, after being held in Maine, Mr. Islam- a life-long British citizen- was then transferred to Logan International Airport in Boston, where the Massachusetts Port Authority said he would be put on a flight to Washington.

Instead, he was subsequently deported back to his home in London.[152]

Yusuf Islam was born Stephen Demetre Georgiou in London to a Greek Cypriot father and Swedish mother.[153] In the 1970s, he took the stage name Cat Stevens and had a string of global musical chart-topping hits during that decade, including *Wild World* and *Morning Has Broken*.[154] He had officially left his music career behind in the late 1970s after his conversion to Islam. He would also later become a teacher and an advocate for his new faith, founding a Muslim school in London in 1983. In 1998, his institution became the first Muslim school in Great Britain to receive government support on the same basis as Christian, Jewish and other religious schools within the United Kingdom.[155]

Throughout his life, Yusuf Islam has also donated, both personally and through his charities, money to victims of the September 11 tragedies and for victims of the AIDS pandemic within Africa.[156] Upon his return to Great Britain after his September 2004 deportation, Yusuf Islam told a crowded press conference in London that he was "shocked and slightly amused" that American officials had determined that he was on a terrorist watch list and was not allowed to enter the United States. Mr. Islam said that he was a victim of an "unjust and arbitrary system," and that he has consistently denounced terrorism in numerous speeches and even on his own official global website.[157]

In regards to the No-Fly list, the former pop singer was allegedly in the same league as (the late) United States Senator Edward M. Kennedy, who apparently also once shared a name with someone on the No-Fly list and who had also been told several times that he could not fly on airplanes as well.[158] Before his death in August 2009, Democratic senator Ted Kennedy had once told the Senate Judiciary Committee that he had been stopped and questioned at airports on the East Coast five (5) times in March 2004 because his name appeared on the government's secretive No-Fly list.[159] Furthermore, Senator Kennedy had stated that he had to personally enlist the help of then-Homeland Security Secretary Tom Ridge to get his name removed from the list.[160] Federal air security officials said that the initial error that led to the scrutiny of the former senior Democratic senator from Massachusetts should not have happened and even they had acknowledged in the past that the No-Fly list was imperfect.

However, privately, many American government officials were embarrassed that it took a United States senator and his entire Senate staff "more than three weeks to get his name removed"[161] from the No-Fly list. As in the case of both Yusuf Islam and (the late) Senator Ted Kennedy, most of the other people ensnared within the No-Fly list debate have absolutely no links to terrorism whatsoever. Similarly, at least one other person said that he was simply once told by government officials that he would need to "have his name legally changed to avoid the problem in the future."[162]

Subsequently, the case of Yusuf Islam would become humorous fodder for newspaper editorial pages and late-night talk show monologues shortly thereafter. The *Washington Post* once commented that in the case of Cat Stevens and the No-Fly list, what the government was "missing was common sense."[163] The *Pittsburgh Post-Gazette* newspaper called the fiasco a "ridiculous overreaction."[164]

"What did federal authorities think he was going to do? Threaten to sing *Peace Train* over and over until certain demands were met?" said the Post-Gazette newspaper editorial. "Here was someone who was traveling with his daughter and had been to the United States several times, most recently in May [of that year], when he met with officials of the [George W. Bush] White House Office of Faith-Based and Community Initiatives to discuss philanthropic work."[165]

Other notable global political figures also spoke up against the United States' arbitrary and secretive denial of Yusuf Islam's entry into the United States. On September 22, 2004, then-British Foreign Secretary Mr. Jack Straw personally told then-United States Secretary of State Colin Powell that the action against Yusuf Islam "should not have been taken."[166] A final validation to this injustice occurred on November 10, 2004 when Yusuf Islam was presented with the *Man of Peace* award by former Russian leader Mikhail Gorbachev at the opening of a meeting of Nobel Peace Prize laureates in Rome, Italy.[167]

The Gorbachev Foundation said that the peace award was for Yusuf Islam's dedication to "promoting peace and condemning terrorism..." Past winners of the Gorbachev Foundation *Man of Peace* Award have included Italian film director Roberto Benigni, winner of the 1998 Best Actor Academy Award for his critically acclaimed movie, *Life is Beautiful (La Vita è Bella)*. The Gorbachev Foundation *Man of Peace* Award is given annually "to a distinguished personage of culture and entertainment for peace messages, fraternity and integration between nations."[168] At the presentation of the peace prize, Mikhail Gorbachev kissed Yusuf Islam on both cheeks and praised him for standing by his convictions despite these personal hardships.

"Cat Stevens' life has not been simple," said Mr. Gorbachev. "Every person who takes a critical stance to make the world a better place ... has a difficult life."[169] In summing up the receipt of this prestigious international peace award and his own ordeal in the United States, the former Cat Stevens told reporters that "perhaps it's part of the irony that sometimes you have to go through a test in order to achieve a prize...So maybe that's a symbol. Today I'm receiving a prize for peace, which is actually, I would say, a bit more descriptive of my ideas and my aims in life."[170]

With the poetic justice quite clear in this case, *The Miami Herald* newspaper called the awarding of the Gorbachev Foundation *Man of Peace* award to Yusuf Islam (the artist formerly known as Cat Stevens) to quite simply be "sweet vindication."[171]

CHAPTER FOUR: HISTORICAL ROOTS OF MUSLIM PACIFISM

"He who is not merciful to others will not be treated mercifully...Have mercy on those here on earth, and the One there in Heaven will have mercy on you..."[1]

-Prophet Muhammad

Salaam, *Shalom,* and Peace. Linguistically speaking, any nominally-trained translator anywhere around the world would be able to tell you the simple fact that each one of these three aforementioned words means exactly (and empirically) the same thing within their respective Arabic, Hebrew and English languages.

Whether you are saying '*Assalamu alaikum*' to a Muslim friend in Islamabad or '*Shalom aleichem*' to a Jewish buddy in Tel Aviv; in both cases, you are simply stating the same respective traditional Abrahamic religious greeting of peace and salutations for both Islam and Judaism, universally translated around the world as: "May peace be with you". Similarly, most academics, historians and linguists would also jointly concur that the etymological origins of the Arabic word *Islam* emanates from the linguistic Arabic root word *sa-la-ma* meaning 'peace'. Finalizing the chronological Abrahamic triumvirate begun by Judaism and Christianity, the 1400-year-old monotheistic religion of Islam is probably the most blatantly misunderstood of the three major Abrahamic religions in existence today.

From its universally-shared monotheistic concept of God (and 'The Golden Rule') to current hot-button geopolitical issues like women/minority rights, the (overused) terminology of *jihad* and the overall basic Muslim concept of 'humanity'; a general holistic understanding of certain major mainstream teachings of Islam (within their appropriate historical and geopolitical contexts) can help to provide some necessary contextual frameworks for a millennial

Muslim sociopolitical ethos firmly found within an ethical philosophy called Islamic Pacifism.

By officially calling for sweeping global legal and sociopolitical reforms within the greater Muslim world, this book shall also hopefully illuminate our own equilibriums back towards a 'purpose-driven' spiritual egalitarian ethos aimed at helping to guide young 21st-century millennial Muslim girls and boys of all races to dedicate their lives to peace and nonviolence by using our Islamic teachings for the sole purpose of helping humanity progress forward.

The Islamic Concept of God and 'The Golden Rule'

On any given day, if you walk into a bookstore anywhere around the world and open up a copy of the Arabic version of the Holy Bible, you would clearly see that millions of Arab Christians around the world translate the English word 'God' as the word 'Allah' within each one of their respective Arabic translations of the numerous editions of the Bible. As such, if there remains anyone in the world (with over three cumulative brain cells) who would ever say that 'Dios' is only the God of the Spanish or that 'Dieu' and 'Gott' are exclusively the gods of the French and Germans, respectively; such patently absurd statements would be dismissed worldwide as being completely nonsensical on literally every objective intellectual level. Even so, former United States President George W. Bush still managed to cause some controversy within certain American right-wing evangelical Christian political circles when he stated publicly during a January 2008 interview with Al-Arabiya television satellite network that everyone in the world, "whether they be Muslim, Christian, or any other religion, prays to the same God."

"That's what I believe," said President Bush at the time. "I believe that Islam is a great religion that preaches peace," he further stated during the globally-televised 2008 interview.[2]

Just as 'Dieu' and 'Dios' are simply the French and Spanish translations for the word 'God', for any rational person to state that the word 'Allah' is somehow exclusively the 'God of the Muslims' is simply a disingenuous argument and factually wrong on every intellectual plane. These people are merely duplicitously trying to advance an inaccurate 'clash of civilizations' dogmatic mantra meant to burn bridges and only dissuade people from completing a holistic understanding of the monotheistic religion of Islam. In highlighting our divinely common human origins, Mahatma Gandhi had once said on the issue of God that, "Islam... believes in the brotherhood of man. But you will permit me to point out that it is not the brotherhood of Muslims only, but universal brotherhood... The Allah of Islam is the same God of Christians and the Ishwar of Hindus."[3]

To analyze the concept of our one shared 'God' of the three major Abrahamic religions, American Muslim academic and scholar Dr. Umar Faruq Abd-Allah of the Nawawi Foundation in Chicago once wrote extensively about the historical and linguistic origins of the word 'Allah' in a 2004 academic journal article entitled "One God, Many Names". The central thesis of his journal article was to prove that any objective student of linguistic etymology and/or comparative religions would overwhelmingly concur on the basic mainstream academic and historically-accurate thesis that all three major Abrahamic world religions (Judaism, Christianity and Islam) all worship the same one monotheistic God of Abraham.

"Etymologically, *Allāh* comes from the same root as the Biblical words *Elāhîm*, *hā-Elāhîm*, and *hā-Elôh* (all meaning 'God') invoked by the Hebrew prophets and the Aramaic and Syriac *Alāhā* ('God') used by John the Baptist and Jesus. *Elāhîm* derives from *elôh* (Hebrew for 'god'), and *Alāhā* is an emphatic form of *alāh* (Aramaic/Syriac for 'god'), while *Allāh* is connected to *ilāh* (Arabic for 'god')." He concluded that: "All three of these Semitic words for 'god' – *elôh*, *alāh*, and *ilāh* – are etymologically equivalent" words meaning the exact same thing.[4]

He also reinforced his etymological thesis by saying that the "fundamental linguistic meaning of the three Abrahamic cognates for God- *Elāhîm* [from the Old Testament], *Alāhā* [used by John the Baptist and Jesus] and *Allāh* [from Islamic traditions]" are linguistically the same root word meaning 'the One who is worshipped.'[5] Furthering the historical thesis that Islam is the chronologically-last of the Abrahamic religious triumvirate, the academic journal article also noted that the Quran calls Islam the 'religion of Abraham' (*millat Ibrahim* in Arabic) when highlighting the following Quranic verse: "Then we revealed unto you [Muhammad] that you follow the religion of Abraham, who did not belong to those associating false gods with [the one true] God." (16:23)[6]

Additionally, the fundamental thesis that Muslims worship the same God of Abraham is so central to basic Islamic teachings that Muslims specifically invoke salutations upon Abraham and his family within each one of our five (5) daily prayers (known in Arabic as *salat*) and during many of the traditional ceremonial rites tied to the annual religious pilgrimages to Mecca (known as the *Hajj*). Finally, the House of Abraham (known in Arabic as the *Ka'aba*) within the ethereal center of the Islamic holy city of Mecca is well-known to all Muslims worldwide as being historically proven to be "tied to the Abrahamic story at every point."[7]

Since the social science of 'etymology' is the empirical study of the linguistic history of words, academics and scholars can trace the origins and development of words from a particular language and often use comparisons with other cognate words from related languages and dialects to find similarities. According to etymological academic consensus, the Semitic words *Allāh* (God in the Quran), the Old Testament *Elāhîm* (God) and the Aramaic/Syriac New Testament *Alāhā* (God) are "etymological cognates";[8] which simply means that all three words have a common etymological origin. Thus, from an academic perspective, all Jews, Christians and Muslims should therefore have no difficulty agreeing that we all worship the same monotheistic God of Abraham; despite our differences in theology and unique ritual practices in the worship of that same one God that we all share today.

The legendary sufi poet known as Rumi once highlighted our common human origins when he wrote: "All these religions…All this singing…One song…The differences are just illusion and vanity."[9] On the concept of religious supremacist narratives and exclusive claims of a monopoly on the issue of 'salvation', Professor Scott Alexander of the Catholic Theological Union (the largest Roman Catholic graduate school in America) once wrote on this subject: "The Bible and the Quran strongly oppose the notion that any one society or community ought to dominate or oppress another. In particular, [both] the Bible and Quran stand against those who would claim that there is something inherent in any group identity (be it that of Israel's 'chosen-ness', salvation in the body of Christ, or membership in the *ummah* of Muhammad) that makes its members superior to others."[10]

Within our own basic Islamic teachings, every living Muslim is reminded every day within several places of the Quran to show love, compassion and respect to the followers of other religions in respect to their freedom to worship God:

> ***"Do not dispute with the people of the Book (Jews and Christians) but in the best of manners, excepting those of***

them who commit oppression, and say (to them): 'We believe in what was revealed to us and what was revealed to you. Our God and your God is One, and we are a people in (willing) submission to Him...'" (29:46)

"Say (all of you): 'We believe in God and what was revealed to Abraham, Ishmael, Isaac, Jacob, and the tribes of Israel and what was given unto Moses and to Jesus and what was given to all the prophets from their Lord. We draw no distinctions between any of them [the prophets], and we are a people who submit themselves [willingly] to God...'" (2:136)

These (and hundreds of other) scriptural verses calling for interfaith compassion and mercy throughout the Quran have been conveniently overlooked by polemicists on both sides and remembering these basic teachings can help to re-inform our own respective individual global pacifist *ethe* (plural of ethos) for sustained interfaith dialogue between all religious traditions currently in worldly existence today.

Moving along, we should also remember the well-known ethical foundations of 'The Golden Rule' principle and its shared religious foundational adages of 'Love Thy God' and 'Love Thy Neighbor' which inherently reside within the vibrant nucleus (aka Ten Commandments) of any major world religion in order to also help advance our human conversation. Most every person knows that the basic philosophical ethic of 'reciprocity' (more commonly referred to as 'The Golden Rule') is a very simple humanitarian ethos where the well-known Golden Rule adage of '*Do Unto Others*' can best be summarized simply as the following:

"Treat all other human beings only in ways that you would like to be treated in the exact same situation."

On June 11, 1963, our own American president John F. Kennedy appealed to this global 'Golden Rule' principle during a major anti-segregation speech that he delivered at the time of the first black students' enrollment at the University of Alabama.[11] During this major June 1963 anti-segregation speech, President Kennedy bravely asked white Southerners to consider what it would be like to be treated as second-class citizens within their own country simply because of their skin color. Using the very basic foundations of the 'Golden Rule' principle, President Kennedy asked white Americans to simply imagine themselves as being 'black in America' - and being told that they could not vote, attend better public schools, eat at most public restaurants or even sit at the front of the bus-simply because of their skin color. In the conclusion of his speech, President Kennedy appealed one last time to the 'Golden Rule' principle by reminding all of us Americans that the "heart of the question is ... whether we are going to treat our fellow Americans as we want to be treated [ourselves]."[12]

Moving this discussion to the world of comparative religions, to highlight the overall transcendental universalism of its humanitarian message, we can see a brief sampling below of basic 'Golden Rule' teachings from some of the major world religions currently in existence today:

Buddhism: *"Hurt not others in ways that you yourself would find hurtful..."* (Udana Varga, 5:18)

Christianity: *"All things whatsoever you would that mean should do to you, do you even so to them, for this is the law and the prophets..."* (Matthew 7:12)

Confucianism: *"If there is one maxim that ought to be acted upon throughout one's whole life, surely it is the maxim of loving-kindness. Do not unto others what you would not have them do unto you..."* (Analects 15:23)

Hinduism: *"This is the sum of duty: do nothing unto others what would cause you pain if done unto you..."* (Mahabharata, 5:1517)

Islam: *"Love for humanity what you love for yourself..."*[13] (*Hadith* of Prophet Muhammad)

"Hurt no one so that no one may hurt you..." (Prophet Muhammad, The Farewell Sermon)

Judaism: *"What is hateful to you, do not unto your fellow man. This is the whole Torah; all the rest is commentary..."* (*Talmud*, Shabbat 31a; *Tobit* 4:15)

Taoism: *"Regard your neighbor's gain as your own gain, and your neighbor's loss as your own loss..."* (T'ai Shang Kan-Ying P'ien, 213-218)

Zoroastrianism: *"That nature alone is good which refrains from doing unto others what it would not do itself..."*[14] (Dadistan-I Dinik, 94:5)

Again, since Islam and Muslims are a vibrant part of the global religious tapestry of different faiths across the globe, we should all remember that this transcendental concept of 'loving' the entirety of God's creation is a central teaching of Islam and should serve as a principal guiding light for modern-day Muslims who are simply trying to make meaningful societal contributions each and every day of their lives. As mentioned earlier in this book, in response to Pope Benedict XVI's controversial September 2006 speech about Islam at Regensburg University in Germany, an official letter called *'A Common Word Between Us and You'* was a global interfaith declaration subsequently signed onto by over 140 international Muslim religious scholars from diverse schools of thought (both Sunni and Shia) who jointly issued this open letter to Pope Benedict urging "mutual understanding" between Christianity and Islam based directly on the aforementioned Golden Rule teachings of 'Love thy God' and 'Love thy Neighbor'.

Sadly though, for my millennial Muslim sisters and brothers living in the 21st century today, these loving and divine basic 'Golden Rule' teachings of Islam have been completely lost by a vocal few within our global community. For this reason, it might behoove us to learn about the powerful non-violent legacies of some influential Muslim pacifist giants from our recent historical past.

Muslim Pacifists in Modern History

Lest I be accused of inventing a new philosophical sociopolitical ethos called 'Islamic Pacifism', by taking a very simple and brief cursory look back at the lives of some influential Muslim pacifist giants of our recent historical past, we can see that this phenomenon of Islamic Pacifism has been around for some time. By doing so, we can also clearly show that our central thesis of Islamic Pacifism is simply the continuation of a long-standing Muslim message of love, compassion and nonviolence that our world has seen many times before. Especially during the 19th and 20th centuries within Central and South Asia, there have been influential Islamic pacifists who have used their proud Muslim sociopolitical ethos of nonviolence in helping to bring about positive social change within their respective societies. Whilst simultaneously praying five times a day towards Mecca, these pacifist visionaries saw absolutely no contradiction whatsoever in practicing their religion as proud Muslims and also furthering their categorical belief in nonviolence towards all of humanity.

From Sheikh Kunta Haji peacefully pushing back the Russian Communist empire for the millions of women and children of Chechnya in the 19th century to Abdul Ghaffar Khan (better known as the 'Frontier Gandhi') advocating for nonviolent political resistance in the Pashtun tribal areas of modern-day Pakistan (alongside his dear friend and legendary pacifist contemporary, Mahatma Gandhi); these luminary Muslim pacifist leaders from many different walks of life and national backgrounds have popped up throughout modern human history in their legendary attempts at making the world a better place to live for all.

Sheikh Kunta Haji (Chechnya)

Kunta Haji (born Kunta-haji Kishiev) was a Chechen Muslim mystical shepherd who in 1849 started to advocate nonviolent resistance "to the ongoing Russian domination" of his native Chechnya.[15] After his forced exile from the Caucasus, Sheikh Kunta Haji returned to Chechnya twelve years later in 1861 and again peacefully continued his Islamic teachings of nonviolence until his arrest by Russian communist authorities in 1864.

During his esteemed lifetime of teaching Islamic nonviolence, it is estimated that Kunta Haji's active supporters numbered "over 20,000 in Chechnya alone" and his passive followers numbered in the "hundreds of thousands" around the rest of the region as well. Amidst the bloody half-century of the Caucasian War (also known as the Russian Conquest of the Caucasus) between 1817 and 1864, the Russian empire sought to annex much of the predominantly-Muslim North Caucausus through these bloody wars waged by three different Russian Czars (including Alexander I, Nicholas I and Alexander II).

Throughout these decades of widespread bloodshed and senseless murder, Sheikh Kunta Haji was one of the leading Muslim pacifist political leaders of the Caucasus who consistently reminded the people of his country that:

> ***"War—it is savagery...Remove yourself from anything that hints of war..."***

In later writings to his native Chechnya from the Muslim holy city of Mecca, Sheikh Kunta Haji continued his Islamic pacifist teachings by writing to his countrymen:

> ***"Defeat the evil man by your goodness and love... Defeat the greedy with your generosity...Defeat the treacherous with your sincerity...Defeat the infidel with your fidelity..."***[16]

Almost fifty years before Mahatma Gandhi would ever come into the global spotlight with his own pacifist philosophy of *Satyagraha* (Sanskrit for "holding firmly to the truth") during the British colonial rule of India, Sheikh Kunta Haji of Chechnya was already practicing his own form of Islamic pacifism for the freedom of his own people more than half a century earlier in Central Asia. Because of his lifetime dedication to Islamic pacifism, it was widely reported that Sheikh Kunta Haji "was reconfigured as the Chechen Gandhi" by the Muslim people of the Russian Caucasus[17] regions during the 1990s; almost one hundred years after he had left this world.

Abdul Ghaffar Khan (also known as 'The Frontier Gandhi')

In March 2005, I was honored to give a keynote speech in my home state at the University of Illinois at Urbana-Champaign and was even more humbled by the fact that the person who was officially introducing me to the college audience that evening was Professor Rajmohan Gandhi; a former Indian politician and well-known grandson of the legendary pacifist, Mahatma Gandhi. In addition to being a lifelong peace activist like his well-known grandfather, Professor Rajmohan Gandhi had also written the seminal biography on the life of Abdul Ghaffar Khan; the famous Muslim pacifist contemporary of Mahatma Gandhi known around as the world as 'The Frontier Gandhi' and the 'Nonviolent *Badshah* [King] of the Pashtuns' within the geographical region known today as modern-day Afghanistan and Pakistan.

In a December 7, 2001 column for *The New York Times* entitled "The Peacemaker of the Pashtun Past", Karl Meyer of the World Policy Journal wrote that Abdul Ghaffar Khan was "renowned as 'the Frontier Gandhi'...His [Muslim pacifist] followers...all had to swear: 'I shall never use violence. I shall not retaliate or take revenge, and shall forgive anyone who indulges in oppression and excesses against me.'"[18] Furthermore, for over two decades of his life, "Ghaffar and his [supporters] dominated the North-West Frontier [Province of modern-day Pakistan and Afghanistan] without resort to violence, enduring prison and torture." In response to this political campaign of Islamic pacifism, Abdul Ghaffar Khan's dear friend and pacifist contemporary, Mahatma Gandhi, once called Khan's non-violent political feat "a miracle".[19] In Professor Rajmohan Gandhi's seminal biography entitled *Ghaffar Khan: Nonviolent Badshah of the Pashtuns*, one of the central theses of the important life history of this Islamic pacifist was the notion that:

"To this Muslim, forgiveness was [an integral] part of Islam."[20]

"There is nothing surprising about a Muslim like me subscribing to nonviolence," once said Abdul Ghaffar Khan during a personal meeting with Mahatma Gandhi in 1931. "It was followed fourteen hundred years ago by the Prophet [Muhammad], all the time he was in Mecca...But we [Muslims] had so forgotten it that when Mahatma Gandhi placed it before us, we thought he was sponsoring a new creed or a novel weapon."[21] For Abdul Ghaffar Khan, this pacifist doctrine of Islamic nonviolence (or *adam tashaddud* in his native Pushto language) was considered to be the "twin of patience [or perseverance], a virtue stressed again and again in the Quran." A true sociopolitical visionary during his lifetime, in response to the blatant historical mistreatment of Muslim women within our own Islamic societies, Ghaffar Khan was once known to have said to all the women of his region: "In the Holy Qur'an, you have an equal [human] share with men...You are today oppressed because we men have ignored the commands of God and the Prophet [Muhammad]...Today, we are the followers of [tribal] custom and we oppress you."[22]

Mahatma Gandhi was once known to have famously said that, "I claim to have as much regard in my heart for Islam and other religions as for my own." Furthermore, during a personal conversation between the two dear pacifist friends, Mahatma Gandhi once told Abdul Ghaffar Khan:

"Look, nonviolence is not for cowards...It is for the brave."[23]

To exemplify the profound impact of Abdul Ghaffar Khan's life on the millions of people of South Asia, in a June 19, 1947 personal conversation with his own grand-niece, Mahatma Gandhi once uttered these amazing words about the Islamic pacifist known around the world as Abdul Ghaffar Khan: "I cannot sleep...The thought of him has robbed me of my sleep...I cannot cease thinking of Badshah Khan...He is a prodigy...I am seeing more and more of his deeply spiritual nature daily...He has patience, faith and nonviolence joined in true humility...He is a man of penance, also of illumination, with love for all and hatred for none."[24]

At a time when there was great communal bloodshed between Hindus, Muslims and Sikhs during the fight for independence from British colonial rule, Abdul Ghaffar Khan always commanded nonviolence to India's Muslim populations in the name of Islam and the Holy Quran. "If you plant a slap after having been provoked by a slap, then what is the difference between the followers of the Quran and the evildoer?" once asked Badshah Khan on the need to peacefully respond to any grievance in the name of the basic Islamic ethical teachings of forgiveness, mercy, and compassion. In 1984, on speaking to the pure divine simplicity of his own Islamic pacifism, the ninety-four-year-old Abdul Ghaffar Khan once said as he tapped his own chest: "What else can I do...if Allah has placed this feeling [of love] for all people inside here?"

At 6:55 in the morning on January 20, 1988, the Muslim pacifist giant known as Abdul Ghaffar Khan (aka 'The Frontier Gandhi') took his last breath at the astounding age of 98. During his funeral processional, tens of thousands of respectful mourners accompanied the coffin of Badshah Khan as it crossed the Durand Line (the modern-day border between Afghanistan and Pakistan). Because of his enormous influence, the funeral service for Ghaffar Khan included the "first ever visit to Pakistan by India's prime minister in nearly three decades" after the estranged rival governments set aside their differences to honor this pacifist giant. The late Indian prime minister Rajiv Gandhi immediately delayed a flight to an international summit in Stockholm and the Pakistani government "issued without question an emergency visa so that he could visit" Peshawar where Abdul Ghaffar Khan's body lay in state.[25]

Similarly, even though the president of Pakistan at the time- the late General Zia-ul Haq (who would later be killed in a plane bombing that same year in August 1988)- had himself personally imprisoned Ghaffar Khan at one point during his life, he had also rushed to Khan's funeral service in Peshawar as well. "History knows very few persons who spent nearly a century in pursuit of a mission they cherished," said General Zia in a letter of condolence to Ghaffar Khan's family. He further wrote that, "May Allah bless his soul and grant fortitude to his bereaved family and followers" in bearing this gigantic loss of the South Asian pacifist legend.

"The funeral procession [of Abdul Ghaffar Khan]...was an event with few parallels in history," wrote Professor Rajmohan Gandhi in his biography. "The caravan of cars, buses, trucks and other vehicles carrying his followers, friends and admirers was endless...A sea of humanity greeted them in Jalalabad, [Afghanistan]."

"This was, so to say, a caravan of peace."[26]

Although he lived within a turbulent region known for civil war and unnecessary violent bloodshed, when asked about facing the imminent possibility of death, Abdul Ghaffar Khan was known to have once smiled and simply replied: "If I die, I will be with God; if I live, God will be with me...You know that I have always been an adherent of nonviolence...I regard nonviolence as love and violence as hate."

"His Islam seemed to be of the most natural kind," wrote Professor Rajmohan Gandhi in *Ghaffar Khan: Nonviolent Badshah of the Pashtuns*. "Unfazed [by violent detractors], Badshah Khan was content having his 'Muslim-ness' confirmed in his own heart, in his prayers, in his practices and in the Holy Book that he treasured...Again and again, he insisted that the Prophet's chief demand of a Muslim was [simply] the service of fellow human beings."[27] Professor Gandhi further highlighted Abdul Ghaffar Khan's Islamic pacifist legacy when he also noted that "one of those [people] motivated by Ghaffar Khan's realistic nonviolence was the Palestinian-born academic and [Christian peace] activist, Mubarak Awad."

As a Christian pacifist himself, Mr. Mubarak Awad once noted that Ghaffar Khan's pacifist legacy of practicing "Islam and nonviolence showed that it was not for the weak" and truly for the brave. Directly because of Abdul Ghaffar Khan's legacy of Islamic pacifism, Mr. Mubarak Awad ultimately decided to dedicate the remainder of his own life to becoming a Palestinian Christian pacifist and then later started "a [global] network called Nonviolence International to promote social change and international peace." For him, the life of this historical Muslim pacifist named Abdul Ghaffar Khan showed that "prayer in whatever language or form was addressed to the one and the same God".

Whether one is a Muslim, Christian, Hindu or Jewish pacifist, the tremendous ninety-eight-year human legacy of global pacifism exemplified by Abdul

Ghaffar Khan showed our world that "the naturalness of his Islam, his directness, his rejection of violence and revenge and his readiness to cooperate with non-Muslims add up to a valuable legacy for our angry times." Named in 1957 as Amnesty International's 'Prisoner of the Year' for his nonviolent protests, the world-renowned human rights organization said at the time that, "His example symbolizes the suffering of upwards of a million people all over the world who are in prison [simply] for their conscience." As the grandson of Mahatma Gandhi and the seminal biographer of Abdul Ghaffar Khan, my dear friend Professor Rajmohan Gandhi finally noted that the most important legacy of the Islamic pacifist known as Abdul Ghaffar Khan was the simple historical fact that "his bridge-building life is a [direct] refutation of the clash-of-civilizations theory."[28]

In summarizing the overall historical significance of the amazing life of Abdul Ghaffar Khan, *The Washington Post* once noted that his life exemplifies the greater need to tell the world "about an Islamic practitioner of pacifism at a moment when few in the West understand its effectiveness and fewer still associate it with anything Islamic."

Finally, the *Christian Science Monitor* once beautifully summarized the overall global contribution of this Muslim pacifist giant quite perfectly when it simply stated:

"The essence of Khan's story…is that the true nature of Islam is nonviolent."[29]

<u>Mr. Jawdat Said</u> (Egypt)

Although little known in the Western world, Egyptian intellectual (and Islamic pacifist philosopher) Jawdat Said has been propagating a vision of Islam "free from violence" for nearly the last 50 years. Through his lifelong dedication to nonviolence, his academic books and writings have been widely read and discussed by Islamic sociopolitical thinkers, intellectuals, and philosophers around the Muslim world for years. First published in 1966, his seminal book *The Doctrine of the First Son of Adam: The Problem of Violence in the Islamic World* was the first publication in modern Islamic sociopolitical thought to present a foundational concept of nonviolence as its central thesis. Now in its fifth edition, the book is still readily available around the world today.

Mr. Jawdat Said was born in Syria in 1931 and moved to Egypt at a young age to study Arabic language at the prestigious Al-Azhar University[30] in Cairo;

one of the most respected centers of educational learning within the entire Muslim world today. Even during his early days in Cairo, Mr. Said had warned against the negative effects of the violence being carried out by the so-called 'Islamic movement' within Egypt and wrote his 1966 book "as a direct response [and challenge] to the writings of Sayyid Qutb, who died in 1966 and is considered the father of [the modern] militant Islamist" movement most notably personified by the infamous likes of Al-Qaeda, Osama bin Laden and Ayman Al-Zawahiri.[31] Similarly, many other prominent Muslims around the Islamic world during that initial period had also turned against the controversial Sayyid Qutb- including even Hasan al-Hudaybi- the leader of the Egyptian Muslim Brotherhood at the time.

In the introduction to his book *The Doctrine of the First Son of Adam*, Mr. Jawdat Said places himself within the tradition of other enlightened Islamic political reformers such as Abd al-Rahman al-Kawakibi (who died in 1902), Algerian writer Malik bin-Nabi (who wrote the book *The Conditions of Renaissance*) and Dr. Muhammad 'Allama' Iqbal- the legendary philosophical luminary who is well-known around the world for being the eventual 'spiritual father' for the modern-day nation of Pakistan. According to Mr. Said, all of these visionary Islamic philosophers shared in common an emphasis on the concept of peaceful 'reformation' within our modern Muslim societies. Unlike our current Muslim political pathology which seems to blame all of our sociopolitical woes on colonial imperialism, these brave Muslim philosophers and sociopolitical thinkers had promoted a culture of 'self-criticism' and analyzed our Muslim world problems *vis-à-vis* our own self-inflicted political failings and human fallibilities throughout the history of our modern times.

Through his cogent Islamic analysis of the historical story of Adam's sons- Cain and Abel- Mr. Jawdat Said showed that the concept of 'nonviolence' within Islam was actually a "divine commandment" exemplified by this story. To prove that this sociopolitical ethos of Islamic pacifism was firmly embedded within the Holy Quran, Mr. Said showed that in Chapter 5 (verses 27-31), one can easily read how the "God-fearing Abel" even refused to defend himself physically against his own brother; although in the end, Cain would end up murdering his own pacifist brother. Thus, like Jawdat Said and other Islamic pacifists around the world, many Muslim thinkers and philosophers see this is as an ultimate quest for mankind to react "like Adam's younger son, who did not even defend himself physically against the attacks of his brother."

This historical act of pacifist non-violence exhibited by Adam's younger son represents, in Jawdat Said's view: "A position to be aspired to by all mankind and adhering to it is one of God's commandments" of nonviolence.[32] Additionally, he also refers to the stories of various other prophets within the Quran to point out that the only charge that they were ever accused of was their belief in the one God of all creation. None of them-he felt it should be noted- attempted to spread their prophetic ideas by means of illegal violence or unjust murder. According to Mr. Said, he saw these prophetic parables as a clear indication that the practice of murderous violence is inherently incompatible with the basic core teachings of Islam and the Quran. In his 1988 book entitled *Read: For The Lord Your God is Benevolent*, he further supported this central thesis of a millennial Islam 'free from violence' by developing an important approach to the interpretation of the Holy Quran. He rightfully pointed out that the various different interpretations of the actual text of our holy book presented a challenge even for the early followers and closest companions of the Prophet Muhammad.

Within his 1988 book, Mr. Said quotes from the fourth Caliph of Islam (Ali ibn Abi Talib) who during a disagreement with his opponents (the Kharijites) demanded that they should disregard using the sacred texts to resolve the dispute because "each group had its own way of interpreting" the scripture in their favor. Instead, the caliph rightfully promoted the use of logical human reasoning (known as *ijtihad* in Arabic) to find a peaceful resolution to their sociopolitical grievances at the time. As a result of this sociopolitical philosophy of Islamic pacifism, the Egyptian philosopher Jawdat Said's works about 'Muslim non-violence' have become a part of a series of positive philosophical writings that can help to serve as a future guidepost for all millennial Muslims around the world and faithfully present a positive Islamic 'audacity of hope' for our future generations of Muslim youth that completely disavows violence and condemns murder anywhere in the world. Through the teachings of these Islamic pacifist giants from our recent human historical past, the future generations of our human race can "use [our] God-given ability to reason"[33] and help bring some much-needed peace back here upon our war-torn planet.

Pluralism within Islam

Interfaith advocates and religious leaders promoting pluralistic dialogue have always emphasized a core foundation of shared beliefs, commonly-held values and overarching societal concerns to find common ground between observant members of all major world religions. Professor John Donohue, director of the Center for the Study of the Modern Arab World at St. Joseph's University noted that during the 1950s and 1960s, global interfaith dialogue was "promoted as a method for joining forces during the Cold War to fight communism" and during the "late 1960s and 1970s, the [interfaith] emphasis shifted to social issues... [and in] the 1980s and 1990s, human rights took center stage" as these examples of cooperation led to an increased recognition on all sides of the religious velvet rope that positive and constructive methods of interfaith cooperation have become a global necessity today.[34]

Professor John Esposito of Georgetown University's Alwaleed bin Talal Center for Christian-Muslim Understanding (ACMCU) highlights that true interfaith dialogue "requires self-criticism...that no religion has been perfect throughout history and that all religions have something to learn from other religions."[35] Thankfully, Dr. Esposito notes that "both Islam and Christianity have shared beliefs that provide a basis for mutual understanding and cooperation." Both religious traditions "recognize and worship God as Creator, sustainer and Judge" and similarly, they also share a belief in common prophets, moral responsibility and ultimate accountability for all of humanity. The Quran proclaims that "We believe what has been sent down to us, and we believe what has been sent to you. Our God and your God is one, and to Him we submit." (28:46). According to religious scholar Professor John Hick, many passages in both the Quran and Bible "imply that the confirmation of prior revelations in present revelation means that all are worshipping the same God."[36]

Dr. Farid Esack, a former visiting professor of Islamic studies at Harvard Divinity School, once defined the modern phenomenon of religious pluralism as "the creation of an environment in which everyone is safe and free to be human and to serve God" in peace and harmony. He calls for a consistent application of basic human ethical morality that asserts the right of every human being to experience justice and be free from oppression, tyranny and conflict. Professor Esack bases his pluralistic philosophy of interfaith cooperation and peaceful coexistence on four major verses of the Quran (23:52, 5:5, 5:47 and 22:40) which "recognize the People of the Book as part of the Muslim community because they were recipients of divine [Abrahamic] revelation."[37] Additionally, it is noted that this interfaith union of Christians, Jews and Muslims lived within a single community under the Constitution of Medina; which has been considered to be "the first known political document asserting religious freedom" for all religions during the Prophet's time. Similarly, other future historical stretches of interfaith harmony beginning with the "track record of fairness and justice that occurred under Muslim rule, including the Jewish Golden Age and second Caliph Umar ib al-Khattab's guarantee of Christian personal property rights and safety for the [Christian] inhabitants of Jerusalem" are all very good examples of peaceful interfaith coexistence and religious pluralism to occur throughout early Islamic history.

Also, millions of Muslim pluralists around the world point to the famous verse in the Quran which states quite clearly that, "There is no compulsion in religion" (2:256) as a direct challenge and empirical contradiction to myopic religious worldviews that divide the world into two absolute spheres of Islam and the 'Other'. Professor Esposito of Georgetown University also points to "Tunisian scholar and leader of the Renaissance Party, Rashid al-Ghannoushi who believes that the Quranic principle that 'there is no compulsion in religion' should serve as the basis for religious, cultural, political and ideological pluralism"[38] amongst people of different belief systems.

On the issue of diversity, it should also be noted that our Islamic holy book clearly states that God deliberately made humanity into different races and nations so that "you may know one another" and that "the most honored among you in the eyes of God is the one who is the most righteous" (49:13) and not based on some notion of racial or ethnic superiority. To this point, the late Dr. Fathi Osman- former senior scholar at the University of Southern California's Center for Muslim-Jewish Engagement- had always argued that diversity was an integral part of divine creation and rather than abolishing diversity around the world, he had believed that the aforementioned passage "encourages people to learn to handle their differences intellectually, morally and behaviorally, both within a single community and between multiple [religious] communities." To illustrate this point further, he also pointed to the consistent use of the term 'Children of Adam' (17:70) given to all human beings as "God's conferring honor and dignity upon all of humanity."[39]

Concededly, there are both good and bad aspects of 'religious pluralism' as it stands today. Professor John Esposito of Georgetown University notes that, on the one hand, the absurdity of "Osama bin Laden's declarations of unending global jihad against 'Christian Crusaders' and 'Zionists' and other militant exclusivist theologies emanating from some religious leaders" in some Muslim countries represent the "worst of Islamic extremism". Similarly, he also points out that ultra-conservative right-wing Christian "denunciations of Islam as a violent and militant religion" with the portrayals of the Prophet Muhammad as "demonic" by extremist voices of the 'Christian Right' like Pat Robertson, the late Jerry Falwell and Franklin Graham also "serve only to promote bigotry, inaccurate information and intolerance"[40] about Islam and Muslims. Only when we take away the microphones from the bizarrely vocal right-wing extremist minority elements on both sides of the global divide will we ever be able to replace this ungodly rhetoric with the truly enlightened divine teachings of pluralism, tolerance and peaceful coexistence among people of all faiths.

What The Hell Is A '*Jihad*' Anyway?

As God as my witness, I have literally been asked this aforementioned (and precisely-worded) question above hundreds and thousands of times throughout my short life thus far. To be sure, the Arabic word of *jihad* has become so bloody overused throughout the world that it has virtually (and practically) lost the entirety of its multi-faceted texture and etymological meaning today. Spanning the definitional global spectrum between an introspective internal self-reflective 'struggle' state of nirvana to an external physical (and/or violent) military 'holy war'; there is simply no single word within the entirety of the Arabic lexicon dictionary today which has garnered more international controversy within our global *zeitgeist* than the five-letter Arabic word of *jihad*.

The absurdity of the global linguistic debate obsessively fixated around the word *jihad* alone has reached such bizarrely epic global proportions that many Muslims even refuse to innocently utter the word out loud in the fear that some domestic government surveillance device is surreptitiously monitoring them and will flag them for further scrutiny simply for uttering that five-letter word. Nonetheless, because of both our own internal Muslim dinosaur extremists like Osama bin Laden and outside non-Muslim racist Islamophobes (who believe that innocent things like praying towards Mecca represent a type of 'holy war');

it is my personal belief that the overused word of *jihad* has effectively lost all of its meaning today.

That's right, I said it.

In my opinion, because of its blatant misuse by everyone and their octogenarian grandmothers, the word *jihad* now simultaneously means nothing (and everything) to any reasonably objective global observer around the world. Both sloppily used by Muslim extremists to declare some perverted (and fictitious) vision of a 'cosmic war' (hat tip to my Facebook friend, author Reza Aslan of *No God But God*) and also simultaneously (and sloppily) used by racist Islamophobes who use it to casually label and demonize anything pertaining to Muslims as *jihad*; this one single Arabic word has sadly devolved into nothing more than the bloody maxim *du jour* for both sides of the sinister 'clash of civilizations' organizational cabal worldwide.

Linguistically speaking, most academics of Islam would concur that the origin of the word *jihad* comes from the Arabic root word *ja-ha-da*, which literally means to 'struggle' as found within any Arabic dictionary today. From the historical birth of Islam, Muslim scholars and academics of linguistics/etymology tied this definitional 'struggle' to our own individualistic internal self-reflective struggles within our own respective 'lower self' (what Sigmund Freud referred to as the human 'ego'). To the contrary, since the late 20th century, the word *jihad* has also gained remarkable political currency as more of a violent *modus operandi*; used by global resistance, liberation and terrorist movements alike to 'legitimize' their cause and motivate their politically-ideological followers without having to justify their murderous actions beyond uttering that one simple word.

Thus, it is between these divinely polar opposites of godly internal 'self-purification struggle' and ungodly 'violent holy war' that the modern-day linguistic (and semantic) battle for the word *jihad* currently takes place within the ethereal global marketplace of ideas. In addressing this ongoing global definitional battle, world-renowned Islamic studies professor John Esposito of the Edmund A. Walsh School of Foreign Service at Georgetown University once highlighted that "the two broad definitions of *jihad*, [both] non-violent and violent, are contrasted in a well-known Prophetic tradition (*hadith*)." Once called "the most influential Islamic scholar in the United States" by the *International Herald Tribune*, Professor Esposito explained this well-known *hadith* where Muslim tradition reported that when the Prophet Muhammad once returned home from a battle with belligerent pagan warriors who had attacked them, he proceed to inform his followers upon their return to their homes and families that:

"We return from the lesser jihad to the greater jihad."[41]

According to his academic analysis, from the plainly clear textual reading of this prophetic *hadith*; past and future generations of all global Muslims are directly taught by the Prophet himself that the 'greater *jihad*' is the more difficult, more rewarded and more important internal self-reflective struggle that we each fight every single day against our own individualistic mortal pitfalls; including our own ego, selfishness, arrogance, greed and overall personal evils. To be sure, like many other words within any human language, the concept of *jihad* is still a concept with multiple historical meanings that have been used and abused throughout our fallible human history. Although we will continue to have global debates both within (and outside) the global Muslim community as to what the word *jihad* 'really' means for the remainder of the 21st century, we millennial Muslims can certainly all agree and must also remember to teach our children one far-overlooked (and very elementary) religious aspect of basic Islamic teachings that the global *jihad* debate very conveniently overlooks far too often. This very basic concept of great religious importance should be emphasized over and over again to every living Muslim man, woman and child breathing our shared oxygen today.

This basic Muslim concept is very simple: ***'Suicide' is absolutely forbidden in Islam.***

Despite all of our global differences, the one thing that all Muslims (ranging from self-proclaimed hippies like myself to extremist zealots) would all ultimately concede unanimously is that Islam as a religion categorically forbids 'suicide' by any living human being; with no exceptions whatsoever. Whether a person deliberately overdoses alone on sleeping pills listening to their Nirvana album or whether they deliberately blow themselves up in a pizzeria in the Middle East murdering scores of other innocent human beings; in either case, any knowledgeable Muslim (with over three total brain cells) would admittedly concede that both of these cases of 'suicide' would be against every basic theological teaching of Islam and thus, completely forbidden (or *haram* in Arabic) for any living Muslim; with absolutely zero exceptions whatsoever.

Since the religion of Islam teaches us that only God shall ultimately be the lawful taker of any human life; we must again rededicate ourselves to teaching and reminding our next generations of Muslim youth worldwide never to despair and commit 'suicide' because of any life situation whatsoever. As we will clearly see from some basic Islamic teachings, the mortal sin of 'suicide' is one of the gravest, most enormous and categorically unforgivable sins within the basic teachings and mainstream beliefs of our religion. To illustrate how completely (and absolutely) forbidden the concept of 'suicide' is within basic Islamic teachings; the Prophet Muhammad once told his followers quite categorically on the issue of suicide:

> ***"He who commits suicide by throttling shall keep on throttling himself in the Hellfire and he who commits suicide by stabbing himself shall keep on stabbing himself in the Hellfire."***[42]

As anyone can clearly see from this very simple prophetic saying, any Muslim who commits suicide (in any form whatsoever) will be punished with that same exact suicidal methodology for the remainder of their eternal afterlife. This basic prophetic logic also teaches us that for any Muslim person who might ever contemplate blowing themselves up (along with other innocent people) anywhere around the world; you can probably forget the ridiculous vision of Osama's promised '72 mythical virgins' and instead imagine perpetually blowing yourself up over and over again within the lowest (and hottest) rungs of hellfire's inferno for the remaining entirety of your afterlife. Again, to be abundantly clear, it should be shouted from the rooftops and minarets of the world that Islam completely (and categorically) forbids suicide; *with absolutely no exceptions whatsoever.* Furthermore, for any logical and rational human being alive, since suicide is completely forbidden in Islam, then it would also make sense (using basic logical deduction) that any 'suicide bombing' which also murders others would be even more detestable to every basic Muslim value and Islamic ethical teaching in existence today.

Nonetheless, the now-dead Osama bin Laden and his zombie pawns always continued to play their '72 virgin' trump card as their primary political propaganda recruitment tool to recruit unsuspecting impressionable Muslim youngsters throughout the world. Just imagine for one moment that seventy-one (71) divinely angelic virginal sirens are gently massaging the cankerous illiterate feet of a murderous suicide bomber as he reclines on an ethereal floating golden chaise eating heavenly seedless grapes from the translucent hand of the 72nd virgin handmaiden; all as some kind of 'reward' for both committing suicide and simultaneously murdering innocent men, women and children at the same time.

Please give me a break, Osama.

Every living Muslim alive knows the fact that every form of personal suicide (including any 'suicide bombing' which takes the lives of other innocent human beings) is completely *haram* (or forbidden) within Islam and the teachings of our last prophet. "The strong is not the one who overcomes the people by his strength, but the strong is the one who controls himself while in anger" is a well-known saying[43] by the Prophet Muhammad addressing how human beings must compose themselves during times of anger, violence or oppression. Within the Quran itself, most academics agree that there is one major passage that appears relevant to suicide:

> ***"O you who believe...And do not kill yourselves; for God has been merciful toward you...And if any do that... then We will burn him in fire..."** (4:29-30)*

Even though most academics say that the subject of suicide is explicitly mentioned only once within the Quran, a vast number of prophetic sayings (or *hadith*) and mainstream Islamic legal sciences "frequently, clearly and absolutely prohibits suicide [in all of its forms]."[44] As mentioned earlier, the Islamic theological punishment for self-slaughter consists of the "unending repetition of the act by which the suicide was committed." Professor John Esposito of Georgetown University sadly noted though that, "Many commentators, however, have been reluctant to say that a person who commits suicide is condemned eternally to hell" even though that is the clear religious punishment for suicide (of any form) within the basic mainstream teachings of Islam.[45] To reiterate this point further, the concept of 'suicide' is also considered to be one of the 'enormous' sins within supplemental Islamic law, according to *Reliance of the Traveler*; a respected classical manual of mainstream Islamic sacred law. Dealing specifically with the issue of suicide, this historical treatise of Islamic law mentions that the Prophet once told his followers a story where:

> ***"Of those before you, there was once a wounded [Muslim] man who could not bear it, so he took a knife and cut his arm, and bled until he died....[In response], Allah said, 'My slave has taken his life before I have, so I forbid him from Paradise...'"***[46]

As clearly highlighted by this Islamic parable, the concepts of both 'suicide' and 'despair' are against every basic Islamic teaching which is firmly embedded around the foundational notion of an all-merciful God who shall ultimately be the one and only divine taker of any human life. Again reiterating the complete prohibition of suicide and the perpetual eternal damnation for the taking of one's own life, it was also reported that the Prophet once told his followers:

> ***"Whoever kills himself with poison will abide forever in the fire of hell, poison in hand, perpetually drinking from it."***[47]

Historically, both Sunni and Shia Muslims have overwhelmingly forbidden 'sacrificial religious suicide' and acts of terrorism as a whole. For example, the Nizari Ismailis, popularly called the 'Assassins' (from the Arabic *Hashasheen* defined by some as 'hashish users')- who in the 11th and 12th centuries were notorious for sending suicidal kamikaze assassin squads against their political enemies- were summarily "rejected by mainstream Islam as fanatics"[48] during the Middle Ages of Islamic civilization. Such was the rejection of the Assassins as fanatics that some historians even pointed to the fact that the word 'assassin' may have been derived because of the hit-men's use of hashish during their stealth missions. However, according to British author Edward Burman, "Many scholars have argued, and demonstrated convincingly, that the attribution of the epithet 'hashish eaters' or 'hashish takers' is a misnomer derived from enemies of the Ismailis and was never used by Muslim chroniclers or sources....It was therefore used in a pejorative sense of 'enemies' or 'disreputable people'. This sense of the term survived into modern times with the common Egyptian usage of the term Hashasheen in the 1930s to mean simply 'noisy' or 'riotous'."[49]

As in any other religious tradition throughout human history, sacred scripture and religious tradition has been used and abused, interpreted and misinterpreted, to justify resistance and liberation struggles, extremism and terrorism, holy and unholy wars since time immemorial. As the next generation of millennial Muslims, we must help to teach the youth of our respective societies to never commit suicide under any circumstances and to patiently persevere throughout life with a deeply profound sense of *sabr* (Arabic for "patience" or "perseverance") when faced with the challenging dilemmas facing our modern times. Whether you are an orphaned 'slumdog' living in Bombay or serving lavishly within the sultanate of Brunei, as peaceful mainstream Muslims, we can help to reclaim the medieval back-pedaling within our current Islamic sociopolitical thought by reawakening the slumber of a Muslim ethic known historically in Arabic as *fada'il al-sabr*, which literally means "the excellences or virtues of patience and perseverance".[50]

Verse 110 of Chapter 16 of the Holy Quran is one of the numerous passages of the Muslim holy book which glorifies the concept of 'patience' or 'perseverance' as a positive form of a peaceful *jihad*: "As for those who after persecution fled their homes and strove actively (*jahadu*) and were patient (*sabaru*) to the last, your Lord will be forgiving and merciful to them on the day when every soul will come pleading to itself." (110:16) The subject of patience and perseverance is further enhanced by a ninth-century work where it was reported that the Prophet Muhammad was once found to be crying in a contemplative state by some of his closest companions. When asked by his companions as to why he was crying, the prophet simply replied by telling them that the tears were caused because, "I am reflecting on the last of my community and the tribulations that they will face...But the patient from among them who arrives will be given the reward of two martyrs [*shahidayn* in Arabic]."[51]

This basic Islamic tradition clearly shows that the patient Muslim woman or man who perseveres peacefully will be given twice the reward of someone who would ever aspire to become a 'military' martyr on a battlefield. Another very famous prophetic *hadith* tradition clearly states that, "The greatest *jihad* is to speak the word of truth to a tyrant."[52] Thus, as millennial Muslims, it again becomes our moral imperative to turn our spiritual gazes inward towards a self-reflective (and nonviolent) sociopolitical paradigm firmly embedded within the central egalitarian ethical teachings of 'love and compassion' found clearly within the basics of our beloved Islamic faith.

For those extremist terrorist skeptics out there who still insist on maintaining violent methodologies to achieve their own perverted political agendas, a brief overview on the Islamic laws of military 'rules of engagement' (or 'ethics of war') should quickly prove that Al-Qaeda and their brainless cronies are so ridiculously far outside of the legal bounds of Islam that even our own Prophet would probably shed a tear if he were alive today. Although Islam (as revealed to the Prophet Muhammad in 7th century Arabia) did historically allow for a physical, outward and military *jihad* in a self-defensive posture against outside violent aggression, the religion of Islam itself is also equally as clear and categorical about the legal 'rules of engagement' for how any 'just war' would be governed within the strict legal parameters of an 'ethics of war'.

First of all, like modern international law today, the Islamic paradigm of military 'rules of engagement' revolves around the established legal doctrine of 'proportionality' and also absolutely outlaws the killing of any innocent man, woman or child (aka civilians) who are active non-combatants to any military conflict at hand. If some violent knucklehead jihadists like the late Osama bin Laden could simply distort (and cherry-pick) aspects of Islam to justify their ungodly violence, then Islamic teachings can also be equally used as their pacifist kryptonite antidote to discredit their abhorrent acts of murder and promote a counter-ideology of Islamic Pacifism for the hearts and minds of future generations of young Muslim girls and boys across the globe.

"If anyone kills a human being unjustly…it shall be as though he has killed all of mankind…If anyone saves a life, it shall be as though he has saved the lives of all of mankind," is the penultimate Quranic verse (5:32) dealing with the concept of unjust murder and its divine punishment within Islamic teachings. Additionally, another verse of the Quran highlights the story of the prophet once discovering the body of a slain woman on a battlefield which caused him to "frown with anger."[53] These legal attitudes prompted a distinct code of conduct (or 'ethics of war') within Islamic legal traditions which include some of the following clear and basic Islamic 'rules of engagement' (which are similar to other Abrahamic religions' strict guidelines for a 'just war'):

- **No killing of women, children, the elderly and other innocents** —these might include hermits, monks, or other religious leaders who are deemed noncombatants;
- **No wanton killing of livestock and animals**;
- **No burning or destruction of trees and orchards**; and,
- **No destruction of water wells**.

To highlight the importance of these basic Islamic rules of engagement, the first caliph named Abu Bakr formulated this same detailed set of rules for Islamic 'rules of engagement' during wartime during his administration as well. For example, during a military campaign against the invading Byzantine Empire, the first caliph (or *khalifa* in Arabic) of Islam explicitly gave the following instructions to a Muslim army setting out for Syria:

> ***"Stop, O people; that I may give you ten rules for your guidance in the battlefield. Do not commit treachery or deviate from the right path. You must not mutilate dead bodies. Neither kill a child, nor a woman, nor an aged man. Bring no harm to the trees, nor burn them with fire, especially those which are fruitful. Slay not any of the enemy's flock, save for your food. You are likely to pass by people who have devoted their lives to monastic services [monks, priests and rabbis]; you are to leave them alone in peace..."***[54]

Quite frankly; since it is virtually impossible to meet and fulfill all of these Islamic legal restrictions and strict requirements for a 'just war'; it would virtually impossible to Islamically justify all of these stringent legal requirements above necessary for the moral application of an outward manifestation of a physical militaristic 'just war'.

Maybe that was the point all along, Osama.

Additionally, any prospective violent *jihadi* recruit should also be reminded of these words promoting non-violence that the Prophet Muhammad uttered when discussing the pitfalls of succumbing to one's politics of rage:

> ***"You are neither hard-hearted nor of fierce character, nor one who shouts in the markets. You do not return evil for evil, but excuse and forgive..."*[55]**

Within another famous prophetic saying on the subject, he also once said that, "The most excellent type of *jihad* is to practice *jihad* against your own self and your own desires for the sake of Allah."[56] He also again once stated that, "The strong is not the one who overcomes people with his strength, but the strong is the one who controls himself while in anger."[57]

Thus, since most global Muslims worldwide would agree that the mainstream Islamic consensus understanding of *jihad* is an 'integral' self-reflective struggle faced by all human beings against our own 'lower selves' (or egos); we can thus help to remove the venom from the spooky 'J-word' by creating a global movement of a 'love *jihad*' led by young Muslim writers, thinkers, public intellectuals and sociopolitical leaders around the world. Together, we can officially 'retire' the overused militaristic violent connotation of this beautiful word from within our casual conversations and shared minutiae of modern public political lexicons. As devout practicing Muslims trying to conquer our own inner (and greater) *jihad*, we can become closer to the Divine simply by focusing on bettering ourselves internally and then making sure that no other human beings ever have to suffer needlessly because of our own shortcomings. As taught by Islam, the concept of 'salvation' is achieved only though God's mercy and a lifetime dedicated to self-improvement and greater social justice- not miraculously attained by pressing one little red detonator button on a suicide bomb-vest somewhere within a crowded metropolitan city square.

Let this journey of a 'love *jihad*' preaching Islamic nonviolence until the end of time be our serene message of universal brotherhood and sisterhood aimed at awakening ourselves from the lazy slumber of the seemingly never-ending stretch of our shared 'Muslim *Malaise*'.

Our 'Muslim *Malaise*'

Within the general abstract, the overall concept behind the French word *malaise* is usually understood to be a general sense of 'depression' or 'painful unease'. Understanding both the nuances of the individual modern-day politics of most of the 56 Muslim-majority countries worldwide and the additional sociopolitical challenges for the 25+ million person Muslim Diaspora in the West (namely within the United States and European Union); the one recurring sociopolitical thesis that has recurred consistently throughout my professional travels within the heart of our three-dimensional geopolitical chessboard is that our current Muslim community of over 1.57 billion men, women and children are not yet able (or willing) to collectively awaken from the generational slumber of our collective sociopolitical 'Muslim *Malaise*'.

For it does not take a rocket scientist to see quite clearly that we Muslims have been the political laughing stock of the world (in terms of geopolitical issues) from the early beginnings of the 20th century. Whether we are talking about despotic oil baron families being propped up as autocratic political regimes in the Persian Gulf or our collective global inability to find a just, lasting, equitable and final political (note: not military) peaceful solution to the Israeli/Palestinian question; empirically speaking, our global Islamic community has tended to be on the 'short end of the political stick' in terms of the average Muslim man, woman or child upon the streets of Cairo, Gaza, Paris, Islamabad or Jakarta.

For these and many other reasons, we have sadly passed along our previous generation's 'Muslim *Malaise*' in terms of geopolitical baggage, unspeakable poverty, internal extremism, pandemic illiteracy, sectarian violence and astronomical infant mortality rates across the Muslim world over the last one hundred years alone. To highlight this point, according to the Population Reference Bureau (PRB), the war-torn Muslim nations of Afghanistan, Somalia, Pakistan and Iraq are currently four of the worst countries within the bottom one-third of global nations with the highest infant mortality rates in the entire world.[58] With seemingly perpetual civil wars and autocratic regimes who continue to rule the plurality of our 56 Muslim-majority countries around the world, it should then come as little surprise to any reasonable observer that the collective pathos of Muslim citizens within these not-so-free societies would then probably revolve itself around the politics of despair and rage. It is from within this specter of a shared desperation and 'politics of rage' that you then begin to see fringe criminal (and pathological) minority elements who then decide to grab their megaphones and proceed to 'cherry-pick' facets of the shared religion of their respective peoples in order to further their own perverted hateful political agendas. Truthfully, they have done this in order to advance their own near-sighted right-wing political agenda which every sensible Muslim knows is a complete violation of the truly peaceful teachings of Islam sent down to the Prophet Muhammad within the sands of Arabia over fourteen hundred years ago.

Even so, reclusive millionaire cave-dwelling terrorists have unfortunately been able to present their hate-filled 'political cherries' to the rest of the world within these last few years in a depressingly successful manner. Because of this phenomenon, it then becomes the moral and religious imperative upon the remainder of our next generation of Muslim youth to help reclaim Islam's true culture of humanity by showing to the rest of the world the vast magnificence of our diverse peaceful cherry tree (minus Osama's cancerous cherries) in order to help bring humankind back together for the advancement of all people of every color, religion, and ethnicity around the world.

Even though you are no longer alive to hear this message, Osama; it is still important to note that our love-filled egalitarian Muslim cherries will always taste a lot better than your ungodly hate-filled ones that you tried to poison us with during your lifetime of murderous infamy.

Welcome to the 'Post-Osama' Era

To every young Muslim girl or boy throughout the planet who will eventually become our respected teachers, doctors, public intellectuals and political leaders of tomorrow; you can personally help to improve your own respective Muslim societies through the basic ethos of Islamic Pacifism and embarking upon a 'love *jihad*' by calling for sweeping sociopolitical, human rights and legal reforms within your 56 Muslim-majority countries where you live and breathe every day. Some of these major sweeping reforms within the Muslim world which will be discussed in detail later in this book include the following:

1) ***Improve women's rights*** *within your countries within every legal and political arena;*
2) ***Abolish the death penalty*** *within your Muslim nations;*
3) *Protect the* ***religious freedom of every human being*** *around the entire world;*
4) *Call for a comprehensive* ***global moratorium on sectarianism*** *within Islam to end the global Sunni / Shia conflict; and*

5) ***Call-out our own autocratic political regimes*** *within our so-called 'Muslim' nations for any continued violations of international human rights law.*

As the next generation of young millennial Muslims, we must always primarily remember that both Islam and the world will both outlive us tomorrow and that our own numbered days on this earthly plane are numbered and quickly fleeting. In the short time span that we all have remaining to share this beautiful planet, let us give every young Muslim girl and boy a true 'audacity of hope' for a better future based on a higher Islamic moral and ethical standard where we promise to help protect every living human being from ever going hungry or needlessly dying on any given day. As proud and practicing Muslims, let us also continue to pray five (5) times a day towards Mecca, fast from food and drink during the holy month of Ramadan and donate generous amounts of *zakat* (or charity) to the poor; which will all help to make our respective local grassroots societies a better place to live for everyone. Finally, let us all truly exemplify the Quranic adage where the Prophet Muhammad (peace be upon him) was told that we as sincere Muslims must show the world Islam's true central essence of being a "mercy to mankind." (21:107)

The legendary Sufi mystical poet (and scholar of Sunni Islam) Maulana Jalaluddin Rumi once said that, "Conventional opinion is the ruin of our souls." Since challenging conventional wisdom is essential to the advancement of any enlightened human society; if you remember nothing else, please make sure that you truly remember that the central 'love and compassion' egalitarian ethical teachings of Islam should be the driving force in successfully pursuing a purpose-filled life down the straight path. Let us also sincerely rededicate our lives to a completely peaceful global coexistence with every other member of the human race (regardless of their color, religion or race) in a way that God would be proud of us.

This is how we can successfully give birth to a new 'Post-Osama' sociopolitical Muslim millennial era by rhetorically spitting in the face of the terrorist cave-dweller who is thankfully no longer roaming our beloved earth. Similarly, to our sisters and brothers of all other races and religions, in addition to the categorical belief within Islamic Pacifism of the unconditional equality of all humanity; if you also believe that: **1) All murder is ungodly, 2) All racism**

is devilish, and 3) All wars are crimes; then you are also one step closer to joining our universal movement towards reviving the slumbering gentle giant of global pacifism. Whether you are a Christian pacifist, Jewish pacifist, Buddhist pacifist, Hindu pacifist or secular pacifist, our international community of colorless pacifists of all backgrounds can help reclaim the esteemed flag of the 'Global Religious Left' starting from this very day onward.

Together, we can all help to recalibrate our skewed equilibrium from teetering to the brink of apocalyptic warfare; with this humanitarian ethos based solely on the undying principle that religion will now only be used for 'good' from this point forward in our shared human history. Remembering that we all share the religious foundations of the 'Golden Rule' principle, we must move forward within our lives affirming the true equality of all people and by always remembering that only he (or she) who is without sin has the moral authority to cast the first (or any) stone. Having said that, only when we fully accept our own respective human fallibilities as imperfect and mortal human beings will we ever have the silent lucidity to see all other people (especially those who are different from us) in that same loving light of Zen-like equality.

Similarly, if you were completely sick and tired of a cave-dwelling, bobble-headed cartoon caricature terrorist named Osama bin Laden representing all Muslims and the illustrious fabric of 21st century millennial Islam; simply put; we must again 'clean our own house' first before we can ever expect to have any rightful credibility with the rest of the international community of modern nations on any political matter. Until we are successful in implementing some of the major sweeping global sociopolitical, human rights and legal reforms mentioned above, we will never successfully awaken ourselves from the shared slumber of our collective 'Muslim *Malaise*'.

Until that one fine day, we in the global Muslim community will simply continue to be the political laughing stock of the world.

As an irreverently imperfect interpreter of global maladies, let it be pledged from this day onward that we will all live meaningful lives dedicated to cleaning the stain of extremism from our own respective ranks within the global marketplace of ideas. In our Abrahamic sisters' and brothers' own respective philosophical traditions of a 'purpose-drive life' and *tikkun olam* (Hebrew for 'repairing the world'), let us utilize *Islamic Pacifism* to help supplement the recalibration of our sociopolitical compasses seeking to help redefine a diversely vibrant 21st-century Islam secured within a basic humanitarian ethical foundation. Finally, as we all jointly embark upon our own respective spiritual (and quixotic) life journeys towards the final unreachable quest for human enlightenment, let us also continue to earnestly pray the devil back to hell each and every day by continuing to call for an international human *détente* or a 'millennial farewell to arms'. By successfully reawakening the slumbering gentle giant of 'global pacifism', people of all colors, religions and nationalities can do their own small part in helping to slightly recalibrate the divine course of human history during these final few remaining days that we all have left to share together before each one of us inevitably leaves this mortal earth and ultimately discover ourselves finally knocking on heaven's door.

CHAPTER FIVE: UNGODLY TERROR: BALI, MADRID, LONDON AND MUMBAI

"This is [simply] a mass murder..."

-Prime Minister Jose Maria Aznar of Spain

During the busy morning rush hour of March 11, 2004, more than ten different bombs choreographically exploded inside four (4) different commuter passenger trains almost simultaneously in a coordinated terrorist attack in Madrid, Spain; which killed over 191 innocent people and staggeringly wounded over 1,800 others by the time the smoke would clear that day.[1] In terms of its socio-political seismic scale, the 3/11 Madrid train bombings was the single deadliest terrorist attack inside all of Europe since the tragedy of the 1988 terrorist bombing of Pan Am World Airways Flight 103; which killed over 270 innocent souls over Lockerbie, Scotland nearly sixteen years earlier on December 21, 1988.[2] "This is [simply] a mass murder," said Prime Minister Jose Maria Aznar immediately after the 3/11 Madrid train attacks in his solemn vow to find the murderous criminals responsible for this horrendous attack. According to then-Prime Minister Aznar: "March 11, 2004 now holds its place in the history of infamy"[3] for the people of Spain.

Beginning at six o'clock in the morning on that fateful day, the four different commuter trains left their respective train platforms within fifteen (15) minutes of each other from the Alcala de Henares train station (about 12 kilometers [7 miles] from the center of Madrid).[4] Spanish police investigators would later determine that as each of the four trains would respectively passed through the Alcala train station; the Madrid attackers had then each placed bags or backpacks containing over 22 pounds (10 kg) of bomb-laden explosives onto different passenger cars of each of their four respective trains on that morning in question.[5] When the first train stopped at the nearby Atocha train station at 6:39 am on that March morning, three (3) different bombs exploded within three different carriages of that train; killing over 34 people instantly.[6] Almost simultaneously thereafter, two other bombs exploded aboard the second train, waiting right outside the same Atocha station.[7] At 6:41am and 6:42am (respectively), the third and fourth trains exploded at other Madrid train stations throughout the city.[8] According to Spanish police investigators, each one of the four train bombs was remotely detonated via mobile cell phones.[9]

Needless to say, these coordinated terrorist attacks immediately caused massive chaos and confusion at Madrid's train stations on that otherwise lovely March morning in 2004. A local Spanish commuter (and eyewitness) from another train platform at the time of the bomb explosions once told BBC World News that, "People started to scream and run, some bumping into each other. I saw people with blood pouring from them, people on the ground."[10] Another eyewitness said that "there were pieces of train in the street and dead people trapped in the twisted iron" amidst the bloody carnage.[11]

With the 3/11 Madrid train attacks occurring a mere three days before Spain's 2004 national presidential election, the Spanish government wasted no time in immediately blaming the terrorist attack on ETA (*Euskadi Ta Askatasuna* or "Basque Homeland and Freedom" in English); a nationalistic Basque separatist organization known for its anti-government violence in the past.[12] In referencing to them as the primary suspects in the 3/11 Madrid train bombings, Spanish Interior Minister Angel Acebes told BBC World News at the time that, "There is no doubt ETA is responsible."[13]

"ETA had been looking for a massacre...Unfortunately, today it achieved its goal."[14] At the time, so certain was the global community of ETA's responsibility that the United Nations Security Council even immediately passed an emergency resolution condemning ETA for the 3/11 Madrid train attacks. In fairness, some other global experts at the time did state publicly that the 3/11 attacks did not fit ETA's usual criminal style (or *modus operandi*); adding that this specific group usually gave a warning <u>before</u> any of their previous terrorist attacks in the past.[15]

One day after the attacks, on March 12, 2004, Spanish police officials located a 'suspicious' van in an isolated area near the city of Madrid. According to *The New York Times*, Spanish law enforcement officials apparently found bomb detonators and an audio cassette tape with "Quranic verses" inside of the suspicious van in question.[16] Shortly after this van discovery, the Brigade of Abu Hafs al-Masri (an Al-Qaeda affiliated group) official claimed responsibility for the 3/11 Madrid train attacks in what it referred to as "Operation Death Trains."[17] In their public global statement sent to London's *Al-Quds al-Arabi* newspaper, the terrorist group claimed that one of its "death squads" had destroyed "one of the pillars of the crusade alliance, Spain."[18] According to their email letter sent to the British Arabic newspaper: "This is part of settling old accounts with Spain, the crusader, and America's ally in its war against Islam."[19] The letter sent by the suspicious group concluded by ominously asking the Spanish people: "[Spanish Prime Minister] Aznar, where is America? Who will protect you, Britain, Japan, Italy and others from us?"[20]

Since this letter could not immediately be authenticated at the time in any meaningful manner by the Spanish government, the office of Prime Minster Jose Maria Aznar still publicly maintained that "there are more possibilities that it's ETA [responsible more] than any other organization."[21] Just another three days later, the ruling conservative-right Spanish government of Prime Minister Jose Maria Aznar lost in the March 2004 national general elections in Spain when millions of Spanish citizens politically retaliated against the ruling conservative political parties because they felt collectively misled by their government's continued claims that ETA was the culprit of the 3/11 Madrid train attacks.[22]

Nonetheless, Spanish police and law enforcement officials continued to earnestly look for the real terrorist culprits of the 3/11 Madrid train attacks. *The New York Times* reported that Spanish government officials eventually came to believe that the train bombings were "carried out by a group of North African Islamists that intersected with a band of petty criminals whose ringleader, Jamal Ahmidan, had become radicalized in a Moroccan jail."[23] One month after the bombings in April 2004, "Seven [7] of the main suspects, including Mr. [Jamal] Ahmidan, blew themselves up [and died] in a Madrid apartment when they were surrounded by the police [during the tense standoff] three weeks after the attacks...Four other [suspects] are believed to have fled" the scene of the standoff at the apartment building.[24]

Shortly thereafter, the Spanish Parliament would ultimately set up an official governmental commission to investigate the 3/11 Madrid train bombings; with more than 30 people testifying during the five-month-long official government inquiry.[25] Since that time, more than seventy (70) other different suspected individuals have been arrested in direct connection for their respective roles in the 3/11 Madrid train bombings.[26] In November 2007, over seventeen (17) people were convicted by a Spanish court for their criminal roles in the tragic 3/11 Madrid terrorist train bombings.[27] During the same November 2007 legal verdict, the three-judge Spanish tribunal court additionally acquitted a total of seven other major suspects and the 17 aforementioned convicted criminals were found guilty of lesser criminal charges related to the attacks; including belonging to an officially-designated terrorist organization. The prison jail-sentences for the convicted 3/11 Madrid terrorists ranged from 3 years to almost 43,000 years; although under Spanish law, the maximum anyone is legally forced to serve is forty (40) consecutive calendar years in prison.[28] Additionally, one defendant was released during the criminal trial for a lack of evidence.

In response to the 3/11 Madrid train bombings, the largest Islamic commission in Spain issued a public decree against Al-Qaeda and Osama bin Laden on behalf of the country's nearly 230,000 Muslims highlighting their anti-terror stance and thanked the Spanish society at large for drawing a line between Islam and terror. "We are going to issue a *fatwa* [religious decree] against Osama bin Laden," said the late Mansour Escudero, who used to lead the Federation of Islamic religious entities (known as the 'Feeri') and who was also once co-secretary general of the Spanish government-created commission on Muslims. This government commission applauded Spanish-based imams for condemning all acts of terrorism at Friday prayers around the nation.

"We have called on [Spanish] imams to make a formal declaration condemning terrorism and for a special prayer for all the victims of terrorism," the late Mr. Escudero once told *Agence-France Presse* (AFP) about the Spanish Muslim initiative. He had also drawn up a document designed to "thank the Spanish people and the government for their attitude towards Muslims" since the 3/11 attacks, in particular for not taking "disproportionate measures similar to those which the September 11 attacks sparked in the United States" against American Muslims.[29] The Spanish people "feel deep and strong solidarity with the victims and their loved ones who have shown an exemplary attitude by never pointing a finger at the country's Muslim population but on the contrary, could tell the difference between terrorists and the Muslim people," another secretary general of the commission, Riay Tatary, once told private Spanish radio station *Cadena Ser*.[30]

The five-page Spanish Muslim anti-terrorism *fatwa* declared that "the terrorist acts" of Al-Qaeda and its leader Osama Bin Laden "are totally forbidden and the object of strong condemnation" by Muslims everywhere. The Spanish fatwa was issued by the Islamic Commission of Spain, created by the government in 1991 to be the representative of the country's Muslim minority. The Islamic religious edict finally said that people like Osama bin Laden are completely "outside of Islam", adding that he, Al-Qaeda and all those "who try to justify terrorism by basing it on the Noble Quran are outside Islam" as well. Finally, the prominent commission of Spanish Muslim leaders rightfully concluded that given the group's support for terrorism, Osama bin Laden and Al-Qaeda "must not be considered Muslims nor treated as such."[31]

7/7 London Bombings (July 2005)

During the busy morning commuter rush hour on the morning of July 7, 2005, four young British men each individually boarded a train for King's Cross railway station on the edge of central London knowing that they were each beginning the final day of their lives. Tragically for the rest of London, thousands of other British commuters and citizens had no way of knowing that these casually-dressed young men were each carrying over 10 pounds (5 kilograms) of bomb explosives within their respective bags or backpacks on that otherwise lovely day in London in July 2005.[32] According to British authorities, official government closed-circuit television (CCTV) cameras caught each of the four men on video when they each respectively reached King's Cross railway station on the morning of July 7, 2005; apparently hugging each other as if they were "happy, even euphoric."[33] From the King's Cross train station, these four young British men would then spread out onto four different London train lines and ultimately cause the greatest terrorist attack to ever hit the soil of the United Kingdom.

At 8:50 in the morning on that day, three (3) different trains on the London Underground (or 'Tube') network exploded almost simultaneously in a coordinated terrorist attack.[34] About one hour later, an explosion decimated one of London's famous red double-decker commuter buses.[35] By ten o'clock in the morning on that fateful day, over 52 innocent people were dead and more than 770 others were injured.[36]

The first train involved in the 7/7 London bombings was the Piccadilly line train (Number 331) traveling to the Russell Square underground Tube station. On this first train, one of the four bombers (Germaine Lindsey, Age: 19) placed a bag full of explosives in the train's front carriage, according to official British government and media reports. On this first train, at least twenty-six (26) people were instantly killed and more than 340 people were injured in the first (and most deadly) of the four 7/7 bombings in London that day.[37] Almost simultaneously, the second train (Number 204 Circle line train) traveling to Aldgate station was destroyed by the second bomber (Shehzad Tanweer, Age: 22); killing at least seven (7) people and injuring 171 others.[38] Another man (Mohammad Sidique Khan, Age: 30) boarded the third train (Number 216 train to Paddington station) where his bomb would ultimately kill six (6) other innocent commuters and injuring over 160 other commuters at the Edgeware Road Station.[39] At 9:47 am, the fourth bomber (Hasib Mir Hussain, Age: 18) ultimately struck when a red double-decker commuter bus passed nearby at the British Medical Association in Tavistock Square. During this fourth final explosion, the bomb exploded on the upper-deck of the bus; killing at least thirteen (13) people instantly and injuring more than 110 people in the surrounding area.[40]

When the smoke finally cleared in London at the end of that day, BBC World News would officially report that over fifty-two (52) people were killed in total during the July 7, 2005 London terrorist attacks.[41] In addition to the 52 people killed, every single one of the four (4) bombers also killed themselves in the suicide terrorist attacks that day inside Great Britain. Within six days of the July 7th bombings, British police and law enforcement agencies had investigated the criminal 'profiles' of the four 7/7 bombers; young British Muslim men ranging from the ages of 18 to 30. According to most official media reports, these were apparently ordinary British men- with one man being a teacher's assistant and another man being a student of art.[42] Friends and associates of the four bombers said that they saw no serious signs of extremist tendencies, but in some cases, they did notice that the men gravitated towards "out of character" solitary isolation as the days grew closer to the 7/7 London attacks.[43]

The eldest of the four terrorists, 30-year-old Mohammad Sidique Khan, ultimately provided more insight about their terrorist plan through a videotaped 'last will and testament' which was aired on *Al Jazeera* television news network in September 2005.[44] In this video, Mohammad Sidique Khan prayed for martyrdom and spoke of his motivation for committing these acts of terrorism. According to the final "Report of the Official Account of the Bombings in London on 7th July 2005" commissioned by the British government, some relevant excerpts from the Khan video included: "Your democratically-elected governments continuously perpetuate atrocities against my people all over the world. And your support of them makes you directly responsible, just as I am directly responsible for protecting and avenging my Muslim brothers and sisters...Until we feel security, you will be our targets...And until you stop the bombing, gassing, imprisonment and torture of my people we will not stop this fight...We are at war and I am a solider...Now you too will taste the reality of this situation."[45]

In conclusion, the video continued to praise similar global terrorists like "Osama Bin Laden, Dr. Ayman al-Zawahiri and Abu Musab al-Zarqawi."[46] Less than two months later, in September 2005, Ayman al-Zawahri, Al-Qaeda's global second-in-command, praised the 7/7 London terrorist attacks in a televised video aired on *Al-Jazeera* and spoke of 7/7 as part of Al-Qaeda's greater global strategy.[47] "I talk to you today about the blessed London battle which came as a slap to the face of the tyrannical, crusader British arrogance... It's a sip from the glass that the Muslims have been drinking from" everyday of their lives.[48]

"This blessed battle has transferred — like its glorious predecessors in New York, Washington, and Madrid — the battle to the enemies' land, after many centuries of the battle being on our [Muslim] land and after [Western] troops have occupied our land in Chechnya, Afghanistan, Iraq and Palestine," continued al-Zawahiri in this September 2005 video.[49] According to British law enforcement and government officials, the United Kingdom could not immediately confirm (or authenticate) al-Zawahri's claim that Al-Qaeda had planned the 7/7 attacks, but did note that the 7/7 London attacks were operationally in-line with Al-Qaeda's overall ideology and criminal methodology.[50] As of September 2009, no other person had yet been arrested or criminally charged in direct connection with the 7/7 London terrorist bombings. Notwithstanding the ongoing criminal investigation, an official British governmental committee did publicly praise the rescue-and-relief efforts of the emergency workers, first-responders, police officers, and ordinary brave British citizens who courageously helped the injured victims of the horrifying July 7, 2005 terrorist attacks in London, England.[51]

In direct response to the 7/7 London bombings, nearly 500 British Muslim clerics, scholars and *imams* (or prayer leaders) issued a global *fatwa* condemning terrorism and religious extremism. As reported by BBC World News, the British *fatwa* against terrorism reads in part:[52]

> ***"Islam strictly, strongly and severely condemns the use of violence and the destruction of innocent lives...***
>
> ***"There is neither place nor justification in Islam for extremism, fanaticism or terrorism. Suicide bombings, which killed and injured innocent people in London, are haram - vehemently prohibited in Islam- and those who committed these barbaric acts in London are criminals not martyrs...***
>
> ***"Such acts, as perpetrated in London, are crimes against all of humanity and contrary to the teachings of Islam...***
>
> ***"The Holy Quran declares:***
>
> ***'Whoever kills a human being, then it is as though he has killed all mankind; and whoever saves a human life, it is as though he had saved all mankind.' (Surah al-Maidah (5), verse 32).***
>
> ***"Islam's position is clear and unequivocal: [the] murder of one soul is the murder of the whole of humanity; he who shows no respect for human life is an enemy of humanity."***

In conclusion, the British *fatwa* against terrorism stated quite clearly: "We pray for the defeat of extremism and terrorism in the world."[53]

The Bali Nightclub Bombings (October 2005)

On the tropical evening of October 1, 2005, several popular holiday resorts and tourist nightclubs in Bali, Indonesia once again became the tragic victims of senseless terrorist bombings. Bomb explosions rocked two (2) outdoor beach resorts at Jimbaran Bay; a scenic beachfront which offers a serene horizon view of the setting evening sun over Southeast Asia.[54] Almost instantly, more additional bombs simultaneously exploded at the shopping area hub at Kuta, Indonesia; about 30 kilometers (19 miles) away from tranquil Jimbaran Bay.[55] After the carnage was over, the 2005 Bali nightclub bombings would kill a total of at least 26 people and injured over 102 others; according to official Indonesian hospital and government reports.[56]

"The ground [was] just covered in blood, people walking around with arms missing," said Australian eyewitness and journalist Sean Mulcahy, who at the time of the Bali bomb blasts, happened to be immediately next door to one of the restaurants that was bombed in the shopping town of Kuta.[57] Indonesian police officials would later find that the bombers' explosive bomb-vests were packed with 'ball bearings'; a bomb-making explosive technique used to cause maximum human casualties.[58] In addition to native Indonesian victims, many foreign tourists and visitors were also killed as well. According to official reports from Bali, among the dead casualties were Australian, South Korean, American, Japanese, and British nationals, tourists and citizens.

Even more astonishing was the fact that Indonesian media outlets reported that police officials had also found many other unexploded bombs around the Bali area and were thankfully able to successfully diffuse them at the time.[59] Indonesian President Susilo Bambang Yudhoyono immediately condemned the Bali attacks on behalf of all Indonesian people on national television airwaves around the country shortly after the bombings. "These were clearly acts of terrorism because the victims were indiscriminately chosen and the targets were public areas…As president and on behalf of the Republic of Indonesia, I strongly condemn these inhuman acts," President Yudhoyono said to his countrymen during his public address to the nation.[60] In terms of assessing the devastating sociopolitical impact of the Bali attacks on the peace-loving people of

Indonesia, an Australian tourist and eyewitness to the Bali bombings told the Australian Broadcasting Corporation (ABC) that, "The Balinese were just devastated...All the taxi drivers were just saying sorry, and, you know, they were more heartbroken than we are, I suppose, because it just . . . ruins them more than it ruins us."[61]

Although no terrorist group immediately claimed responsibility for the Bali nightclub attacks, official Indonesian suspicions quickly arose that the bombings were probably the work of the group called *Jemaah Islamiyah* (better known as 'JI'); which has been ideologically (and materially) linked with Al-Qaeda in the past. In the past, JI has proudly claimed responsibility for similar terrorist bombings over seven years earlier on October 12, 2002 at another Kuta, Indonesia nightclub;[62] where over 201 people were tragically killed on that tropical evening.[63]

Getting back to the more recent 2005 Bali nightclub bombings, Indonesian law enforcement investigators would later find the severed heads of the three (3) suicide bombers at the crime scenes, but were unable to immediately identify their remains.[64] According to official reports, the suicide bombers' torsos and legs had been completely blown off by the explosive bomb-vests strapped to their chests; their respective heads and feet were to be found a few yards away from the blast sites.[65] Soon after the terrorist bombings, Indonesian police accused two major JI leaders- Azahari bin Husin and Noordin Mohamed Top- of being the masterminds of the 2005 Bali nightclub attacks.[66] Azhari Bin Husin was nicknamed 'Demolition Man' within JI because of his bomb-making skills and Noordin Top was known internally as the 'Moneyman' because of his ability to recruit bombers and financiers for their ungodly terrorist attacks.[67] Both of these men were highly-wanted criminal fugitives within Indonesia and had eluded police capture for years by primarily hiding in densely-populated areas; as they were both suspected of being behind the 2002 Kuta nightclub bombings and other suicide attacks in Jakarta in 2003 and 2004, respectively.[68]

On November 9, 2005, as police surrounded Azahari Bin Husin's hideout on the Indonesian island of Java, the 'Demolition Man' decided to blow himself up to avoid arrest and prosecution; additionally killing two other wanted militants who were holed up inside with him during the 10-day-long standoff with Indonesian police authorities.[69] Over the next one calendar year, four other men were tried and found guilty for their respective criminal involvement in the 2005 Bali nightclub bombings. These four men were found guilty of crimes ranging from supplying bomb-making equipment to transferring a video of Noordin Top onto a computer disk and giving shelter to designated terrorist Noordin Top.[70] It is interesting to note that none of these convicted Bali terrorist criminals received more than eighteen (18) years in prison as a jail sentence.[71] Up until the 2009 Jakarta hotel bombings at the Ritz-Carlton and J.W. Marriott hotels, the fugitive terrorist Noordin Top continued to remain at-large and on-the-run from Indonesian police authorities. Leading up to the 2009 Jakarta hotel bombings, many global political analysts also believed that Noordin Top may have subsequently broken away from *Jemaah Islamiyah* (JI) to form his own independent terrorist splinter group.[72] Our world would again hear the name of Noordin Top once more over four years later as he would later emerge as the prime mastermind terrorist suspect of the 2009 Jakarta 'Five-Star' hotel bombings analyzed later in this chapter.[73]

Only two days after the Bali bombings, the diverse Muslim community in Indonesia reacted swiftly to the bombings in Bali saying that the great majority of Muslims are against terrorism and condemned the bombings in the strongest terms. In a televised press conference, Mr. Kiai Haj Hasyim Muzadi, president of Indonesia's largest Muslim organization Nahdlatul Ulama (NU), offered his condolences and publicly condemned the "use of Islam as an ideology to carry out things which are totally against humanity and the essence of Islam."[74] He further emphasized that, "Terrorism has nothing to do with Islam" and invited Indonesians of all religions to fight terrorism together "hand-in-hand."[75] Also, Mr. Syafii Maarif, former president of the second leading Muslim organization in the country said that, "These bloody actions go against humanity and against the values of Islam...These terrorists define themselves as Muslims but it is unacceptable. No religion could ever excuse such a bloody action against fellow humans."[76] Several well-known Indonesian scholars of Islam also urged the terrorists to "cut off their identity as Muslims because their actions only tarnish the good image of Islam" and violate its basic ethical principles.[77]

Meanwhile, the country's most influential Muslim leader and former Indonesian president, Mr. Abdurrahman Wahid summed up the sentiments of his nation when he expressed his support and solidarity in the fight against terrorism and the urgency of "stopping extremist activities" by not speaking out against the "cowardly action conducted by certain extremists"[78] who distort basic Islamic teachings to further their own political agenda.

2005 Amman Hotel Bombings (November 2005)

During an otherwise beautiful desert winter evening, three nearly-simultaneous bomb explosions rocked foreign-owned hotels killing at least 56 people and injuring over 100 others in Amman, Jordan on that one single night alone.[79] On November 9, 2005, the Grand Hyatt Amman, Amman Days Inn and Amman-Radisson Blu (formerly SAS) hotels- all popular with affluent Jordanians/expatriates and international tourists- were rocked by these bombings on that one evening alone in late November 2005.[80]

At the Amman Radisson-Blu Hotel, over 250 wedding guests were already enjoying the wedding of Mr. Ashraf al-Khaled and Mrs. Nadia al-Alami on that picturesque November evening. Wedding guests and eyewitnesses remember seeing the proud bride and groom standing with their respective fathers, smiling for family photographs inside of the hotel's main foyer and lobby. The wedding party of nearly 300 guests then joyously began to enter the main wedding ballroom of the Amman Radisson-Blu hotel to the sounds of music and laughter all around their wedding party.

"I remember seeing my mum and dad clapping and laughing and smiling... It was wonderful," remembered the proud bride, Mrs. Nadia al-Alami.[81]

But that is when everything changed forever; all too suddenly.

What nobody at the wedding party knew was that two (2) suicide bombers- an Iraqi husband and wife 'team' - were already inside the main wedding ballroom with the intent of destroying the entire Radisson-Blu hotel in Amman.[82] "The music ended and I remember looking behind me and seeing my sister fixing my dress," recalled the bride to BBC World News shortly after the bombings. "Then I felt the hotel shake...I saw my father with his hands clasped to his heart, his eyes rolling....Then [the groom] Ashraf covered me with his body."[83] Only moments later, both of the two proud respective fathers (of both the bride and groom) were tragically killed.[84] Even more tragic was the fact that the bride's mother would also later die because of her extensive injuries from the hotel bombing that night. When the bomb initially went off, the groom (Ashraf al-Khaled) merely thought that the loud explosion was nearby fireworks for their wedding celebration.[85]

But then he saw all of the blood.

"I could see my father-in-law had died....I went to my [own] father, he was near the door, my mum was there screaming and calling for help...He was already dead; I saw his brain outside his head," the groom told reporters shortly after the terrorist attack. "I went inside and saw a lot of bodies on the floor, it was a big mess, everything was white at our wedding, but it all turned red because of the blood," he remembered about his wedding night in November 2005.[86] Bravely though, the groom would also later tell the Associated Press (AP) that terrorism would never win and that these acts do not hurt anyone more than Muslims and Arabs around the world themselves.

"The world has to know [that] this has nothing to do with Islam...We should show people all over the world that this is not Islam because this cannot help us as Arabs or as Muslims."[87]

Nearby at the Grand Hyatt hotel in Amman on that same evening, the bomb which had just simultaneously exploded there inside of the main hotel lobby created "a huge ball of fire [that shot] up to the ceiling and then everything went black," according to a French United Nations (UN) official at the scene.[88] Scores of restaurant dinner guests and hotel staff at the Grand Hyatt immediately began to help each other move the dead and injured victims safely outside of the hotel's perimeter.[89] According to official reports, two senior Palestinian political officials were among the confirmed dead victims.[90] The most notable casualty of the Amman Grand Hyatt hotel bombing was Mr. Moustapha Akkad, a Syrian film producer and Hollywood director who was best known for producing the *Halloween* horror movie series and directing the globally-acclaimed motion pictures *Muhammad: Messenger of God* and *Lion of the Desert* (starring two-time Academy Award winning actor, Anthony Quinn). Even sadder, both Mr. Akkad and his daughter (Rima Akkad Monla) were both killed together that evening from the bomb blast at the Grand Hyatt hotel.[91] Relatives of another Grand Hyatt hotel bombing victim would later tell the *Washington Post* about the powerful resilience of her fellow Jordanian citizens and how the peaceful citizens of Amman were not going to be scared by terrorists of any kind.

"We want to make it known loud and clear that this is not Islam," said Merissa Khurma, press attaché for the Jordanian Embassy in Washington DC to the *Washington Post* shortly after the attacks. "And we will reclaim Islam back from those who hijacked it."[92] Ms. Khurma again echoed these same powerful sentiments during a November 2005 commentary for National Public Radio (NPR) when she said that, "I grew up [as] a Muslim in Amman, and this is not the Islam [that] I know." She concluded by saying: "Life will never be the same."

"This is our 9/11."[93]

Soon thereafter, Al-Qaeda in Iraq issued a public statement claiming full responsibility for the 2005 Amman hotel bombings; linking them to the US-led war and occupation in Iraq.[94] In their public statement, the group stated that Jordan was the target that evening because the city of Amman was "a filthy place for the traitors" and "a center for prostitution."[95]

"The Jordanian despot turned [the chosen hotels into] a backyard garden for the enemies of the religion, Jews and crusaders,"[96] said the statement. Though this claim of responsibility could not be immediately authenticated by the Jordanian government, it did resonate with already mounting suspicions of Al-Qaeda amongst average Jordanians on the streets of Amman. Furthermore, Jordanian government and law enforcement officials in Amman had immediately suspected the hotel bombings to be the infamous work of the notorious terrorist Abu Musab al-Zarqawi; a Jordanian national who was the leader of 'Al-Qaeda in Iraq' and was already a wanted criminal for his connections with other terrorist attacks and unsolved murders within the country of Jordan.[97]

As the people of his country mourned together, King Abdullah II of Jordan immediately promised that his country would pursue the terrorist masterminds behind the 2005 Amman hotel attacks. "We will pull them from their holes and bring them to justice," said King Abdullah shortly after the Amman bombings.[98] Similarly, hundreds of thousands of peaceful Jordanian citizens echoed the King's message of peace as they lowered national flags to half-mast and peacefully marched in the streets of Amman against terrorism.[99]

"Zarqawi! From Amman; We say to you: '*You are a coward!*'" thousands chanted in the streets of Amman during their peaceful counter-terrorism protests around the country.[100] According to official media and government reports, over 250,000+ people joined anti-terrorism protests and peaceful marches within cities throughout Jordan (and the greater Middle East) in direct response to the tragic November 2005 Amman hotel bombings.[101]

In the meantime, the police investigation would soon reveal that at least four of the hotel suicide bombers had entered into Jordan from Iraq less than one week before the bombings; using fake passports and travel documents to cross the porous Iraq/Jordan border. An Iraqi woman- Mrs. Sajida Mubarak Atrous Al-Rishawi- was soon arrested after police raided the apartment that she shared with her husband and two other bombers that they had jointly rented a mere two days before the November 2005 Amman hotel bombings.[102] At the time, Jordanian police officials on the scene stated that Mrs. Al-Rishawi was fast asleep when she was arrested and shockingly was still wearing her suicide bomb-vest as she slept on her bed.[103]

In a taped confession aired on Jordanian national television, Mrs. Sajida Al-Rishawi proceeded to confess that a certain 'driver' had transported the suicide bombers from Iraq to Jordan. She further confessed that this 'driver' was the overall mastermind in the planning of the Amman hotel attacks; providing each of the bombers with explosive belts and explaining how to operate their explosive bomb-vests.[104] She and her husband were assigned to bomb the Radisson-Blu hotel wedding party. According to reports, the husband-and-wife team strapped suicide vests underneath their fancy wedding attire and proceeded to enter the main hotel ballroom for the nearly 300-person wedding. When her bomb vest apparently did not explode upon detonation, Mrs. Al-Rishawi's husband then immediately pushed her outside of the wedding ballroom and detonated his own bomb-vest instead.[105] Mrs. Al-Rishawi had immediately become a prime suspect on that same evening of the bombing when Jordanian police were alerted about a potential female criminal suspect running from the scene of the crime at the nearby Radisson-Blu hotel.[106]

Al-Qaeda in Iraq's later public statement claiming responsibility would also mention an unnamed woman (Mrs. Al-Rishawi) who "chose to accompany her husband to his martyrdom."[107] Furthermore, Jordanian police would also find what they believed to be the severed remains of the three (3) other male suicide bombers at the Grand Hyatt, Days Inn, and Radisson-Blu hotels around Amman that evening.[108] Soon thereafter, more than 120 people were subsequently arrested by Jordanian police authorities in direct connection with the Amman hotel attacks; including twelve (12) other primary terrorism 'suspects'.[109]

In her five-month-long criminal trial, Mrs. Sajida Al-Rishawi was legally tried for her criminal role in the 2005 Amman hotel terrorist bombings. Not surprisingly, she changed her story in court several times, now stating that she never wanted to participate in the hotel attacks and that she ran away without trying to detonate her bomb-vest.[110] Now pleading innocence, she would also later claim that her earlier videotaped confession was given 'under duress'.[111] Furthermore, she finally stated that she had only married her husband (and fellow hotel bomber) only a few days before the attacks itself.[112] Nonetheless, Mrs. Sajida Al-Risahwi was found guilty by a Jordanian court and sentenced to death in September 2006. Additionally, six other criminal defendants were at-large but were tried in absentia; and all seven (7) total criminal defendants were sentenced to death by hanging.[113] Similarly, the notorious terrorist Abu Musab Al-Zarqawi was also tried in absentia, but the Jordanian court dropped these criminal charges after Al-Zarqawi was killed by a U.S. airstrike in June 2006.[114] By this verdict, Mrs. Sajida Al-Rishawi became the first woman ever sentenced to death for terrorism charges in Jordan.[115] Subsequently, Jordan's highest court again upheld her death sentence in a January 2007 appeal hearing.[116]

As mentioned previously, Abu Musab al-Zarqawi, the infamous terrorist mastermind of the 2005 Amman hotel bombings, would be killed by an allied air-strike in Baquba, Iraq (north of Baghdad) a few months later on June 7, 2006 ending his reign of terror.[117]

The Assassination of Benazir Bhutto (December 2007)

The late Benazir Bhutto will always be historically remembered as the woman who successfully made history by becoming Pakistan's first female Prime Minister – twice.[118] She followed in the famous political footsteps of her father, former Prime Minister Zulfikar Ali Bhutto, when she was herself elected to the prime ministerial position in both 1988 and again in 1993.[119] Despite her strong educational background and her impressive electoral victories within a male-dominated Muslim society of over 172 million people (sixth largest population in the world), Mrs. Benazir Bhutto's political career was controversial; to say the least. Because both of her political tenures were greatly mired by widespread ruthless corruption, bribery and murder, she was ultimately dismissed as Prime Minister of Pakistan from both of her elected terms by Pakistan's president on these widespread charges of political corruption. Such were the Shakespearean depths of Mrs. Bhutto's own turbulent political life that when Mrs. Bhutto's own brother and political rival- Mr. Murtaza Bhutto- was murdered during a gun battle with police in September 1996; she was accused by many, including her own mother, of ordering the killing; and her husband Asif Ali

Zardari was tried in Pakistani court for his complicity in the murder of his own brother-in-law.[120]

Furthermore, Swiss lawyers announced a June 1998 legal indictment against both Mrs. Bhutto and her husband on money-laundering charges relating to illegal misuse of Swiss bank accounts. In April 1999, Mrs. Bhutto was sentenced by a Pakistani court in Rawalpindi to up to five (5) years in prison and she was further legally banned from holding any elected political office in Pakistan ever again.[121] Although she had always publicly maintained that these corruption and murder allegations were untrue and politically motivated,[122] Mrs. Bhutto subsequently exiled herself to London (and later Dubai) in 1999 and became a high-priced regular on the international speaking circuit.[123]

Nearly one decade later, General Pervez Musharraf, the Pakistani soft dictator who had taken the presidency through a 1999 bloodless military coup, felt his executive power waning towards the end of his soft-dictatorial term. Sensing a neutralizing political ally in Benazir Bhutto, in October 2007, Mrs. Bhutto was allowed to return to Pakistan when General Musharraf granted her amnesty from her political and legal corruption charges. Of course, this was in direct exchange for her 'political support' as a legitimizing neutral ally for his dictatorial military regime and their fight against internal religious militancy within Pakistan itself.[124] Shortly upon her return to Pakistan in October 2007, Mrs. Bhutto soon regained her prominent political position within the country as a potential future presidential candidate and thousands of people flocked to her traveling political entourages as they traveled by bus and train throughout the country to campaign for her Pakistan Peoples Party (PPP) in nationwide elections.[125] Even so, it is also important for everyone to remember that Mrs. Benazir Bhutto was still as hated within Pakistan as she was loved; if not even more.

Mrs. Benazir Bhutto would escape her first assassination attempt in Karachi, Pakistan shortly after her arrival back from Dubai in October 2007 when her convoy and parade route was bombed by two different suicide bombers.[126] Although Mrs. Bhutto narrowly survived this first major assassination attempt against her life, more than 123 innocent Pakistani men, women and children (on her welcoming parade route) were tragically killed by this bombing attack on that October evening in 2007.[127]

Less than two months later, on December 27, 2007, Mrs. Benazir Bhutto would attend her last political rally ever in the city of Rawalpindi; the garrison sister-city of Pakistan's capital of Islamabad. On that particular December day, as Mrs. Bhutto was standing atop the sunroof of her armored vehicle-smiling and waving to the crowded masses through the open-roof escape hatch atop of her armored escort vehicle- a nearby armed assassin shot at her twice at close-range from only a few feet away.[128] Mrs. Bhutto initially escaped the would-be assassin's bullets, but a nearby secondary bomb detonated a massive explosion in the park only moments later; killing over twenty-one innocent bystanders at the Rawalpindi political rally.[129]

After frantically being rushed by ambulance, former Pakistani Prime Minister Benazir Bhutto succumbed to her injuries and later died at a near-by hospital in Rawalpindi that same day on December 27, 2007.[130]

Absolute chaos and confusion erupted immediately within Pakistan as the societal debate quickly raged on why Mrs. Bhutto was killed which led to widespread allegations of corruption, conspiracy theories and political cover-ups against Pakistani authorities (especially directed at Pakistan's own tin-pot dictator, Pervez Musharraf).[131] Initial media reports stated that Mrs. Bhutto had died when the initial assassin's bullets had struck her in the head and that two attackers were involved in the assassination – one for the gunshots and one for the subsequent bomb explosion- inside the Rawalpindi park on that December day.[132] Later official government reports would indicate that Mrs. Bhutto had not died from the initial assassin gunshots, but was actually killed from traumatic head injuries sustained during the massive secondary bomb blast. These other official reports in Pakistan also stated that there was only one (1) lone assassin who was responsible for the entire event.[133]

This is where the whole political 'blame game' began within Pakistan.

President Pervez Musharraf wasted no time at all in immediately pointing his finger on the Bhutto assassination towards the Pakistani Taliban leader named Baitullah Mehsud; who would later deny any involvement in Benazir's December 2007 political assassination. In turn, millions of Pakistani citizens collectively raised their middle fingers to the dictator and directly blamed Musharraf himself for orchestrating the whole Bhutto assassination.[134] Ultimately, even Al-Qaeda jumped into the political fray by claiming responsibility on some Internet websites and some Pakistani (and American) government officials would later agree that the Taliban (and/or their local Al-Qaeda affiliates within Pakistan) were most probably responsible for the Bhutto assassination.[135]

At around the same time, the most haunting (and disconcerting) historical fact was that Mrs. Benazir Bhutto herself had stated before her untimely death that she would personally hold General Pervez Musharraf responsible for any future assassination attempts on her life. In a now-famous October 2007 Bhutto personal e-mail read on-air live by CNN television anchor Wolf Blitzer, Mrs. Bhutto was quoted as saying to a friend that she would "hold Musharraf [personally] responsible" if she were ever to be assassinated for his failure to authorize adequate security guard details for her political rallies within Pakistan.[136]

Coming as little surprise, given the empirical (and historical) facts that she was an overtly-corrupt politician during her own elected political tenures who was once nicknamed a 'kleptocrat in an Hermes scarf'[137] and he was a two-star soft dictator general; most knowledgeable Pakistan experts conceded that Mrs. Bhutto was probably jeopardizing (and endangering) her own life by even returning to Pakistan in 2007 and especially by entering into an unholy political alliance with a two-star dictator like Pervez Musharraf.

"When you have the criminal and corrupt in the same [political] camp, it makes for dangerous bedfellows," I was quoted as saying in a December 27, 2007 article for TIME Magazine immediately following Mrs. Bhutto's assassination that same day. "In a sense, Benazir knew she was on a martyrdom mission. She was willing to give up her life for democracy."[138]

Shortly after her assassination, detectives from the United Kingdom soon confirmed what President Musharraf's administration had later found – that Mrs. Bhutto had not actually died from the two gunshots- but rather from the severe traumatic head injuries that she sustained from the aftershocks of the huge secondary bomb blast in Rawalpindi on that day in December 2007.[139] Her own PPP political party later rejected General Musharraf's findings and immediately called for an independent official United Nations (UN) inquiry into her assassination; claiming that Musharraf's government had not provided Mrs. Benazir Bhutto with enough adequate security. [140]

Even prominent Americans at the time, including then-Senator (and now Vice President) Joseph Biden, personally implored General Pervez Musharraf to provide the re-aspiring political leader with heavier security details upon her return to Pakistan from Dubai.[141] In February 2008, two men confessed to Pakistani authorities to helping the assassin/suicide-bomber acquire his bomb-vest (and pistol) and also driving him to the Rawalpindi park where Mrs. Bhutto was going to be holding her last political rally.[142] The head of the official Pakistani police investigation, Chaudhry Abdul Majid, once told BBC World News that the assassin's "motive for attacking Bhutto was that she was coming to Pakistan at the behest of a foreign power."[143]

On the international stage, the United Nations had also officially launched their own internal investigation into the Bhutto assassination later in July 2009. This official six-month probe was to investigate 'the facts and circumstances' of the Benazir Bhutto assassination and they were tasked with presenting their official report to the UN Security Council and United Nations Secretary-General, Mr. Ban Ki-moon. At the time, Pakistan's Interior Minister, Rehman Malik, said that an independent UN investigation was ultimately necessary to finding out the complete truth about the Benazir Bhutto assassination.

"Obviously, there might be some actors within Pakistan or within the region, but we want really to expose the whole conspiracy, because we think that this was a kind of a beginning of an attempt to 'Balkanize' [the country of] Pakistan," he once told BBC World News about the importance of an official outside UN inquiry.[144] Although the December 2007 Benazir Bhutto assassination will always share seismic political parallels with the November 1963 John F. Kennedy assassination (in terms of its overall effect on the respective nations of Pakistan and the United States), it seems as though the perpetual finger-pointing and 'blame game' will sadly continue onwards within Pakistan for many years to come.

One thing is to be made clear though; although we may never truly know the real masterminds or culprits responsible for the December 2007 political assassination of former Pakistani prime minister Benazir Bhutto; her ongoing political legacy will now forever be seen through the historical lens of being a political 'martyr for democracy' when she bravely gave up her own life for the political well-being of over 172 million women and children of Pakistan.[145] To properly and quickly sum up the overall political madness within Pakistan in the devastating aftermath of the December 2007 political assassination of former two-time prime minister Mrs. Benazir Bhutto, I believe that the legendary American journalist Edward R. Murrow would probably have said it best:

"Good night, Benazir ... And good luck, Pakistan..."[146]

Islamabad Marriott Bombing (September 2008)

The five-star Marriott hotel in Pakistan's capital city of Islamabad has always been unique – it was prized for its heavy security and was one of the few places within Pakistan where foreign dignitaries were safely housed during official visits to the nation. Immediately inside of the main Marriott hotel lobby, their hallways included high-end boutique stores, spacious hotel room suites and a delicious 'Dynasty' restaurant that served a fusion of Pakistani-Cantonese Chinese cuisine. Tall regal doormen and security guards stood at the front-glass doors of the 5-star luxury hotel's gates, dressed lavishly in red Mughal-style *shirwani* suits and wearing white *kullahs* (ceremonial turbans with a fan on top), greeting every dignitary, expatriate and/or foreign diplomat who frequently graced the Islamabad Marriott with their loyal patronage.[147] Additionally, the Islamabad Marriott hotel is also less than one mile away from both Pakistan's Senate and Parliament buildings and the hotel is also in very close proximity to both the Prime Minister and President's governmental offices as well.

The trusted Islamabad Marriott security guards were also quite well-known around Pakistan for their overall skill and bravery- in January 2007- a hotel security guard stopped a potential suicide bomber from entering the hotel premises and was bravely killed himself when the suicide bomber exploded his bomb-vest just outside of the Marriott hotel's front entrance.[148] Even so, September 21, 2008 was a different day altogether for the Islamabad Marriott in Pakistan.

That warm September evening during the middle of the Muslim holy month of Ramadan, while hotel and restaurant guests were opening their Ramadan fasts with communal *iftar* dinners around 8pm on that picturesque Saturday evening; a group of suicide bombers drove a truck packed with explosives into the hotel's front security gates in one of the worst terrorist attacks that Pakistan has ever seen to date.[149] When the smoke finally cleared, hotel officials estimated that the explosion had killed at least 53 people, injured 266 others and left firefighters combating the fiery blazes for up to twelve additional hours well into the next morning.[150] Most notably, among the 53 fatalities who were killed that evening at the Islamabad Marriott included the Czech Republic's Ambassador to Pakistan; Mr. Ivo Zdarek.[151]

Hotel video surveillance footage from the Marriott security cameras showed the suicide bombers ramming their truck against the hotel security barricades before bomb-sniffing dogs started barking loudly at the security guards to alert them of the imminent bomb threat.[152] According to some media and eyewitness reports, there was one small initial 'mini-explosion' which occurred inside the truck cab; causing the truck to light on fire. Almost immediately thereafter, the black-and-white surveillance video footage of the Marriott goes completely blank; because the entire Marriott hotel's security cameras have now been obliterated by the second massive bomb explosion which killed over 53 hotel guests, including Ambassador Zdarek.[153]

According to Pakistani authorities, the suicide truck-bomb contained over 1,300 pounds of bomb explosives made up mainly of aluminum powder; which would accelerate subsequent fires and raise the overall temperature of the 'back-draft' fire blaze upwards of 725 degrees Fahrenheit.[154] In terms of sheer explosive magnitude, local police investigators later found that the second major hotel bomb blast had shattered windows several thousands of feet away and also caused a 30-foot-deep (and 50-foot-wide) enormous crater in the earth which jeopardized the Marriott's entire architectural structural integrity and caused possible danger of a complete building collapse.[155] Intelligence and police officials in Pakistan had also later stated that the bomb blast would have been much worse had it not been for the Marriott's security systems in place throughout the perimeter of the hotel.[156]

For instance, according to government officials, if the truck bomb had gotten past the initial hotel gate barricades and was allowed to drive directly into the main hotel lobby; thousands of people could have been potentially killed that night in September 2008. Mr. Shah Hussain, a hotel waiter and eyewitness to the Islamabad Marriott bombing- whose white tunic was stained with the blood of victims that he personally carried to the hospital- said immediately after the bomb blasts: "Thank God that they were stopped at the gates...If they got any closer, or even inside, nothing would have survived...The building would have collapsed and we all would have been killed."[157]

Pakistani President Asif Ali Zardari- widower of the late former prime minister Mrs. Benazir Bhutto- immediately condemned the terrorist attacks in a televised national address to the country immediately after the Islamabad Marriott bombing. "Make this pain your strength," said President Zardari. "This is a menace, a cancer in Pakistan which we will eliminate...We will not be scared of these cowards."[158] Although Pakistani police authorities officially continued to investigate and arrest relevant suspects for questioning,[159] no known terrorist group had immediately claimed responsibility for this September 2008 Islamabad Marriott hotel bombing. Though the proverbial fingers were immediately pointed at the usual suspects - Al-Qaeda and the Taliban- the government of Pakistan would later say that a smaller Al-Qaeda-linked group called *Lashkar-e-Jhangvi* was probably responsible for this attack and subsequently arrested a suspected member of this group in August 2009 for his complicity in the September 2008 Marriott hotel bombing.[160]

In the wake of this dastardly 2008 Islamabad Marriott terrorist bombing, the famous 5-star luxury hotel would immediately start to clean up and rebuild itself. Only three months after the Ramadan bombing- with a 14-foot high 'blast wall' covering where the bombs had blasted away the front of the hotel- the five-star Islamabad Marriott luxury hotel was reopened for regular business once again.[161] The prestigious hotel invited foreign diplomats and other international VIPs to a 'High Tea' in the main hotel ballroom on December 28, 2008. Islamabad Marriott hotel owner Mr. Sadruddin Hashwani started the ceremony by lighting candles in front of pictures of hotel employees who were tragically killed in the September 2008 attack only three months earlier.

"I have now made this hotel into a fortress," said Mr. Hashwani with tears in his eyes. "My heart bleeds today while remembering these great soldiers, who did not let the bombers enter the hotel."[162] Highlighting the heartbreaking legacy of the September 2008 Islamabad Marriott bombing, the hotel's assistant manager (Mr. Mohammad Asif) summed up the heartbreaking situation within Pakistan perfectly when he said:

"Every day, we will remember those who died...But we will go on..."[163]

2008 Mumbai Hotel Attacks (November 2008)

Many people around the world are not aware that the Indian metropolitan city of Mumbai (formerly known as Bombay) currently ranks immediately behind New York City as the 5th largest metropolitan city in the entire world. In November 2008, over 19.2 million citizens of all religions, castes and ethnicities watched in horror as part of the metropolitan city's virtual 'five-star district' reeled from the aftermath of the deadly terrorist attacks which claimed the lives of almost 170 innocent people and wounded at least 300 more.[164]

Beginning on the evening of November 26, 2008, nine different gunmen spread across the city of Mumbai on a three-day killing rampage; targeting two separate luxury hotels and other historical and cultural landmarks around the city formerly known as Bombay. Four different major attacks across the city of Mumbai began almost simultaneously at 9:20pm on the evening of November 26, 2008; stressing already thin Indian police resources and sending a coordinated shiver down Mumbai's collective back.

At the famous century-old Taj Mahal Palace hotel, seven different gunmen shot innocent dinner guests and razed a part of the hotel to the ground during their killing spree.[165] At least three (3) of these Taj hotel terrorist gunmen were immediately killed, along with other hotel guests and police commandos; including the Chief of Mumbai's Terrorism Police, Mr. Hemant Karkare.[166] The remaining gunmen within the Taj hotel continued to hold hostages within that luxury hotel (and fired indiscriminately at police) until well into the next day.[167] Almost simultaneously, several other terrorist gunmen rounded up hotel guests and threw hand grenades inside the famous Oberoi-Trident Hotel in Mumbai around the same time as the Taj hotel terrorist siege. Located near the Bombay Stock Exchange and popular with foreign tourists, business people and wealthy VIPs, the Oberoi-Trident hotel immediately became a second battleground as India's National Security Guard exchanged massive gunfire with the armed terrorists; killing two (2) of the Oberoi-Trident terrorist gunmen.[168] According to media reports, many hotel guests were also barricaded within their hotel rooms at the Oberoi-Trident hotel for over two whole days before police could safely rescue them to safety after the long shooting stand-off.

At virtually the same time, several rifle-packing gunmen began to indiscriminately throw hand grenades and shoot train passengers with automatic weapons at the Chhatrapati Shivaji Terminus (CST) train station in central Mumbai. At the historic train station, over ten people were eventually killed (and at least 30 were injured) at this crime scene at Mumbai's most well-known train station. The historic CST train station in Bombay was completed over one hundred years ago in 1888 and was once named a UNESCO world heritage site because of its famous Victorian gothic architecture. As of today, the CST train station still proudly remains active as one of the country's busiest railway stations inside all of India.[169]

Next, several armed gunmen would storm the Nariman House business and residential complex within the city of Mumbai. This building complex is home to the Jewish *Chabad Lubavitch* outreach center, where many Jewish and Israeli visitors would often come to pray, study and attend religious community events during their time in Bombay. Unfortunately, over eight people were killed in this dastardly terrorist attack, including a respected young rabbi, his wife and young baby, along with two of the terrorist gunmen at yet another horrifying Mumbai terrorism crime scene.[170] Adding insult to injury, several terrorist gunmen also attacked the famous Café Leopold; a popular famous tourist watering hole since 1871. British patron Harnish Patel described "continuous firing" and told BBC World News after the attack that, "[the gunman] saw me and a number of others at the back, and then he just opened fire on us," killing two people standing right next to him inside the famous Mumbai cafe. Four other terrorist gunmen also opened fire at the Cama and Albless Hospital, built in the 1880s as a charity hospital for poor women and children.[171]

These shameful horrific terrorist attacks indiscriminately claimed Hindu, Muslim, Jewish, Sikh and Christian victims alike as the terrorist gunmen indiscriminately killed people of all religions and nationalities during these ungodly terrorist attacks. Mrs. Nafisa Qureshi, a 23-year-old Muslim citizen of Mumbai, helplessly held her own six-year-old daughter in her arms as her baby daughter later died of a gunshot wound to her back. "She was writhing in pain and bled to death in my arms . . . I lost consciousness after that,"[172] said Mrs. Qureshi during the criminal trial of the lone surviving Mumbai gunman.

21-year-old defendant Mohammad Ajmal Qasab, the lone-surviving Mumbai terrorist gunman, did not even look up as a 10-year-old child named Devika Rotawan testified clearly and calmly that a gunman had shot her in the leg during the November 2008 Mumbai terrorist attacks.[173] Not surprisingly, both India and the United States did not waste much time in accusing neighboring Pakistan of being (at least) complicit in the Mumbai attacks; but Pakistani President Asif Ali Zardari and the Pakistani government have always vehemently denied any responsibility whatsoever.[174] Indian police were finally successful in arresting the lone-surviving member of the ten-man (10) terrorist gunman group; Mohammad Ajmal Qasab, a 21-year-old Pakistani villager and officially charged him with 'waging war on India.' Each one of the rest of the ten Mumbai terrorist gunmen was eventually killed by Indian police security forces during their respective shooting stand-offs at the different Mumbai crime scenes.

Initially, 21-year-old Ajmal Qasab pled innocent to the charges despite his earlier confessions of being a member of the Pakistani extremist group

Lashkar-e-Taiba (better known as 'LeT') and despite further mountains of video surveillance and photographic evidence against him. For example, in one of the most infamously-timeless journalistic photographs of the November 2008 Mumbai attacks, the young Mr. Qasab was caught on film holding a large automatic machine-gun and calmly walking through a train station during the terrorist siege.

Finally, in June 2009, the government of Pakistan finally (and officially) admitted that some of the gunmen were indeed Pakistani citizens. During the trial of the lone surviving gunman, he managed to shock even his own defense lawyers by surprisingly changing his own plea and now pleading guilty to over eighty-six (86) criminal counts of terrorism.[175] At a special court hearing covered extensively by South Asian (and the greater global) media, Ajmal Qasab stood up at that time and stated to the judge very simply:

"Sir, I plead guilty to my crime[s]."[176]

Qasab then continued to give a full confession,[177] including a detailed explanation of how the Mumbai terrorists were trained – through a network of *Lashkar-e-Taiba* (LeT) training camps and safe-houses inside Pakistan- and other details about the Mumbai attacks. He also gave the full names of the other Mumbai attackers and also subsequently described in detail the specific roles of each respective terrorist[178] and also provided information about their respective crime-scene locations. At the time, the criminal trial of Qasab within India was so legally unconventional that the presiding judge in Mumbai decided to adjourn the court as he met personally with both prosecution and defense lawyers to discuss how to move forward during those unconventional legal proceedings.[179]

In September 2009, Pakistani authorities placed under house-arrest the leader of an Islamist group suspected of playing a key role in the November 2008 Mumbai terror attacks. Hafiz Muhammad Saeed, the founder and leader of *Lashkar-e-Taiba* (LeT) was placed under 'house arrest' and forbidden from leaving his home by Pakistani authorities pursuant to governmental police orders. At virtually the same time, Pakistani Interior Minister Mr. Rehman Malik also officially announced that his government would also indict an additional seven (7) terrorism suspects for their complicity in the November 2008 Mumbai terrorist attacks; finally helping to bridge some of the diplomatic (and legal) impasses between neighboring India and Pakistan after the tragedy of Mumbai.[180]

Mumbai (formerly known as Bombay) is well-known around the world as the financial capital of India and also as the birthplace of the global movie phenomenon known as "Bollywood". In many ways, the city formerly known as Bombay is central to the sociopolitical heartbeat of our world's largest vibrant democracy within India. Many people may be surprised to learn that there are currently over 1.1 billion people who live in India today, making it the 2nd most-populated country in the world (only behind China's 1.3 billion people).[181] As the single largest democracy in the world, India's multi-ethnic and multi-religious diversity of over 1.1 billion people has helped it withstand these heinous terrorist attacks amidst the shattered glass windows of the Taj Mahal and Oberoi-Trident hotel lobbies.

Simply put; Bollywood will always trump Al-Qaeda in India.

As an international human rights lawyer who is well-versed within the nuanced sociopolitical history of South Asia; the Mumbai 'Five-Star' terrorist attacks were simply a vile and disgusting disregard for human life and an immoral crime against humanity. Regardless of political grievances or the proverbial South Asian political question of Kashmir, the methodical and intentional targeting of innocent civilians at Western hot-spots, Jewish cultural centers and famous luxury hotels in a diverse multi-ethnic (and multi-religious) metropolitan city like Mumbai can never be justified and should always be condemned by every living person of any color or religion around the world.

In the immediate wake of this horrible tragedy, a symbolic glimmer of hope was on the horizon when BBC World News reported that Muslim leaders in India had decided that "they will not allow the militants to be buried in Muslim graveyards anywhere in the country" shortly after the Mumbai attacks. Mr. Ibrahim Tai, the president of the Indian Muslim Council- which looks after the social and religious affairs of the Muslim community in India- told BBC World News shortly after the Mumbai attacks that the terrorists had "defamed" their religion. "They are not Muslims as they have not followed our religion which teaches us to live in peace…We do not want the bodies of people who have committed an act of terrorism to be buried in our cemeteries," he said.

"These terrorists are a black spot on our religion," continued Mr. Tai. "We will very sternly protest the burial of these terrorists in our cemetery."[182]

A black spot, indeed.

2009 Jakarta Hotel Bombings (July 2009)

With over 17,508 islands, the Southeast Asian country of Indonesia is well-known around the globe as the largest island archipelago in the world.[183] With a diversely multi-ethnic (and multi-religious) population of over 240.2 million people, it also currently ranks as the 4th most-populated country on earth and has sadly been no stranger to global terrorism itself in the past. From the horrific 2002 Bali nightclub bombings (which killed over 201 people) to a 2003 bombing at the J.W. Marriott Hotel in the capital city of Jakarta (which killed over 12 people and was one of the two sites of the more-recent July 2009 hotel terrorist attack); the nation of Indonesia has sadly had to face the challenge of being one of the largest and most vibrant multi-ethnic (and multi-religious) democracies within our world today.

At around 7:45am local time on Friday, July 17, 2009, two near-simultaneous bomb explosions rocked through both the neighboring Ritz-Carlton and J.W. Marriott hotels in downtown Jakarta during the morning breakfast hour; killing at least six people and injuring over 50 others, according to an Indonesian presidential spokesman.[184]

"I looked out my window and I saw a huge cloud of brownish smoke go up," said Australian journalist (and eyewitness) Greg Woolstencroft during a live telephone interview[185] from Jakarta with CNN's *Anderson Cooper 360* shortly after the Ritz-Carlton hotel blast; where he had once lived himself for over one year. "I grabbed my iPhone to go downstairs ... and then the second bomb went off at the Ritz-Carlton, so I then ran around to the Ritz-Carlton and I was able to find that there had been a massive bomb that went off in this ... restaurant area...and the explosion had blown out both sides of the hotel," continued Mr. Woolstencroft during the same interview with Anderson Cooper immediately after the hotel blasts. "I found inside the body of what appears to be a suicide bomber... it looked like someone who had been a suicide bomber or someone who had been very, very close to the explosion," Mr. Woolstencroft further said during the same CNN evening broadcast.[186]

At this point, this is where the Indonesian terrorist group *Jemaah Islamiyah* (JI) most probably came into the picture yet again. According to the International Crisis Group (ICG), the group called *Jemaah Islamiyah* (JI) is again a Southeast-Asian terrorist organization based in Indonesia which has remained active and dangerous throughout the years with the 2002 Bali nightclub bombings and other acts of terrorism;[187] despite the mid-August 2003 arrest of Riduan Isamuddin (better known by his *nom de guerre,* 'Hambali'), one of its top terrorist operatives who was once dubbed the 'Osama bin Laden of Southeast Asia'.[188] He was also one of the fourteen (14) 'key' terrorists that were held in CIA secret prisons (also known as 'black sites') before being moved to the notorious Guantanamo Bay prison in Cuba in late 2006.[189]

The more interesting counterterrorism debate at the time of this more-recent 2009 Jakarta 'five-star' hotel attacks at the Ritz-Carlton and J.W. Marriott hotels actually revolved around the *modus operandi* of these attacks and how they actually differed in criminal methodology from both the 2003 Jakarta Marriott bombings (at the exact same hotel) and the 2002 Bali nightclub bombings in nearby Kuta, Indonesia. According to international media reports, the August 2003 Marriott hotel bombings in Jakarta occurred when a suicide bomber[190] drove an explosives-laden car directly into the hotel taxi stand; detonating it just outside the front glass doors of the main hotel lobby. The earlier August 2003 car-bomb exploded through the hotel's front entrance, blowing out the walls and shattering windows, severely damaging five (5) entire floors of the American-owned luxury hotel chain. Furthermore, the explosives and methodology used in this earlier August 2003 deadly blast were similar to those used in the first Bali terrorist bombings, which had occurred only a year earlier in October 2002.

According to my dear friend and former CNN Washington Deputy Bureau Chief John Towriss who had once lived in Indonesia, the Jakarta Marriott had beefed up their overall hotel security[191] in light of the August 2003 bombing, making it virtually impossible now for people to again drive up to the hotel's front entrance in bomb-laden vehicles. Both the Ritz-Carlton and J.W. Marriott hotels in Jakarta had also jointly set up enhanced metal detector systems and thick concrete barricades to prevent future potential car-bombers from driving up to the front lobbies of their luxury hotels ever again. If so, it had soon become quite clear soon thereafter that the terrorists had slightly altered their criminal *modus operandi* to achieve their sinister operational terrorist ends in this most-recent July 2009 version of the Jakarta hotel terrorist attacks.

"I just don't know how someone could get in there with a bomb, given the level of security and screening that people have to go through," said eyewitness and Australian journalist Greg Woolstencroft; who lived across the street from both hotels at the time of the blasts in July 2009. Mr. Woolstencroft also highlighted the impeccable (and improved) security at both luxury hotels; mentioning heavily-armed security guards and enhanced metal detector screening centers to search people, bags and vehicles before anyone could possibly ever enter the secured perimeter of these fine luxury hotels in Jakarta. Thus, if a terrorist could no longer feasibly drive a car-bomb to the front entrance of either one of these two luxury hotels (because of the new cement barricades and/or armed checkpoints) AND a person could not walk into the hotel with a bomb inside of a backpack (since it would presumably be found at the enhanced front-entrance metal detector screening centers); the only rational (and chilling) conclusion was that the July 2009 bombings was probably (at least partially) aided by an 'inside job' with either hotel employees (or checked-in hotel guests) at both of these luxury hotels.

As someone who has actually stayed in both four-star and five-star hotels within the Muslim world and beyond, I have seen firsthand the enhanced security measures in place at these fine international luxury hotels; which include impenetrable cement barricades preventing cars from driving to front entrances and enhanced state-of-the-art metal detector bomb screening centers at the front door entrances of these four- and five-star luxury hotels around the world. Having said that; we should always remember that this was not the first time that we have tragically seen high-caliber Western 'luxury hotels' being targeted within the Muslim world and beyond by global terrorists. In addition to the aforementioned September 2008 Islamabad Marriott bombing in Pakistan (which killed over 53 people) and the November 2008 Mumbai terrorist attacks at the Taj Mahal and Oberoi-Trident hotels in India (which killed over 173 people); it has become quite clear that high-caliber Western 'luxury hotels' around the world have now sadly become prime targets for acts of terrorism. Since high-profile Westerners, rich businesspersons and influential expatriates frequent many of these four- and five-star luxury hotels, many potential terrorists now seem to relish having these 'Western' targets within their own backyards.

With Western luxury hotels becoming prime potential targets for international terrorism, the Office of Intelligence and Analysis at the U.S. Department of Homeland Security (DHS) and the FBI simultaneously released a 'Joint Homeland Security Note' in September 2009 to raise security awareness regarding "terrorist interest in targeting luxury hotels"[192] around the world.

According to the DHS/FBI September 2009 joint intelligence report, Western luxury hotels are "attractive targets for terrorists because of the substantial number of people present to include VIPs and tourists." The American intelligence report further added that, "Hotels generally lack the robust perimeter security necessary to prevent access by terrorists, and regular delivery of products and services offer venues or opportunities to penetrate protective measures." The joint DHS/FBI intelligence report also clearly concludes that they "are not aware of any threat to luxury hotels in the United States, but analysis of historical reporting, previous attacks abroad, and thwarted plots provide some insight into the tactics used by terrorists against [luxury] hotels"[193] (emphasis added).

A slight sigh of collective relief for the 240 million people of Indonesia occurred on September 17, 2009, when Indonesian Special Forces police commando units raided a known terrorist hide-out and finally killed the notorious Indonesian terrorist mastermind known as Noordin Muhammed Top; striking at the heart of the Indonesian terrorist network behind a deadly terror campaign of many suicide attacks within Indonesia, including the Bali nightclub bombings in 2002. According to the Associated Press (AP), Noordin Top had eluded capture for more than seven (7) years on the run. He was tracked down to a safe-house in the city of Solo in central Java, a so-called "breeding ground for militant Islam," where an overnight siege stand-off and hours-long gunfight ended at dawn with a massive explosion during the early morning hours.[194]

In addition to the dead body of Noordin Top, Indonesian law enforcement officials also found the bodies of four (4) other suspected terrorists recovered from the burned-out house; including an alleged explosives expert (named Bagus Budi Pranato) believed to have manufactured the bombs used by the suicide attackers in the July 2009 hotel attacks on the J.W. Marriott and Ritz-Carlton hotels. Even with the eventual death of Noordin Top, the tragedy of the 2009 Jakarta hotel bombings at the Ritz-Carlton and J.W. Marriott hotels has already sadly transpired within our shared modern human historical timeline. Like with the Bali nightclub bombings, these hundreds of millions of peaceful Indonesians should know that the entire world's condolences and prayers were with the 240 million wonderful people of Indonesia as they mourned this terrorist attack within two of their most popular luxury hotels within their beautiful capital city of Jakarta.

The Terminal Decline of Terrorism: Public Opinion within the Muslim World

Many years after the tragedy of the 9/11 terrorist attacks, the specter of global terrorism still continues to haunt our global conversation today. Having said that, over the years, many global academics and counter-terrorism experts have continued to see a surprising and heartening long-term trend: *Al-Qaeda and its terrorist ideology of 'violent jihad' are in a pronounced decline throughout the Muslim world today.*

"Al-Qaeda is losing its moral argument [with Muslims worldwide] about the killing of innocent civilians," said Dr. Emile Nakhleh, who once headed the Central Intelligence Agency's (CIA) strategic analysis program on political Islam until 2006. "They are finding it harder to recruit…They are finding it harder to raise money," Dr. Nakhleh further added on this positive recent geopolitical trend in public opinion circles.[195]

Former Oxford University professor Dr. Audrey Kurth Cronin, a professor at the National War College in Washington DC, agreed with this overall global assessment of the terminal decline in popularity of Al-Qaeda and likened this decline to previous violent extremist groups, from the Russian 'People's Will' organization to the Irish Republican Army (IRA), during the academic research for her July 2009 book, *How Terrorism Ends*. "I think Al-Qaeda is in the process of imploding,' said Professor Cronin. "This is not necessarily the end…But the trends are in a good direction,"[196] she once noted in a September 2009 article in *The New York Times* on the overall declining popularity of Al-Qaeda within the Muslim world.

In terms of the growing overall unpopularity of terrorism within the Muslim world, most global observers and academic experts would agree that as the number of Al-Qaeda terrorist attacks inside Muslim countries began to increase over the years; this political trend has also subsequently led to plummeting public opinion of Al-Qaeda (and terrorism in general) among majority-Muslim populations around the world. As terrorist groups like Al-Qaeda and their brainless cronies began primarily killing their own Muslim people around the world, it has now become "more and more difficult to romanticize Al-Qaeda as fighting the global hegemons- basically- 'sticking it to the man'," once said Dr. Peter Mandaville, a professor of government and Islamic studies at George Mason University in suburban Washington DC. Professor Mandaville further stated that an increase in the number of global "public recantations (or condemnations of terrorism)" by prominent Islamic scholars and leaders around the world in recent years has also had an overall positive effect in further marginalizing terrorists around the world.

However, most global observers would still agree that the biggest catalyst for plummeting public opinion against terrorism within the Muslim world has been these terrorist bombings increasingly hitting "close to home" and killing more Muslims than anyone else. According to *The New York Times*, public support for terrorist bombings in Jordan plummeted "after three bombs hit hotels in Amman in November 2005, including one at a wedding party" at the Raddison-Blu hotel in the Jordanian capital. In Iraq, the slaughter of innocent Muslim civilians by the group that called itself 'Al-Qaeda in Mesopotamia' prompted "Sunni tribal leaders to make common cause with American Forces." In Pakistan, major terrorist bombings, including the "2007 [assassination terrorist] attack that killed [former Pakistani prime minister] Benazir Bhutto, soured most [Pakistani] people of all social classes on Al-Qaeda-style violence" throughout the Muslim nation.[197]

Furthermore, for all of its nonsensical ungodly talk of a global 'religious war', hundreds of millions of Muslims around the world now know that Al-Qaeda (and people like Osama bin Laden) have offered <u>absolutely nothing</u> in terms of practical solutions for local or national problems: unemployment, illiteracy, poverty, government corruption and poor education. "People [have now] realized [that Osama] bin Laden didn't have anything to offer," Professor Peter Mandaville added on the terminal decline of Al-Qaeda-style terrorism within Muslim world 'public opinion' today.[198] In terms of empirical global public opinion within the Muslim world, we have seen that this terminal decline in public support for terrorism thankfully continues downward as acts of terrorism within Muslim countries (and targeting fellow Muslim citizens) continues to grow. For example, in the seven years between 2002 until 2009 alone, the view that suicide bombings are 'often or sometimes justified' had declined sharply, according to the Pew Global Attitudes Project, from 43 percent to 12 percent in Jordan; from 26 percent to 13 percent in Indonesia; and from 33 percent to a staggeringly low <u>5 percent</u> in Pakistan.[199] Most notably, the Pew study found that **"positive ratings for Osama bin Laden have fallen by half [50%] or more in most of the [Muslim] countries [around the world that] Pew polled"** in this comprehensive 2009 global opinion study.[200]

With these acts of terrorism now transparently and widely discredited within general 'public opinion' inside the Muslim world, the major concern that most counterterrorism officials around the world (both Muslim and non-Muslim alike) now focus their attention is on small splinter groups (or lone-wolf individual terrorists) who are not directly linked to Al-Qaeda or Osama bin Laden at all; but whose criminal profile now fits the young demographic parameters shared by many of the terrorist attackers involved in the aforementioned Bali, Madrid, London and Mumbai attacks after 9/11. "Al-Qaeda's core demographic [group now] is young 'hot-heads' aged 16 to 28," once said Professor Bruce Hoffman of Georgetown University. "I still don't think [that Al-Qaeda] has lost its [full] appeal to that demographic [group of young hot-heads]," he further explained.[201]

Dr. Marc Sageman, a former CIA officer and forensic psychiatrist, has also been at the forefront of those people who have argued that the 'centralized' Al-Qaeda responsible for the September 11, 2001 attacks is "giving way to a generation of dispersed, aspiring terrorists linked largely by the Internet- who still pose a danger, but of a lesser degree."[202] Dr. Sageman has also publicly stated on numerous occasions that the Al-Qaeda threat "was a diminishing problem, and everything I have seen since then has confirmed" the central thesis of the plummeting downward public support inside the Muslim world for what counterterrorism specialists call 'Al-Qaeda Central'.

Again, this proves what even the conservative author Dinesh D'Souza has said about combating extremism: "America should ally with traditional Muslims to defeat the radical Muslims."[203] Even with these positive international trends of downward plummeting global public opinion condemning terrorism within the greater Muslim world; the jointly on-going wars (and quagmires) within both Iraq and Afghanistan now seem to be two of the remaining major 'calling cards' for infamous extremist dinosaurs like Osama bin Laden whose ungodly terrorism has finally left this world for good.

CHAPTER SIX: BOMBS OVER BAGHDAD: THE WARS IN AFGHANISTAN AND IRAQ

"In peace, sons bury their fathers...In war, fathers bury their sons..."

-Herodotus

A mere nine days after September 11, President George W. Bush would officially introduce Al-Qaeda and its mastermind leader- Osama bin Laden- to the American people during a live nationally-televised speech before a joint session of Congress on September 20, 2001. Not long thereafter, the political and military gears of war began to slowly turn inside our country as our American government sought to avenge the single-deadliest terrorist attack to ever hit our soil of the United States of America. "On September the 11th, enemies of freedom committed an act of war against our country," said then-President George W. Bush during his nationally-televised speech before a joint session of Congress nine days after the 9/11 attacks. "The evidence we have gathered [thus far] all points to a collection of loosely affiliated terrorist organizations known as 'Al-Qaeda'...They are some of the murderers indicted for bombing American embassies in Tanzania and Kenya [in 1998] and responsible for [the October 2000] bombing of the USS Cole [which killed 17 American soldiers in a seaport off the coast of Yemen]."[1]

"Al-Qaeda is to terror what the Mafia is to crime," continued former President Bush that evening. "But its goal is not making money, its goal is remaking the world and imposing its radical beliefs on people everywhere...The terrorists practice a fringe form of Islamic extremism that has been rejected by Muslim scholars and the vast majority of Muslim clerics; a fringe movement that perverts the peaceful teachings of Islam."[2] Now directly addressing the ruling Taliban government (and the 28.4 million people) of Afghanistan,[3] President Bush did not mince his words when he next said that: "The Taliban must act and act immediately...They will hand over the terrorists or they will share in their fate."

Shifting his focus to the greater Islamic world, President Bush wanted to make it clear that, "I also want to speak tonight directly to Muslims throughout the world...We respect your faith...It's practiced freely by many millions of Americans and by millions more in countries that America counts as friends... Its teachings are good and peaceful, and those who commit evil in the name of Allah [actually] blaspheme the name of Allah."[4] Our American president then proceeded to outline his political ultimatum to the Taliban governmental regime in Afghanistan during this rhetorical build-up to the 2001 war inside Afghanistan which would ultimately claim the lives of at least "1,478 coalition deaths – 865 Americans, 11 Australians, one Belgian, 219 Britons, 131 Canadians, three Czechs, 25 Danes, 21 Dutch, six Estonians, one Finn, 35 French, 30 Germans, two Hungarians, 20 Italians, three Latvians, one Lithuanian, four Norwegians, 13 Poles, two Portuguese, 11 Romanians, one South Korean, 25 Spaniards, two Swedes, two Turks and one NATO/ISAF"[5] soldiers as of October 2009– in addition to the hundreds of thousands of other innocent Afghani women and children civilians killed during the post-9/11 war in Afghanistan.

"By aiding and abetting [Al-Qaeda and Osama bin Laden], the Taliban regime [in Afghanistan] is committing murder...And tonight, the United States of America makes the following demands on the Taliban [government]:

- ⇨ *Deliver to United States authorities all of the leaders of Al-Qaeda who hide in your land;*
- ⇨ *Release all foreign nationals, including American citizens you have unjustly imprisoned;*
- ⇨ *Protect foreign journalists, diplomats and [humanitarian] aid workers in your country;*
- ⇨ *Close immediately and permanently every terrorist training camp in Afghanistan. And hand over every terrorist and every person and their support structure to appropriate authorities; and*

⇨ *Give the United States full access to terrorist training camps, so we can make sure they are no longer operating.*"

With this major September 2001 nationally-televised congressional speech a mere nine days after 9/11, President George W. Bush would now make it abundantly clear that we were on the verge of war in Afghanistan when he stated ominously towards the end of his speech:

"These demands are not open to negotiation or discussion."[6]

2001 War in Afghanistan: Welcome to the 'Graveyard of Empires'

Historically well-known around the world to global observers as the 'Graveyard of Empires',[7] the central Asian feudal nation-state of Afghanistan has successfully cast off the historical imperialist likes of Alexander the Great, Genghis Khan's Mongol empire, the British Victorian colonial empire and most recently, the USSR Soviet communist empire; who were embarrassingly defeated by the Afghan *mujahideen* during the entire decade of the 1980s. "No outside force has, since the Mongol invasion, ever pacified the entire country [of Afghanistan]... Even Alexander the Great only passed through," once noted former U.S. Secretary of State Henry Kissinger in an October 2009 *Newsweek* magazine article[8] on the historical and regional importance of Afghanistan within our greater geopolitical context. As a strategic geographical crossroads within Central Asia, from its invasion by "Genghis Khan and his two-million strong Mongol hordes to the superpower proxy war [during the 1980s] between the United States and the Soviet Union, Afghanistan's trade routes and land-locked position in the middle of the region have for centuries rendered it vulnerable to invasion by external powers."

According to an official 2009 CATO Institute 'white paper' policy document, although Afghanistan "has endured successive waves of Persian, Greek, Arab, Turk, Mongol, British, and Soviet invaders, no occupying power has ever successfully conquered it...There's a reason why it has been described as the 'graveyard of empires', and unless America scales down its objectives, it risks meeting a similar fate."[9]

Operation 'Enduring Freedom' (formerly known as Operation 'Infinite Justice')

With stellar Rumsfeld-ian political foresight, around September 20, 2001, as American war-planes began to be deployed to the Persian Gulf in the now-inevitable buildup of forces for the war in Afghanistan, everyone would soon learn that the Pentagon's brilliant official code name for the military operation would be the ominously-sounding 'Operation Infinite Justice'.[10]

As columnist Scott Rosenberg rightfully noted in a September 2001 column on the apocalyptical operation code-name: "The words of war keep getting wackier."[11]

Only five days later, on September 25, 2001, then-Secretary of Defense Donald Rumsfeld announced during a Pentagon briefing that what had been originally named 'Operation Infinite Justice' was now going to be known by the less-controversial military code-name 'Operation Enduring Freedom'. According to BBC World News, Mr. Rumsfeld had said that the Bush administration had quickly "reconsidered the original name because, in the Islamic faith, such 'finality' [like 'infinite justice'] is considered something provided only by God."[12] Less than one week earlier, President George W. Bush would again add more political insult-to-injury by running into rhetorical trouble again by using similar 'clash of civilizations' terminology during similar public statements that would offend widespread sensibilities throughout the world.

During unscripted remarks to journalists on the White House lawn only one week earlier, President George W. Bush was quoted as saying in September 2001: "This crusade…this war on terrorism…is going to take a while."[13]

Nice one, Dubya.

Notwithstanding the clearly tone-deaf (and borderline apocalyptic) rhetoric and operational code-names for the post-9/11 war in Afghanistan, the bombs of 'Operation Enduring Freedom' soon began to fall from the skies of Afghanistan shortly thereafter on October 7, 2001. Within the first four days of the coalition bombing campaign alone, it was reported that coalition air-strikes "damaged or destroyed 85 percent of targets throughout Afghanistan," according to U.S. Air Force General Richard Myers, then-chairman of the Joint Chiefs of Staff during a Pentagon press briefing on October 9, 2011.[14] In addition to now moving to day-time bombing raids of targets within Afghanistan (as opposed to the first few evenings of only night-time American bombings), several United

Nations (UN) aid workers were among the first civilian casualties reported in the US-coalition bombing campaign nicknamed 'Operation Enduring Freedom' in Afghanistan.

BBC World News reported that shortly after the bombing campaign began in Afghanistan, the "office of a UN-funded mine-clearing organization was hit... killing four [4] security guards and injuring a fifth [innocent civilian]."[15] Within three days of the commencement of 'Operating Enduring Freedom', American coalition forces had successfully destroyed most of the key strategic military targets within the major Afghani cities of Kabul, Jalalabad, Kandahar and Mazar-e-Sharif. Back at the Pentagon, then-Secretary of Defense Donald Rumsfeld told reporters that when planes were given a task of attacking "emerging targets" and none emerged, it was no surprise that these American planes then returned home to their bases with their bombs completely intact. "We're not running out of targets...Afghanistan is," Secretary Donald Rumsfeld once famously joked[16] to a gaggle of chuckling journalists in October 2001 during the first few weeks of 'Operation Enduring Freedom'. In the next military phase of 'Operation Enduring Freedom', the Bush administration would now focus their laser-sights on targeting Taliban ground forces after having already destroyed much of the Taliban government's infrastructure within the first few weeks of aerial bombardments alone.

During this next phase of the operation, so-called "bunker-busting" (or "Daisy Cutter") bombs were being used against underground tunnel and cave complexes where the Taliban leadership was believed to be hiding throughout Afghanistan. Generally speaking, the "Daisy Cutter" bomb is well-known throughout the world as the largest conventional bomb in use within modern warfare today. According to most estimates, the Daisy Cutter bomb "weighs approximately 15,000 pounds and destroys anything within a 600-yard radius." First used during the Vietnam War, these "huge bombs have since been employed in the [First] Gulf War [in 1991] and most recently in Afghanistan [after 9/11]... Although the 'Daisy Cutter' bomb is not a nuclear weapon, its use in battle has caused controversy because of its terrifying and utterly destructive nature."[17] The Daisy Cutter (whose technical name is BLU-82B) is the largest conventional bomb in existence and is over seventeen (17) feet-long, five (5) feet-in-diameter and "about the size of a Volkswagen Beetle, but much heavier...It contains 12,600 pounds of GX slurry (ammonium nitrate, aluminum powder, and polystyrene), and is so bulky that it cannot even be launched in a conventional method."[18]

To put that into appropriate context, the ammonium nitrate explosives in just one Daisy Cutter bomb is about six times (6x) more deadly than the explosives used in the April 1995 bombing of the Alfred P. Murrah Federal Building in Oklahoma City (which was the deadliest terrorist attack in America before 9/11; killing over 168 and injuring 680 people)[19] by convicted (and eventually executed) American domestic terrorist, Timothy McVeigh. Although the blast from this Daisy Cutter bomb is extremely lethal to targeted human populations, it is still estimated to only have "less than one-thousandth [1/1000th of] the destructive power of the atomic bomb used on Hiroshima [Japan during World War II]."[20]

An Opium (and Heroin) Nation

Within a ruggedly barren central Asian nation of over 27 million people that has been decimated by war, poverty and pandemic drought throughout the centuries, the drug trade phenomenon of 'opium' (and heroin) has come to dominate both the national economy and everyday life inside Afghanistan. To highlight this point, opium is heavily grown in "22 of Afghanistan's 30 provinces" and for poor struggling farmers across the nation, the 'poppy seed' has literally become an economic lifeline within this impoverished country. Opium has been in Afghanistan for centuries, but only became a true national economic force after the end of Afghanistan's 10-year war with the Soviet Union in 1989. With a vibrant drug network that "supplies more than 70% of the world's total opium, the United Nations once estimated that Afghanistan's opium crop dropped by more than 90%" in the one year[21] after 9/11 alone (from the nearly 3,300 metric tons produced only a year earlier in 2000).

Since that time, however, it has become quite clear that the Taliban has either been unable (or unwilling) to enforce this opium ban; which both American and U.N. officials say appears to have been largely a ploy to drive up opium prices skyward by limiting the supply throughout the first few years after 9/11. To illustrate this trend, some United Nations officials have said that for the past several years, Afghan drug rings have been "stockpiling about 60% of their annual opium harvests" within reserve warehouses. These opium reserves, which intelligence sources say were being held in "at least forty (40) warehouses throughout

Afghanistan," have long been a financial safeguard for the Taliban and the Afghan government.[22]

To date, American officials estimate that the opium trade in Afghanistan still continues to net "up to $30 million a year in taxes and tolls" for the Taliban which it has collected from Afghan drug rings around the country. In addition to opium, Afghanistan now also supplies approximately ninety-five percent (95%) of the world's heroin as well.[23] Although the Taliban and drug warlords inside Afghanistan have historically benefited from the drug trade, many foreign affairs experts also point to the fact that even the highest-levels of Afghani government officials and politicians have also personally benefited from the opium and heroin industry as well.

Mr. Ahmed Wali Karzai- the governor of Kandahar province and infamous younger brother of Afghan president Hamid Karzai- had long been suspected by American and European officials of being a major player in the heroin trade inside Afghanistan. According to an October 2008 article in *The New York Times*, the Bush White House once said that they "believed that Ahmed Wali Karzai is involved in drug trafficking, and American officials have repeatedly warned President [Hamid] Karzai that his brother is a political liability."[24] Over the years, numerous scattered reports would further link the younger Karzai brother directly to the Afghanistan heroin drug trade, according to former Administration officials from the White House, State Department and United States Embassy in Kabul.

In direct meetings with Afghan President Hamid Karzai, including a 2006 joint meeting with the United States ambassador and the CIA station chief in Afghanistan (along with their British intelligence counterparts), the Western officials at the private meeting discussed the heroin allegations directly with President Hamid Karzai with their sincere hope that the president "might move his brother out of the country," according to several people who took part in the meeting with President Karzai.[25] "What appears to be a fairly common Afghan public perception of corruption inside their government is a tremendously corrosive element working against establishing long-term confidence in that government — a very serious matter," said former U.S. Lieutenant Gen. David W. Barno, who was commander of coalition military forces in Afghanistan from 2003 to 2005.[26] "That could be problematic strategically for the United States [in Afghanistan]."[27]

Both President Hamid Karzai and his younger brother have always disputed these charges of drug trafficking as being politically motivated and baseless-in-fact. "I am not a drug dealer, I never was and I never will be," said Ahmed Wali Karzai in a published 2008 phone interview.[28]

"I am a victim of vicious politics." On July 12, 2011, Ahmed Wali Karzai was assassinated by his own bodyguard at his home in Kandahar, Afghanistan.[29]

From Tora Bora to 'Operation Anaconda'

According to American intelligence officials, well after midnight one early morning in December 2001, Osama bin Laden sat with a group of his top aides - including members of his elite international '055 Brigade' - in the mountainous region of Tora Bora in eastern Afghanistan.[30] For the next twelve days in December 2001, American and coalition forces would probably come the closest they have ever come to capturing Osama bin Laden alive during this famous two-week battle at Tora Bora. Instead of primarily using American soldiers during this December 2001 famous battle at Tora Bora, American military commanders decided to instead primarily utilize local Afghan fighters (led by local Afghan tribal chieftains) who also had a serious vested interest in rooting out Osama bin Laden and Al-Qaeda from Afghanistan. "We chose to fight using the Afghans who were fighting to regain their own country," former U.S. Army Colonel Rick Thomas once told *The Christian Science Monitor* in March 2002.[31] "Our aims of eliminating Al-Qaeda were similar" to the goals of the local Afghans, continued Colonel Thomas.[32]

So along with a motley crew of nearly 2,500 local Afghan soldiers who were recruited (via local Afghan warlords) for the famous battle; several groups of American, German[33] and British Special Forces flanked their nearly 3,000 Afghan comrades against approximately "1,500 or 1,600 of the best Arab and Chechen fighters in [Osama] bin Laden's terror network."[34] This December 2001 battle of Tora Bora would again probably be the last time that American forces would have an imminent opportunity to capture Osama bin Laden alive before he would ultimately escape from the eastern mountains of Afghanistan over the porous border into neighboring Pakistan.

During the battle of Tora Bora, United States Marine Corps General James N. Mattis (the commander of some 4,000 Marines inside of the Afghan war theater) was quite convinced that with these strong numbers of American coalition and local Afghan forces, they could have successfully surrounded and sealed off Osama bin Laden's cavern lair; as well as deploy more troops to the more-sensitive portions of the largely unpatrolled border with Pakistan. After nearly a week of intense fighting, General Mattis argued strongly that he should be permitted to proceed forward towards the spacious caves of Tora Bora to capture Osama bin Laden.

Strangely, the general's request was turned down.

An American intelligence official inside the Bush administration at the time would later conclude that the refusal of General James Mattis' request to dispatch the Marines - along with their overall failure to commit more U.S. ground forces to Afghanistan generally - was the "gravest error of the [Afghanistan] war" in his opinion.[35] Because of this strategic mistake, many American intelligence officials now estimated that "some 800 Al-Qaeda fighters escaped Tora Bora" in the last few days of fighting. According to reports, other fighters had already escaped or deserted and still others stayed behind to fight, including Osama bin Laden himself.

"You've got to give him credit," said Gary Schroen, a former CIA officer who led the first American paramilitary team into Afghanistan in 2001. "He [Osama bin Laden] stayed in Tora Bora until the bitter end."[36]

By the time the Afghan militias advanced to the last of the Tora Bora caves, no person of any significance remained; only about twenty disheveled young men were taken prisoner on the final day of fighting at Tora Bora on December 17, 2001. According to most American intelligence reports, Osama bin Laden most probably left Tora Bora for the last time on (or around) December 16, 2001. He and his men are believed to have journeyed on horseback directly south out of Tora Bora towards the old Pakistani military outpost of Parachinar just across the Pakistan border.

Then, in the timeless words of Keyser Soze: "And like that...He was gone."[37]

Most global analysts would agree that Tora Bora was the one major event after the 9/11 attacks when United States operatives were "confident [that] they knew precisely where Osama bin Laden was and could have captured or killed him" during that pivotal time period. Some political observers had argued that it was Washington's 'last chance'; even though American Navy Seal special forces would eventually locate and kill Osama bin Laden in an Abbottabad, Pakistan mansion compound in May 2011. Still, some major American government officials within the Bush administration still publicly questioned whether we truly had Osama bin Laden within our grasp at Tora Bora ten years earlier in 2001. "We don't know to this day whether Mr. [Osama] bin Laden was at Tora Bora," wrote retired U.S. General Tommy Franks in an October 2004 opinion editorial for *The New York Times*. According to General Franks (who was the lead American military commander at Tora Bora), "some reliable intelligence sources said he was [there]; others indicated he was [already] in Pakistan at the time; still others suggested he was in Kashmir…Tora Bora was teeming with Taliban and Qaeda operatives, many of whom were killed or captured."

"[B]ut Mr. bin Laden was never within our grasp," claimed General Franks at the time.[38] It was not until Spring 2005 that the Pentagon- after a Freedom of Information Act (FOIA) request- publicly released a document to the Associated Press (AP) which stated that Pentagon investigators did officially believe that Osama bin Laden was indeed present at Tora Bora and "that he [ultimately] escaped" from the fierce battle to live to see another day.[39]

'Operation Anaconda' was the next code-name given to the next major battle fought in Afghanistan's Shah-i-kot Valley shortly after the battle of Tora Bora. Fought in March 2002, it was the largest American conventional battle since Operation Desert Storm and was also "the highest altitude battle [8,000-12,000 feet] that the United States [had] ever fought"[40] in its entire military history. Over 1,500 coalition soldiers, including special forces "from Australia, Canada, Germany, Denmark, France and Norway, as well as the U.S. and Afghanistan," attacked hundreds of suspected Al-Qaeda and Taliban holdouts in eastern Afghanistan (near Gardez) on the first day of nearly two weeks of intense fighting.[41]

The Anaconda mission was bolstered by the use of a 2,000-pound "thermobaric bomb," designed to deprive underground or mountainous caves of all oxygen sources. According to *TIME* Magazine, one American soldier was killed and more than 16 others were injured as allied forces met unexpectedly fierce resistance on the first day of fighting alone.[42] On Day 2 of Operation Anaconda, American coalition aircraft dropped over 270 bombs on the Taliban and Al-Qaeda hideouts in the region.[43] On Day 3, U.S. ground forces took the lead in the battle as the allied fighting force grew to over 2,000 coalition soldiers. According to media reports, at least seven American soldiers were killed in a firefight on Day 3 after an enemy rocket-propelled grenade (RPG) shot down an MH-47 Chinook helicopter and forced a second American helicopter to land.[44] On Day 5 of Operation Anaconda, many reports claimed that as many as "800 Al-Qaeda and Taliban fighters" were killed by coalition and Afghan security forces on that one single day alone. This high volume of enemy fighters led many global observers to wonder whether Osama bin Laden may have been nearby; but American government officials immediately down-played any such speculation.

"We...know that they are exceedingly well dug in...they are also well supplied,"[45] said then-U.S. Defense Secretary Donald Rumsfeld about the enemy's tenacity during Operation Anaconda in March 2002. When the operation was complete, according to most official reports, there were a total of eight American soldiers and between 100 and 200 Taliban/Al-Qaeda fighters who were killed during the nearly two-week battle[46] in Afghanistan's eastern mountains called code-name 'Operation Anaconda.'

Nation-Building in Afghanistan: Life 'After' the Taliban

Ever since the beginning of the invasion of Afghanistan, the American government's definition of a political 'victory' within Afghanistan (publicly articulated since 2001) had always been "to build [an] Afghan government and security force that can defend itself as economic growth and development takes hold" throughout the country.[47] On November 14, 2001, the United Nations passed Security Council Resolution 1378 which called for a "central role" for the United Nations in establishing a transitional administration and inviting member states to send peacekeeping forces to promote stability and aid delivery throughout Afghanistan.[48]

On December 5, 2001, many different Afghan political factions (not including the Taliban) came together to officially sign the 'Bonn Agreement'[49] in Germany to help layout a political blueprint for the future of Afghanistan. One day later, the Bonn Agreement was also later ultimately endorsed by UN Security Council Resolution 1383 on December 6, 2001.[50] Reportedly forged with substantial Iranian diplomatic help because of Iran's support for the Northern Alliance faction within Afghanistan, the basic parameters of the Bonn Agreement included:

- Forming the **interim administration headed by Hamid Karzai**;
- **Authorizing an international peace-keeping force** to maintain security in Kabul and Northern Alliance forces were also directed

to withdraw from the capital. UN Security Council Resolution 1386 (December 20, 2001) gave formal Security Council authorization for the international peacekeeping force (International Security Assistance Force or ISAF);[51]

- Referring to the need to **cooperate with the international community on counter-narcotics, crime, and terrorism**.

The first national presidential election within Afghanistan (after post-9/11 Taliban rule) was held on October 9, 2004, with an overall voter turnout of 80% around the country. On November 3, 2004, President Hamid Karzai was declared the winner (with 55.4% of the total popular vote) over his seventeen (17) other challengers in the first round of voting; avoiding a potential runoff. Subsequently, parliamentary and provincial council elections were intended for April-May 2005, but were delayed until September 18, 2005.[52]

The Re-Birth of the Taliban and President Obama's War (2006-Present)

Between 2001 and 2006, American forces and Afghan troops fought relatively low levels of insurgent violence by the Taliban. By late 2005, both U.S. and Afghan coalition forces appeared to believe that the combat, coupled with overall political and economic reconstruction, had virtually "ended any [Taliban] insurgency" within the country. However, an increase in Taliban violence beginning in mid-2006 took many global observers by surprise. Several major reasons for this internal deterioration within the nation included: Afghan government corruption and the absence of security forces in many rural areas—as well as the safe-haven enjoyed by militants in neighboring Pakistan; the reticence of some NATO contributors to actively combat insurgents; civilian casualties caused by NATO and U.S. military operations; and the slow pace of economic development within Afghanistan.[53] With this resurgence of the Taliban within Afghanistan, on March 27, 2009, American President Barack Obama announced a new 'comprehensive' strategy which addressed the key factors involved in this resurgence of the Taliban in the three years since 2006.

In one official presidential 'white paper' (an informal term given to a parliamentary policy brief enunciating governmental policy) on the situation within Afghanistan, President Barack Obama laid out his new focus areas dealing with the deteriorating sociopolitical and security situations within Afghanistan. According to President Obama's official March 2009 'white paper' policy document on Afghanistan, the major realistic and achievable objectives for the people of Afghanistan now set forth by the Obama administration included:

- **Disrupting terrorist networks in Afghanistan** and especially Pakistan to degrade any ability they have to plan and launch international terrorist attacks;
- Promoting a more **capable, accountable, and effective government in Afghanistan** that serves the Afghan people and can eventually function, especially regarding internal security, with limited international support;
- Developing **increasingly self-reliant Afghan security forces** that can lead the counterinsurgency and counterterrorism fight with reduced U.S. assistance;
- Assisting efforts to **enhance civilian control and stable constitutional government in neighboring Pakistan** and a vibrant economy that provides opportunity for the people of Pakistan;
- **Involving the international community** to actively assist in addressing these objectives for Afghanistan and Pakistan, with an important leadership role for the United Nations.[54]

In order for coalition forces to successfully achieve these new revised strategic objectives within Afghanistan, the White House clearly stated that it was "the core goal of the U.S…to disrupt, dismantle, and defeat Al-Qaeda and its safe havens in Pakistan, and to prevent their return to Pakistan or Afghanistan."[55] In summarizing his 'key recommendations' for a successfully-revised 'Global Af-Pak Strategy', President Obama and his military advisors outlined the following fifteen major 'white paper' recommendations in order to achieve political stability within Afghanistan and neighboring Pakistan:

1. *Executing and resourcing* **an integrated civilian-military counterinsurgency strategy** *within Afghanistan;*
2. *Resourcing and* **prioritizing civilian assistance** *in Afghanistan;*
3. *Expanding the* **Afghan National Security Forces**: *Army and Police;*
4. **Engaging the Afghan government** *and bolstering its legitimacy;*

5. *Encouraging Afghan government efforts to* **integrate reconcilable insurgents***;*
6. *Including provincial and* **local governments in our capacity-building efforts***;*
7. **Breaking the link between narcotics and the insurgency***;*
8. *Mobilizing* **greater international political support** *of our objectives in Afghanistan;*
9. **Bolstering Afghanistan-Pakistan cooperation***;*
10. *Engaging and* **focusing Islamabad** *on the common threat;*
11. *Assisting* **Pakistan's capability to fight extremists***;*
12. *Increasing and* **broadening assistance in Pakistan***;*
13. *Exploring* **other areas of economic cooperation with Pakistan***;*
14. **Strengthening Pakistani government capacity***;*
15. *Asking for* **assistance from allies for Afghanistan and Pakistan**.[56]

In conclusion, the March 2009 Obama administration white paper on Afghanistan did concede that "there are no quick fixes to achieve U.S. national security interests in Afghanistan and Pakistan." Furthermore, understanding that the war in Afghanistan is actually part of a greater regional Af-Pak policy, the Obama White House would go on to state their ultimate goals for the future: "In 2009-2010, the Taliban's momentum must be reversed in Afghanistan and the international community must work with Pakistan to disrupt the threats to security along Pakistan's western border."[57]

The McChrystal Factor: A *Rolling Stone* General

On May 11, 2009, United States Secretary of Defense Robert Gates and Joint Chiefs of Staff Chairman Michael Mullen announced that, in concert with the new U.S. strategy announced in March 2009, the presiding American officer in Afghanistan (General David McKiernan) had been asked to resign and was ultimately replaced by Lt. General Stanley McChrystal- considered by many to be an innovative commander to become head of U.S. special operations in the Afghani theater of war.[58]

At the legendary United States Military Academy at West Point (NY), General Stanley McChrystal's classmates fondly remembered comparing "him to the charismatic renegade played by Steve McQueen in *The Great Escape*" during his time at their alma mater. Known within the military as "a gaunt ascetic who rises at 4:30am, eats one meal a day and jogs for an hour," it was General Stanley McChrystal who had pushed for a "secret joint operation in the tribal region of Pakistan...aimed at capturing or killing Ayman Al-Zawahiri, Osama Bin Laden's [second-in-command]"[59] more than four years earlier in 2005. According to former CIA officials, this proposed secret-ops mission was cancelled "at the last minute" by then-Defense Secretary Donald Rumsfeld because it was deemed to be "too dangerous and based on unreliable intelligence."[60]

However, according to *The Sunday Times* newspaper in London, General Stanley McChrystal's major *coup de grace* would later occur in Iraq at the culmination of a successful June 2006 special forces operation against Abu Musab Al-Zarqawi, the Al-Qaeda terrorist chief inside Iraq. At the time, according to official media reports, Jordanian intelligence agents had successfully identified Al-Zarqawi's clerical adviser, who was then tracked to the terrorist's hideout near Baquba, Iraq (north of Baghdad). After several weeks of close surveillance and observation, American coalition special forces were able to successfully assassinate the most-wanted terrorist in Baquba, Iraq on June 7, 2006.

General Stanley McChrystal, who had himself reportedly made an "eyes-on identification of Zarqawi's body", was personally congratulated by President George W. Bush in a telephone call shortly after the successful special-ops mission. According to *The Sunday Times*, this was McChrystal's second major professional 'coup'; with the first one being the capture by his Joint Special Operations Command (JSOC) forces of Saddam Hussein in Tikrit, Iraq during December 2003.[61]

McChrystal v. Obama: The Bob Woodward Leak and October 2009 London Speech

One of the most significant political developments in the nearly decade-long war within Afghanistan occurred on September 21, 2009 when a confidential 66-page military assessment report on Afghanistan (written by General Stanley McChrystal) was conveniently leaked to legendary *Washington Post* reporter Bob Woodward (who jointly won the 1973 Pulitzer Prize for Public Service with fellow reporter Carl Bernstein for uncovering the infamous Watergate scandal). In an exclusive front-page story in the September 21, 2009 edition of the *Washington Post*, Pulitzer Prize-winning journalist Bob Woodward wrote that, "[T]he top U.S. and NATO commander in Afghanistan [General Stanley McChrystal] warns in an urgent, confidential assessment of the war that he needs more forces within the next year and bluntly states that without them, the eight-year conflict 'will likely result in failure'."[62]

"Failure to gain the initiative and reverse insurgent momentum in the near-term (next 12 months) – while Afghan security capacity matures – risks an outcome where defeating the insurgency is no longer possible," wrote General Stanley McChrystal within this 'secret' assessment sent to the Obama administration via Defense Secretary Robert Gates on August 30, 2009.[63] According to Bob Woodward, General McChrystal concluded the document's five-page 'Commander's Summary' on a note of muted optimism:

"While the situation is serious, success [in Afghanistan] is still achievable."[64]

Furthermore, according to the September 2009 front-page *Washington Post* story on the leaked McChrystal report, General Stanley McChrystal had also apparently asked for "speeding the growth of Afghan security forces... The existing goal is to expand the army from 92,000 to 134,000 by December 2011."[65] Within this classified memo leaked to Bob Woodward, General McChrystal also further outlined his personal desire to see the "Afghan army to grow to 240,000 and the police to 160,000 for a total security force of 400,000;" even though he did not specify when those numbers could be realistically reached on the ground within Afghanistan.[66]

Additionally, General McChrystal officially requested "as many as 40,000 additional [American] troops" on the ground inside of Afghanistan, according to the Associated Press.[67] As of October 2009, there were already over 65,000 U.S. forces in Afghanistan now, along with 40,000 more from [other] NATO countries.[68] Furthermore, General McChrystal also said that the military must play an active role in reconciliation, winning over less committed insurgent fighters inside Afghanistan. According to him, the American coalition forces "require[d] a credible program to offer eligible insurgents reasonable incentives to stop fighting and return to normalcy, possibly including the provision of employment and protection," he further wrote within this confidential memo leaked to Bob Woodward of *The Washington Post*.[69] Toward the end of his classified report, General McChrystal again revisited his ominous central theme. "Failure to provide adequate resources also risks a longer conflict, greater casualties, higher overall costs, and ultimately, a critical loss of political support. Any of these risks, in turn, are likely to result in mission failure," he concluded.[70]

In a high-profile follow-up to this leaked report to *The Washington Post*, General Stanley McChrystal further drew raised eyebrows from within the Obama administration when he gave a very-candid public address in London soon thereafter to the Institute of International and Strategic Studies (IISS) on October 1, 2009.[71] During this controversial October 2009 London speech, General Stanley McChrystal flatly rejected White House proposals (led by Vice President Joe Biden) to switch to a more-detached military strategy in Afghanistan that would be more reliant on "drone missile strikes and special-forces operations" against Al-Qaeda and the Taliban around the country.[72] General McChrystal famously told the London audience in October 2009 that the formula favored by American Vice President Joe Biden would lead to "Chaos-istan."[73]

When asked whether he would support the Obama plan, General McChrystal plainly said: "The short answer is: No."[74]

Professor Bruce Ackerman, an expert on constitutional law at Yale University, immediately publicly commented on the General McChrystal controversy by saying that, "As commanding general, McChrystal has no business making such public pronouncements [which violate American military 'chain-of-command' doctrines]." In speaking further on McChrystal's unconventional October 2009 speech in London, Professor Ackerman added that it was highly unusual for a senior military officer to "pressure the president in public to adopt his [own personal] strategy."[75]

A Muslim Solution for Afghanistan: Fix the 'Durand Line'

Within the nuanced enormity of the regional South Asian political history of both Pakistan and Afghanistan, one of the most pressing regional geopolitical questions has always revolved around the more existential issue about where the true geographic 'border' between Pakistan and Afghanistan actually exists. Along with the rest of the world, the country of Pakistan has always believed that Afghanistan ends (and thus Pakistan begins) where a 1,600-mile-border was drawn on the world map in 1893; at the direction of a British colonial officer named Henry Mortimer Durand, who wanted to define the outer edge of what was then-British India. Until the end of British colonial rule in India (which effectively created Pakistan and India one day apart in August 1947), the people of Afghanistan begrudgingly accepted this map[76] despite the fact that what ultimately came to be known as the 'Durand Line' would cut right through certain Pashtun tribal areas and even villages that they had considered to be part of Afghanistan in the past.[77]

According to the November 12, 1893 official agreement between Henry Mortimer Durand (who would later became British Ambassador to the United States) and King Abdur Rahman Khan of Afghanistan, the signatory parties to the Durand Line Agreement met in Kabul and were "desirous of settling these [border] questions by friendly understanding, and of fixing the limit of their respective spheres of influence, so that for the future there may be no difference of opinion on the subject between the allied Governments" of Britain and Afghanistan.[78] At the time, since the geographical topography of Pakistan was still technically part of 'British India' (Pakistan would not be created until over fifty years later in August 1947), the Durand Line Agreement helped to demarcate the borders between Afghanistan and the colony of British India by stipulating that, "The Government of [British] India will at no time exercise interference in the territories lying beyond this [Durand] line on the side of Afghanistan... and His Highness the Amir [of Afghanistan] will at no time exercise interference in the territories lying beyond this line on the side of [British] India."[79]

As financial compensation for agreeing to draw the official Durand border line between Afghanistan and (modern-day) Pakistan, the King of Afghanistan was to receive a yearly monetary subsidy of 12 *lakh* (1.2 million) rupees from the British colonial government in India.[80] Fast-forwarding to today, the debate over the Afghanistan-Pakistan border has effectively resulted in "one distinct Taliban advantage: the border between Afghanistan and Pakistan barely exists for the Taliban" today.[81] Since the border between Afghanistan and Pakistan virtually does not exist for the myopic Taliban, this extremely porous 'Durand Line' has been the central regional geographic fulcrum of our modern-day global Af-Pak strategy.

In a November 2001 column written for *The New York Times*, Vartan Gregorian of The Carnegie Corporation noted how "the arbitrary [Durand] line the British colonial administration in India drew through 'Pashtunistan' in the 19th century, which still forms much of the modern border, created problems that have still not been resolved [until today] in this volatile border region."[82] Such was the historical Afghani opposition to the Durand Line that "based on its objections to the Durand border, Afghanistan [actually] cast the sole vote against Pakistan's entry into the United Nations" in September 1947.[83]

Furthermore, respected Af-Pak specialist Professor Barnett Rubin of New York University's Center on International Corporation has also extensively written about the historical political divide on the Durand Line issue between Afghanistan and Pakistan. "Immediately [after signing the Durand Line Agreement in 1893,] tensions flared between Afghanistan and Pakistan....Afghanistan claimed that Pakistan was a new state, not a successor to British India, and that all past border treaties had lapsed...A *loya jirga* [Pushto for "grand council"] in Kabul denied that the Durand Line was an international border and called for self-determination of the tribal territories [they referred to] as 'Pashtunistan'."[84]

Thus, although Afghanistan and Pakistan have not officially 'fought any wars' over the 1,600-mile-long Durand Line border between the two countries, it is still nonetheless a historical fact that Afghans did begrudgingly accept the Durand Line even though it cut right through certain historic Pashtun tribal areas and other geographic enclaves that they believed (rightfully or wrongfully) to be an official part of Afghanistan. With these nebulous border regions now having devolved into virtually lawless modern-day 'Wild West' enclaves, in order to promote a final peaceful political solution to the Af-Pak 'border dance', it would diplomatically behoove the entire international community to help secure this significant geographic perimeter between these two key central/south Asian nations once and for all in order to preserve the final official sovereignty and physical safety of these two important countries within Asia known as Afghanistan and Pakistan.

As such, the international community (in direct conjunction with both official governments of Afghanistan and Pakistan) need to appropriate all sufficient funds necessary to help officially fortify this 1,600-mile-border between Pakistan and Afghanistan; once and for all. Concededly, although a 1,600-mile-long 'border wall' along the Durand Line may not be the sole 'trump card' solution to our current Af-Pak geopolitical issues, it would certainly help reduce the number of Taliban (and/or Al-Qaeda) insurgents able to freely pass to-and-fro between the extremely porous Durand border regions. By securing the porous

Swiss-cheese border regions with a fortified concrete 'border wall' instead of random (and scattered) border checkpoint crossings; any terrorist attacks on the shared border wall would result merely in re-constructing crumbled concrete and not in burying innocent human beings who are murdered policing the porous border checkpoints along the Durand Line.

Having said that, it is also important to note that this political suggestion is not the first time that an Af-Pak fortified 'border wall' along the Durand Line has been proposed between Afghanistan and Pakistan by prominent leaders and thought leaders around the world. In September 2005, even then-President of Pakistan (General Pervez Musharraf) brought up the idea of a nearly 2,600 kilometer (1,612 mile) border 'fence' to help the joint security of both Afghanistan and Pakistan. At the time of his 2005 Af-Pak border proposal, his main strategic political blunder was the fact that he proposed this 'border fence' idea first to then-United States Secretary of State Condoleezza Rice, rather than to have "[direct] talks with his Afghan counterpart [President Hamid Karzai], which ha[d] brought Afghan resentment to a boiling point" because of the political snub by the bumbling dictator named General Musharraf.[85]

Not surprisingly, in response to President Musharraf's bungled border proposal, Afghan president Hamid Karzai immediately rejected the border idea, telling a 2005 press conference in Kabul that "a wall would not deter terrorists... It would, however, have a host of other disadvantages such as dividing tribes and families."[86] Since the key regional Af-Pak players in the region seem unable (or unwilling) to finalize a border solution, for these reasons, it is important for the Durand Line project to be monitored and sponsored by the United Nations and the rest of our international community.

To highlight this important idea further, according to former Saudi Ambassador to the United States- Prince Turki al-Faisal- he once suggested in an October 2009 opinion editorial in *The Washington Post* that, "As long as this border drawn by the British [the Durand Line] is not fixed, Pakistan and Afghanistan will be at loggerheads and always suspicious of one another...A joint development project for the border area, announced by both Pakistan and Afghanistan, and supported by the United States and the world community, will direct people's eyes to the future rather than to the past."[87] Although the Durand Line does effectively split some small Pashtun populations in the lawless tribal regions of both Afghanistan and Pakistan, it is also important to note the empirical fact that the rising third-world country of Pakistan already hosts the most number of total refugees (mainly Afghani Pashtuns) than any other single country on the entire planet.[88]

According to the U.S. Committee for Refugees and Immigrants (USCRI)- one of the oldest and largest refugee rights organizations in America- their 2008 *World Refugee Survey* annual report calculated that "the total number of refugees in the world has increased to more than 14 million" refugees worldwide.[89] Out of the 14 million refugees on the face of the earth today, the nation of Pakistan currently hosts the largest number (and greatest percentage) of refugees in the entire world.

Since nearly 2 million Afghani refugees already currently reside within Pakistan today (the largest single percentage [15%] of the world's refugee population], it should become a moral imperative on the rest of the community of nations to ensure that a peaceful and final political resolution to Af-Pak regional politics is put into place for the greater stability of future generations of Central and South Asian children.

As part of her tremendous work on behalf of global refugees, Hollywood superstar actress (and United Nations goodwill ambassador) Angelina Jolie has spent much of her philanthropic time visiting refugee camps in Pakistan and Tanzania as part of her goodwill ambassadorship for the United Nations High Commissioner for Refugees (UNHCR). According to a 2008 UNHCR survey of displacement trends, there are currently over "42 million uprooted people [around the world] – 15.2 million were refugees, 26 million were internally displaced people [IDPs] and 827,000 were asylum seekers."[90] Ironically enough, the total number of refugees from our two latest American wars (in Afghanistan and Iraq, respectively) currently constitute almost half (50%) of all refugees worldwide. As of today, nearly 1 out of 4 refugees in the world is from Afghanistan; and over 69 countries around the world have accepted Afghan refugees for asylum, UNHCR agency officials had found in 2009.

"I believe we must persuade the world that refugees must not be simply viewed as a burden," said Angelina Jolie during World Refugee Day 2009 in Washington DC. "They are the survivors. And they can bring those qualities to the service of their communities and the countries that shelter them."[91] The official United Nations Convention Relating to the Status of Refugees (known more commonly as the '1951 Refugee Convention') universally defines the term 'refugee' to mean any persons "who are outside their country and cannot return owing to a well-founded fear of persecution because of their race, religion, nationality, political opinion or membership of a particular social group." According to Antonio Guterres- the UN High Commissioner for Refugees[92] since June 2005- because of the war in Afghanistan, the nation of Pakistan currently struggles both politically and economically with the largest refugee population in the world; with about 1.8 million refugees. In addition, the country also has "more than 2 million internally displaced citizens [IDPs]...largely because of the fighting between the Pakistani military and the Taliban since April [2009 in the Swat valley in northwest Pakistan]."[93] At World Refugee Day 2009, UNHCR Chief Antonio Guterres said that internally displaced people "face the same plight [as refugees]...They have lost the same as refugees... [Sadly, t]hey don't have the same international protections granted to refugees [under international law and the 1951 Refugee Convention]."[94]

Slowly making the shift from one quagmire war in Afghanistan to our 'other war' inside of Iraq, it is also important to keep in mind that the single largest refugee crisis of recent time has been the exodus of Iraqi refugees from the violence and instability of their ancestral war-torn homeland. According to the U.S. Committee for Refugees and Immigrants (USCRI), over 2 million Iraqi refugees have been scattered throughout Syria, Jordan, Lebanon, Egypt, Turkey and many other countries since the onset of the 2003 American invasion (and subsequent occupation) of Iraq. Sadly, neither the Iraqi government nor the countries that comprise the coalition forces in Iraq have taken sufficient responsibility for the safety and well-being of these global refugees. While the Bush Administration and the United Kingdom were busy trying to win the Iraq war through military power, they had "provided no leadership toward ensuring the rights and well-being of the [refugee] victims of this war," said USCRI in one of its official reports. Even the European Union- which for the most part warned of the dire humanitarian consequences of the Iraq war- has also done little to help the Iraqi refugees about whom they were so initially concerned.

Ironically, most of the refugees from Iraq have found "relative safety in Syria, a 'rogue nation' according to the [Bush] Administration, and Jordan, one of the United States' closest allies in the region."[95] Whether anyone is talking about the quagmire in Afghanistan or the ongoing war in nearby Iraq, the devastating human toll on these respective civilian populations will leave lasting sociopolitical repercussions on the overall well-being of these fledgling nations and our overall global equilibrium as well. From Al-Qaeda (and their Taliban abettors) to the 'Durand Line' political issue to the largest refugee population crises on our planet, the unstable political situation in Afghanistan is only remotely paralleled by the ongoing catastrophic occupation which has collectively haunted the nearly 30 million people of Iraq since the most recent American invasion of their country which officially began on March 20, 2003.

The 2003 Iraq War: Weapons of Mass Distraction?

After Saddam Hussein's first invasion of Kuwait in 1991, the United Nations immediately passed UN Resolution 687 on April 8, 1991 which clearly called for the government of Iraq to "unconditionally accept the destruction, removal, or rendering harmless, under international supervision, of...all chemical and biological weapons [aka WMDs]."[96] Furthermore, UN Resolution 687 introduced Iraq (and the global community) to the concept of 'weapons inspections' by calling for the Director-General of the International Atomic Energy Agency [IAEA] to "carry out immediate on-site inspection of Iraq's nuclear capabilities [and]... to develop a plan for submission to the Security Council within forty-five [45] days calling for the destruction, removal, or rendering harmless as appropriate of all items listed."[97]

Nearly twelve calendar years later, on March 20, 2003, American and coalition military forces would begin to launch missiles and bombs at targets within Iraq during an early morning bombing campaign in Baghdad to commemorate the official beginning of the 2003 Iraq war. Air-raid sirens were heard in the streets of Baghdad at about 5:30 a.m. local time on March 20, 2003; about ninety minutes[98] after the 48-hour American deadline for Saddam Hussein to step down or face a U.S.-led military attack had elapsed. Less than forty-five minutes after the commencement of the 2003 Iraq war, U.S. President George W. Bush wasted little time in addressing our nation from the Oval Office of The West Wing in a nationally-televised address that lasted just over four minutes in total.

"American and coalition forces are in the early stages of military operations to disarm Iraq, to free its people and to defend the world from grave danger," said President Bush during this four-minute televised address[99] on March 20, 2003 announcing the official beginning of the 2003 Iraq war.

Doctrine of 'Preemptive War': The Article 51 Argument

Within the basic American constitutional legal framework, former New York Governor Mario Cuomo once wrote in a *Los Angeles Times* column that, "The [2003 Iraq] war happened because when Bush first indicated his intention to go to war against Iraq, Congress refused to insist on enforcement of Article I, Section 8 of the [United States] Constitution."

"For more than 200 years, this article [of the Constitution] has spelled out that Congress – not the president – shall have 'the power to declare war'... Because the Constitution cannot be amended by persistent evasion, this constitutional mandate was not erased by the actions of timid Congresses since World War II that allowed eager presidents to start wars in Vietnam and elsewhere without a 'declaration' by Congress."[100]

From the vantage point of customary international law, much of the global legal debate about the technical legality of the war in Iraq revolved around the concept of 'preemptive' military action as defined by Article 51 of the official Charter of the United Nations. Article 51 of Chapter VII of the official United Nations Charter of 1945 provides simply that: "Nothing in the present Charter shall impair the inherent right of individual or collective self-defense if an armed attack occurs against a Member of the United Nations, until the Security Council has taken measures necessary to maintain international peace and security."[101]

These legal requirements were universally acknowledged to legally justify America's invasion of Afghanistan and toppling the Taliban government after the 9/11 terrorist attacks on the U.S. by Al-Qaeda from their sanctuary safe-haven in Afghanistan. To the contrary, since Iraq had nothing to do with the September 11, 2001 attacks on America, many international law experts have strongly debated the legality of a preemptive strike on Iraq; especially in light of the empirical facts that Iraq neither possessed alleged 'weapons of mass destruction' (WMDs) nor presented a 'clear and present danger' of any imminent attack on American soil that had been so self-righteously touted by prominent hawkish neoconservative members of the myopic Bush administration.

Historically speaking, the recognized right of a state to use force for purposes of self-defense has traditionally included the use of preemptive force (like the use of force in anticipation of an imminent attack). For example, Hugo Grotius (known by many as the 'father of international law'), once stated in the 17th century on the doctrine of 'preemption' that: "[I]t be lawful to kill him who is preparing to kill."[102] Having said that, it is still important to note that the demarcated boundaries on the legal doctrine of 'preemption' have still not yet been very well-defined within the international legal arena of our global marketplace of ideas. In addition to Article 51 of Chapter VII of the UN Charter, Article 39 of the same Charter grants the UN Security Council the authority to determine the existence "not only of breaches of the peace or acts of aggression that have already occurred, but also of threats to the peace; and under Article 42 [of the UN Charter], it has the authority to 'take such action by air, sea or land forces as may be necessary to maintain or restore international peace or security.'"[103]

Even though the United Nations Charter of 1945 has given wide legal latitude to nation-states in protecting the sanctity of their national security under Article 51, many international legal experts will continue to debate whether international law should allow "the preemptive use of force by a nation or group of nations" without direct official U.N. Security Council authorization in the future.[104]

'Mission Accomplished' and the Execution of Saddam Hussein

On May 1, 2003, President George W. Bush decided to publicly declare an official end to major fighting in Iraq by giving a historic speech aboard the flight deck of the USS Abraham Lincoln (a *Nimitz*-class Navy aircraft-carrier nicknamed 'Abe') during which he would famously declare an end to "major combat in Iraq" with an ironically-scenic backdrop of the now-infamous **'Mission Accomplished'** banner hanging from the control tower of the USS Lincoln super-carrier battleship.[105];

"[M]y fellow Americans, major combat operations in Iraq have ended," began President Bush during this famous May 2003 speech aboard the USS Lincoln. "In the battle of Iraq, the United States and our allies have prevailed."[106]

"Operation Iraqi Freedom was carried out with a combination of precision and speed and boldness the enemy did not expect and the world had not seen before," continued President Bush during this May 2003 'Mission Accomplished' speech. "In this battle, we have fought for the cause of liberty and for the peace of the world...Your courage, your willingness to face danger for your country and for each other made this day possible."

"Because of you, our nation is more secure. Because of you, the tyrant [Saddam Hussein] has fallen and Iraq is free."[107] Even though the 'Mission Accomplished' speech ended in early 2003, the global controversy and political blame-game over the infamous 'Mission Accomplished' banner continued even several years later here within the political beltway of Washington DC. On the five-year anniversary of the 'Mission Accomplished' speech in May 2008, the Bush White House was still trying to shift explanations about the blatantly tone-deaf banner and eventually said that "the 'Mission Accomplished' phrase referred to the carrier's crew completing their 10-month mission, not the military completing its mission in Iraq."[108]

In a May 2008 article for CBS News, former Bush White House press secretary Dana Perino remarked during the 5-year anniversary of the 'Mission Accomplished' speech that, "President Bush is well aware that the [Mission Accomplished] banner should have been much more specific...and we have certainly paid a price for not being more specific on that banner...And I recognize that the media is going to play this up."[109] In the subsequent years since the global fiasco, both "the [United States] Navy and former White House Press Secretary Scott McClellan have [both] taken the blame in the past" for the monumental 'Mission Accomplished' banner blunder.[110] However, it was only in January 2009 that the world would finally learn the truth about who would ultimately claim final responsibility for the 'Mission Accomplished' political debacle.

On January 13, 2009, former Bush senior counselor Daniel Bartlett would finally admit that he was actually the Bush administration official who had ultimately "signed-off" on the 'Mission Accomplished' banner during an interview on CBS News' *The Early Show* with Harry Smith.

"Quite frankly, yours truly was the guy who actually signed off" on posting the banner, said Dan Bartlett during this January 2009 on-the-record television interview with CBS News. "I regret it to this day, because it did send the wrong message" to the rest of the world.[111] Even so, long-time Republican strategist Ed Rollins still noted that the misleading banner was not the only regrettable image from the famous May 2003 'Mission Accomplished' speech. During the same January 2009 CBS News interview, Mr. Rollins rightfully noted that for the famous May 2003 speech aboard the USS Lincoln, President George W. Bush "flew in on a jet, he had a pilot's outfit on" and also noted that President Bush was too "overly confident" during his two presidential terms. Even during somber press conferences, Mr. Rollins noted to CBS News about President Bush quite flatly that, "There was [simply] no humility there."[112]

Moving onwards, on December 14, 2003, our entire human race was finally able to collectively exhale a sigh of relief as the infamous dictatorial cult of personality known officially as Saddam Hussein Abd al-Majid al-Tikriti was finally captured within a 'spider hole' in a farm hideout near his hometown of Tikrit, Iraq.

"Ladies and gentlemen, we got him," said Paul Bremer, the former civilian head of Iraq's US-led administration during a packed news conference on December 14, 2003. "The tyrant is [now] a prisoner,"[113] continued former Ambassador Bremer. Wasting no time at all, then-President George W. Bush immediately addressed the nation in a televised address and told the global public that Saddam Hussein would now face "the justice he denied to millions."[114]

"In the history of Iraq, a dark and painful era is over. A hopeful day has arrived," continued President Bush on the day of Saddam Hussein's capture in December 2003. According to the Associated Press, Saddam was captured without a shot being fired at 8:30pm local time (1730 GMT) in a fortified farm compound in Adwar, a town about ten miles from his hometown of Tikrit, Iraq. According to international media reports, his underground hideout was little more "than a specially-prepared 'spider-hole', with just enough space for a man to lie down."

According to U.S. Lt. General Ricardo Sanchez- the top US military commander in Iraq at the time- he said that "bricks and dirt camouflaged the entrance" to Saddam's final hiding place near Tikrit. Shortly thereafter, there was massive globally-publicized video footage of the former Iraqi president undergoing a medical examination after he had been captured and which showed a disheveled Saddam with unkempt dark hair and a thick beard which had become increasingly grey. Along with Saddam Hussein and two of his cronies, it was reported that over $750,000 cash (in $100 bills), two AK-47 automatic machine guns and a used taxi-cab were also found in the same farm compound near Tikrit.[115]

Unfortunately, the ultimate capture of Saddam Hussein on December 14, 2003 did little to help the overall safety and security of average Iraqi women and children who were already suffering from the daily traumas of an ongoing war which had been slowly unraveling the sociopolitical landscape of a land where the legendary Tigris and Euphrates rivers converge in a place known since time immemorial as the 'cradle of civilization'. "I am thrilled that Saddam's cult of personality went out not with a roar, but with a [rat-like] whimper," I once wrote in a newpspaer column immediately after the successful capture of Saddam Hussein in December 2003. "With that, I hope that the healthy and constructive criticism of the [Iraq war and] occupation will continue [here] on the [American] home front...For that is the only way to demand the best foreign policy from [our American] administration...One that expedites the full autonomy and self-governance of Iraqis and brings our boys and girls in the [U.S.] armed forces quickly back into their families' loving arms."[116]

Although many pro-war hawks used the Saddam capture to declare a 'victory' in the war in Iraq, I pointed out in my same December 2003 newspaper column that "once the elation from Saddam's capture recedes...We will soon realize that even though we have won the battle of capturing Saddam Hussein... We are still a long way from winning the [Iraq] war."[117] Unlike the infamous former Serbian dictator Slobodan Milosevic (who was better known as the genocidal 'Butcher of the Balkans')[118] who would eventually die of natural causes on March 11, 2006 at the official United Nations war crime tribunal's detention center located in the Scheveningen district[119] of The Hague in The Netherlands; long-time Iraqi dictator Saddam Hussein would never find his way to an international criminal court tribunal and was ultimately executed (via videotaped hanging) inside Iraq on December 30, 2006.

With noticeable "fear in his face", the notorious dictator Saddam Hussein was hanged shortly after 6 am local Iraqi time (10 pm EST), according to Iraq's national security adviser at the time, Dr. Mowaffak al-Rubaie. On Al-Arabiya television, Dr. Rubaie stated that the execution of Saddam Hussein took place at the 5th Division intelligence office in Qadhimiya, Iraq (outside of the heavily-fortified Green Zone and with no American officials present at all).

"This dark page [of Iraq's history] has been turned over," Dr. Rubaie said immediately after the execution. "Saddam is gone...Today Iraq is an Iraq for all the Iraqis, and all the Iraqis are looking forward...The [Saddam Hussein] era has gone forever."[120] According to CNN, the cell-phone viral video recording of Saddam's last moments and execution by hanging was subsequently leaked (and aired globally) on state-run television network Al-Iraqiya several hours after the execution itself. The Internet cell-phone video of the execution showed

Saddam Hussein- dressed in a black overcoat- being led into a room by three masked guards. The Al-Iraqiya video broadcast only showed the execution to the point where the noose was placed over Saddam's head and tightened around his neck. According to official media reports, there was "no audio" that was heard during the duration of the execution video.[121]

Iraq's National Security Adviser, Dr. Rubaie, who personally witnessed the execution of Saddam Hussein, stated that the former dictator seemed "strangely submissive" during the execution process. "He was a broken man," he said. "He was afraid... You could see fear in his face."[122] As with all historical tyrants and political dictators since the beginning of time who all ultimately partake in our shared imminent human mortal fate of death, the world was finally able to exhale slightly on December 30, 2006 when Saddam Hussein Abd al-Majid al-Tikriti finally took his final breath as the longtime political dictator of the 30+ million women and children of the Republic of Iraq nestled within an ancient fertile land once known as Mesopotamia. Although all future generations of Iraq's children would now thankfully be safe from the demonic ghost of Saddam Hussein, the collective gaze of over 30 million Iraqi women and children would now turn towards the haunting ghosts of an infamous torture prison known ominously around the world as 'Father of the Poor' or the 'Place of the Banished'.

The Ghosts of Abu Ghraib Prison

For the remainder of our chequered human history, the current location of the Baghdad Central Prison which stands today will always infamously be known around the world simply as two Arabic words: '*Abu Ghraib*'. Generally translated from Arabic as 'Father of the Poor' or 'Place of the Banished', the notorious Abu Ghraib prison has long sent chills down the spines of Iraqi citizens for the last few generations of Saddam Hussein's rule. After officially changing its name in February 2009, the Baghdad Central Prison[123] attempted to exorcise its own torturous demons with a simple name change which had little effect on the restless souls of those human beings who were tortured within its walls for the entire world to ultimately see and indelibly record into our institutional history books for the remainder of recorded time.

The hundreds of thousands of public photographs (and videos) were profoundly haunting; piles of naked bodies stacked into a pyramid, shackled-andcuffed prisoners wearing black Klan-like hooded costumes and snarling attack dogs cornering naked prisoners within the darkest abysses of Abu Ghraib prison. And then; there were the smiling American soldiers who were bizarrely (and brazenly) posing within many of these Abu Ghraib torture photographs which shocked our global conscience to its very core.

Allegations of severe maltreatment and torturous abuse of Iraqi prisoners by US military and intelligence personnel and contractors at Baghdad's Abu Ghraib prison began emerging in late 2003, prompting the United States Army to launch an official internal army investigation beginning in January 2004.[124] This official American report- known as 'The Taguba Report' (named after U.S. Major General Antonio Taguba)- had ultimately found that our own American soldiers had been committing "grave breaches of humanitarian law" in their inhumane treatment of prisoners in the echoless chambers of Abu Ghraib prison on the western outskirts of Baghdad.[125] According to BBC World News, some prisoners at Abu Ghraib were "reported to have been raped, sodomized and beaten to death....[Many] photographs were taken of bodies, sometimes with US troops grinning and doing 'thumbs-ups' [with a dangling cigarette in their mouth]."[126]

Mainly because of the mountains of photographic and video evidence and scathing official findings of the official 'Taguba Report' - in total- at least seventeen (17) American soldiers and officers - including the camp commandant - were suspended and criminal proceedings were immediately launched against them. For the American (and global) public, the widespread abuse at Abu Ghraib prison officially became public in April 2004 when CBS News Television and *The New Yorker* magazine jointly published graphic details of the physical abuse; including many graphic and sexually-explicit photographs showing guards beating prisoners and forcing them into humiliating and torturous 'stress positions.'[127] Furthermore, an August 2004 official four-member Defense Department panel (chaired by former United States Secretary of Defense James Schlesinger [1973-75]) found that, "Lieutenant General Ricardo S. Sanchez, the former top commander in Iraq, [had] approved the use in Iraq of some severe [illegal] interrogation practices intended to be limited to captives held in Guantánamo Bay and Afghanistan." Moreover, the Schlesinger report further contended that, "by issuing and revising the rules for interrogations in Iraq three [3] times in 30 days, General Sanchez and his legal staff sowed such confusion that interrogators acted in ways that violated the Geneva Conventions, which they understood poorly anyway."[128]

Even the most hawkish Bush administration officials had always repeatedly stated that the Geneva Conventions clearly "applied to all prisoners in Iraq," but relevant passages of the subsequent Abu Ghraib reports said that these interrogation procedures approved by General Sanchez "exceeded the Geneva [Convention] guidelines as well as standard Army doctrines [as outlined in the Uniform Code of Military Justice (UCMJ)]."[129] In May 2004, with over "1,800 new pictures" showing Abu Ghraib prisoners being "raped, prisoners being ridden like animals and other Iraqis being forced to eat pork"[130] and Iraqi women prisoners "forced to bear their [naked] breasts"[131] by American soldiers in official uniform; the collective outrage in America and the rest of the world began to show what really happened behind those ghastly prison bars within the lowest Dante-esque rungs of Abu Ghraib's prison inferno.

"I expected that these pictures would be very hard on the stomach lining and it was significantly worse than anything that I had anticipated," said United States Senator Ron Wyden (D-OR) to journalists and reporters in May 2004 when these 1,800 new pictures officially came to public light. "Take the worst case [scenario] and multiply it several times over,"[132] Senator Wyden of Oregon said after seeing the nearly 2,000 new photographs and videos of widespread torture and sexual abuse at Abu Ghraib prison. Additionally, the official Taguba Report stated that in the three months alone between October 2003 and December 2003, numerous incidents of "sadistic, blatant, and wanton criminal abuses were inflicted on several detainees" at Abu Ghraib prison by American soldiers stationed with the 800th Military Police Brigade at the Abu Ghraib Prison in Baghdad.[133] According to the Taguba Report, these "intentional abuse[s] of detainees by [American] military police personnel" included (but were not limited to) the following egregious acts:

- *Punching, slapping and kicking detainees;*
- *Forcibly arranging detainees in various sexually-explicit positions for photographing;*
- *Forcing naked male detainees to wear women's underwear;*
- *Forcing groups of male detainees to masturbate themselves while being photographed and videotaped;*
- *Using military dogs (without muzzles) to frighten detainees; and*

- *An American male military police (MP) guard having sex with an Iraqi female detainee.*[134]

Since the initial global outcry of the Abu Ghraib prison scandal began in 2004, official courts-martial and legal military proceedings against at least seven (7) American soldiers (of varying ranks) has ultimately resulted since that time. Apparently, even then-Secretary of Defense Donald 'Rummy' Rumsfeld claimed that "he had twice (2x) offered to resign over the [Abu Ghraib] scandal"; but that both of his resignation offers were ultimately rejected by his buddy, President George W. Bush.[135] Even Bush did ultimately condemn the Abu Ghraib prison scandal, but was also roundly "criticized for not apologizing [directly] to the Iraqi people [himself when] he gave interviews to Arabic TV stations, including the US-owned *Al-Hurra* [global satellite television network]."[136]

Even with a questionable military occupation and blatantly systematic 'cruel and unusual punishments' photographed by some of our smiling American soldiers, there has probably been no greater empirical unraveling of civil society (resulting in thousands of innocent human casualties) within Iraq more troubling than the rebirth of sectarian violence between Sunni and Shia Muslim citizens of Iraq since the beginnings of the 2003 American occupation within Iraq.

Sectarianism Gone Wild: Muslim vs. Muslim

Empirically speaking, it would be hard to debate with any reasonable global Muslim observer that there has simply been no greater *fitna* (Arabic for 'division' or 'strife') in the entire 1500 years of Islamic history that has unraveled more of our global Muslim social fabric than the tragic sectarian history between our Sunni and Shia communities around the world since the beginnings of the 7th century. Analogous to the gigantic Catholic/Protestant historical sectarian divide within modern-day Christianity, modern Islamic history has sadly been no stranger to this disgusting sectarian hostility between Sunni and Shia Muslims since the caliphate of Muawiyah I around the calendar year of 661 CE. As stated before, the divine human history of global Muslims has been ravaged by this intra-religious ideological and physical sectarian venom which has been needlessly passed between our two major sects of Islam (and amongst some of its respective followers) for generations over our chequered human historical record.

Very generally speaking, the overall population of the entire global Muslim community (or *ummah* in Arabic) is primarily split into two major branches: Sunni (85-90%) and Shia (10-15%). This sectarian divide within the global Muslim community originated many centuries ago during a dispute soon after the death of the Prophet Muhammad as to who should be the future leader (or *khalifa* in Arabic) of the first post-prophetic Muslim political community. Just like Catholics and Protestants share the fundamental beliefs of Chirstianity, our two major Muslim sectarian communities also share all of the fundamental religious beliefs (or '5 pillars') of Islam including: 1) The 'one-ness' of God, the belief that Muhammad was the last in the great line of God's Abrahamic prophets (along with Adam, Abraham, Moses and Jesus); 2) Our five basic daily prayers (*salat*); 3) Fasting during the month of Ramadan (*saum*); 4) Charity to the poor (*zakat*); and 5) The annual Hajj pilgrimage to Mecca at least once in every Muslim's lifetime.

In modern times, however, there have been greater incremental differences within the doctrines, rituals, laws, and religious organizations of the respective Sunni and Shia communities around the world. In terms of nuanced difference, the word Sunni comes from the Arabic term '*Ahl al-Sunna*', which generally means "the people of the tradition". This tradition generally refers to the basic religious practices set forth by precedent and teachings of the Prophet Muhammad and his closest companions. Like Shia Muslims, Sunni Muslims venerate all of the Abrahamic prophets mentioned in the Quran (including Adam, Abraham, Moses and Jesus) and have special reverence for Muhammad as simply the last of God's divine messengers to ever walk the earth. Thus, for Sunni Muslims, every subsequent Muslim political leader after the life of the Prophet has been seen merely as temporal political figures.

In early Islamic history, Shia Muslims were a political faction named after the "party of Ali" (*Shiat Ali* in Arabic). Immediately after the death of the Prophet Muhammad in the year 632 CE, Shia Muslims believed in the political right of Ali- the cousin and son-in-law of the Prophet Muhammad- and his genealogical descendants to serve as the first *khalifa* (caliph) of the first post-prophetic Islamic community in the world. Even though the prophet's cousin Ali ibn Abi-Talib would ultimately become the fourth (and final) member of *Al-Khulaifa Rashidoon* (the first four 'Rightfully Guided Caliphs' preceded by caliphs Abu

Bakr, Umar ibn Al-Khattab and Uthman ibn Affan, respectively); the fourth caliph (and the Prophet's son-in-law) Ali was subsequently killed in 661 CE during a political power struggle over who should be the next leader of the Muslims after the first four 'Rightly-Guided Caliphs'.

Additionally, it is also significant for Shia Muslims that Ali's two sons (and the Prophet Muhammad's two grandsons) also ultimately sacrificed their lives in order to regain the caliphate – Imam Hussein died on the battlefield opposing a subsequent caliph at the famous Battle of Karbala (in Iraq) in 680 CE and Shia Muslims also believe that the Prophet's other grandson (Imam Hassan) to have been poisoned by political adversaries around the year 670 CE. As a result, he is buried in the famous *Jannatul Baqee* ("Garden of Heavens") cemetery near his beloved grandfather right across the southeast entrance of *Masjid Al-Nabawi* ("The Mosque of the Prophet"); one of Islam's two holiest mosques in Medina, Saudi Arabia.

Fast-forwarding to today, out of the nearly 1.57 billion global Muslims who currently live on the planet today, most estimates find that Shia Muslims represent approximately 120 to 170 million people; roughly about one-tenth (10%) of all global Muslims worldwide.[137] Today, most accounts find that Shia Muslims are probably in the numerical majority in some countries such as Iran, Iraq, Bahrain and- according to some estimates- Yemen. Additionally, there are large Shia communities inside Afghanistan, Azerbaijan, India, Kuwait, Lebanon, Pakistan, Qatar, Syria, Turkey, Saudi Arabia, and the United Arab Emirates (UAE).[138]

Within the tragic historical legacy of our global Sunni/Shia sectarian conflict, the country of Iraq would become the latest modern victim of our deplorable sectarian violence which has plagued our global Muslim community since shortly after the death of Islam's last prophet over a millennium ago. Because of the bloody sectarian violence in Iraq, in October 2006, prominent Sunni and Shia religious and political leaders from Iraq met inside the Muslim holy city of Mecca to sign the official "Mecca Declaration" sponsored by the 57-member Organization of the Islamic Conference (OIC) to call for an immediate stop to sectarian violence in Iraq and around the rest of the world. The Mecca Declaration was signed on October 20, 2006 and the official document directly drew from Islamic religious texts which clearly states that murdering any innocent human being is completely forbidden (or *haram*) within Islam. Moreover, the Mecca Declaration urged the preservation of Iraq's internal unity, protection of all religious holy sites (like Sunni mosques and Shia religious shrines) and called for the immediate release of all "innocent detainees" within Iraq today.[139] Both Sunni and Shia religious leaders from Iraq signed this major 10-point statement of the Mecca Declaration categorically forbidding the following within Iraq and everywhere else: sectarian killings, kidnappings, beheadings, incitement of hatred, attacks on religious sites and the forcing of members of the other sect from their homes.

"The most important point in [the Mecca Declaration] is that the shedding of Sunni and Shia blood is forbidden, forbidden, forbidden," said Sheikh Ahmad Abd al-Ghafour al-Samerrai, the head of the Sunni Waqf Department in Iraq to the BBC News Arabic service shortly after the signing of the Mecca Declaration in October 2006. On the Shia Muslim side, official representatives of Iraqi Prime Minister Nouri Al-Maliki and Iraq's largest Shia party- the Supreme Council for the Islamic Revolution in Iraq- backed the Mecca Declaration, as did the former leader of Iraq's largest Sunni political party as well. Furthermore, according to the Associated Press, an official Iraqi spokesman told the news agency that the Mecca Declaration had also been approved by Iraq's top Shia cleric- Grand Ayatollah Ali al-Sistani- and even the radical militant Shia Iraqi leader Muqtada al-Sadr- whose 'Mehdi Army' militia had been widely blamed for involvement in violent sectarian attacks in Iraq- had also surprisingly approved the principles of the Mecca Declaration.[140]

Even with the significant political accomplishments of the Mecca Declaration and an overall decline in sectarian violence within Iraq, the last few years have still seen some tragic sectarian violence on both sides of the Iraqi political equation. On February 22, 2006, the nation of Iraq was rocked by a treacherous bombing of the Al-Askari shrine in Samarra (north of Baghdad), where two men detonated themselves and blew up the famous golden dome at one of the holiest sites for Shia Muslims during a pre-dawn raid on the famous mosque. According to Jon Brain of BBC World News in Baghdad, the bombing "was almost certainly designed to raise the existing tensions between the majority Shia and minority Sunni populations"[141] within Iraq.

After this infamous February 2006 bombing of the historic golden dome in Samarra, an upsurge in sectarian violence further resulted in as many as "1,300 [deaths]...in the wave of sectarian violence that swept Iraq following the bombing of [the] gold-domed [Al-Askari] shrine in Samarra."[142] In one week alone,

The Washington Post reported that Iraqi officials at Baghdad's main morgue had "logged more than 1,300 deaths" since the attack on the Al-Askari shrine only one week before. Most shockingly, it was reported that most of the murdered Iraqis "had been shot, knifed or garroted, often with their hands tied execution-style behind their back."[143]

In 2007, in continued retaliation for targeting the major Samarra shrine for Shia Muslims, at least three different Sunni mosques near the Iraqi capital of Baghdad were destroyed only one day after the Samarra attack. In the next few weeks alone, there would be a total of six (6) other Sunni mosques that were attacked in direct response to the insurgents who toppled the two minarets of the Samarra shrine a few weeks prior. According to Iraqi officials, several unidentified men traveled to the Hutin mosque in Iskandariya (south of the capital Baghdad) in the early hours of a Thursday morning and planted bombs which caused a huge explosion at the local Sunni mosque. In the town of Mahaweel (also south of Baghdad), Shia insurgents opened fire on the Bashir mosque during the dawn (*fajr*) prayers and forced the mosque's guards to leave and ultimately set fire to the building; according to Iraqi police officials.[144]

Iraq's tragic legacy of sectarian violence would continue well into 2008 and 2009 as the nearly 30+ million people of Iraq neared the culmination of the first decade of their most recent occupation by a foreign military power. A May 2008 report on Iraq by Amnesty International USA found that the overall human rights situation is "disastrous, a climate of impunity has prevailed, the economy is in tatters and the refugee crisis continues to escalate" within the land formerly known as Mesopotamia. Furthermore, an official survey conducted by the World Heath Organization (WHO) in Iraq found that over 21.2 percent of Iraqi women had experienced some form of physical violence. Oxfam International also reported in July 2007 that nearly 70 percent of Iraqis lacked adequate access to safe drinking water and over 43 percent of Iraqis were living on the equivalent of less than one-dollar-per-day. According to major human rights organizations, there are currently over 8 million Iraqis who are in dire need of emergency assistance of some kind.

Similarly, the child malnutrition rates have increased from 19 percent during the period from 1991-2003- when international sanctions were imposed on the country under Saddam Hussein- to over twenty-eight (28%) percent in 2007.[145] Even with Iraq's children going hungry or the women of Iraq being raped on a daily basis, the militant sectarian insurgent thugs (on both sides) have done absolutely nothing to help the overall plight of their own people and instead continued their irreligious massacres on both sides of the sectarian velvet rope.

On April 18, 2008, at least 140 Shia Muslims were killed by a car bomb detonated at a busy marketplace in al-Sadriya, a predominantly Shia district in Baghdad. Only a few weeks earlier, Shia gunmen wearing police uniforms gunned-down over 70 Sunni Muslims near the town of Mosul on March 27, 2008. Survivors of this aforementioned attack stated that the uniformed gunmen "dragged men from their homes, handcuffed and blindfolded them, and then riddled them with bullets."[146] On July 7, 2008, more than 150 Iraqi people were killed (and more than 265 injured) in a suicide car-bomb attack at the main bazaar marketplace in Amerli (a predominantly Shia village in Salahuddin governorate).

According to an official 2009 report on Iraq by Human Rights Watch, "In Baghdad, twin bombings in a crowded commercial district on March 7, 2008, killed as many as 71 people, a June 18 truck bomb in a neighborhood where Sunnis have been displaced by Shia militias killed as many as 63 people, a female suicide bomber targeting Shia pilgrims killed at least 32 people on July 28, and two separate waves of attacks before and during the *Eid al-Fitr* holiday [after Ramadan] in early October killed at least 48 people."[147]

Additionally, international journalists have also been the tragic victims of the senseless bloodshed within Iraq today. According to the Committee to Protect Journalists (CPJ), there have been "at least 122 journalists...and 41 media support staffers [that] have been killed in Iraq since the U.S.-led invasion in March 2003, making it the deadliest [war] conflict for the press in CPJ's 26-year history." CPJ also further noted that "about 85 percent of media deaths have been Iraqi [citizens]."[148]

One of these tragic journalist deaths was 27-year-old Iraqi citizen Shehab Mohammad al-Hiti. As the young newspaper editor of the fledgling *Al-Youm* ("The Day") weekly newspaper in Baghdad, the young 27-year-old newspaper editor was last seen alive "leaving his home in Baghdad's western neighborhood of Al-Jamia to go to the newspaper's offices" one warm Sunday afternoon in October 2007. Later on that same October afternoon, Iraqi police officials had sadly "found the [Sunni] journalist's body...in Baghdad's northeastern Ur neighborhood... [which] is adjacent to Baghdad's 'Sadr City' - controlled by the Mahdi Army- led by radical Shia cleric Muqtada al-Sadr."

"We condemn the killing of Shehab Mohammad al-Hiti and offer his family and colleagues our deepest condolences," said Committee to Protect Journalists (CPJ) Executive Director Joel Simon shortly after the tragic murder of the young 27-year-old Iraqi newspaper editor. "Journalists continue to be killed in Iraq at an alarming rate, underscoring the risks of practicing what has become one of the deadliest professions in the country."[149]

In light of these needless tragedies, the people of Iraq should always remember the noble Islamic teachings of 'love and compassion' encompassed within the Mecca Declaration calling for the complete eradication of all sectarian violence between Sunni and Shia Muslims. It is also important to note the positive trends that both Sunni and Shia religious leaders in Iraq are undertaking by bravely showing their willingness to give up their own lives to help end all sectarian violence in Iraq for the betterment of all Iraqis; regardless of their sect, ethnicity and/or political affiliation. As of August 2009, *The New York Times* reported that Sunni and Shia Muslim clerics in Iraq "have been successfully urging their followers not to retaliate against a fierce campaign of sectarian bombings", especially since Shia Iraqis have accounted for "most of the 566 Iraqis killed" in sectarian violence since American troops pulled out of Iraq's cities on June 30, 2009.

"Let them kill us," said Sheikh Khudair al-Allawi, the imam of an Iraqi mosque bombed in August 2009, in a news article for *The New York Times* shortly after his mosque was attacked. "It's a waste of their time....The sectarian card is an old card and no one is going to play it anymore....We know what they want, and we will just be patient," said the Iraqi imam about the future of any sectarian militant thugs (whether Sunni or Shia) who still continue to indiscriminately kill innocent Muslim women and children within both Sunni mosques and Shia shrines around Iraq on a seemingly daily basis.

The imam added: "But [God willing], they will all go to hell."[150]

The Shoe Heard Around the World: Iraq's Farewell to President George W. Bush

Not since former Soviet leader Nikita Khrushchev once pounded his famous footwear onto a table at an October 1960 United Nations session had we seen a 'shoe' create such a global political firestorm around the world. Over 48 years after Khrushchev's famous footwear incident at the United Nations, on

December 14, 2008, our global political *zeitgeist* would now have an unknown young Iraqi journalist literally 'hurling' himself into the annals of human history with his own rendition of the ongoing historical saga entitled "Shoes Heard Around the World." From YouTube to Facebook, the now-infamous viral Internet video clip showed 29-year-old Iraqi journalist Muntadhar Al-Zaidi standing and hurling both of his shoes at President George W. Bush during his final December 2008 farewell press conference in Iraq and shouting in Arabic as he hurled his Size-10 shoes:

"This is a farewell kiss, you dog....This is from the widows, the orphans and those who were killed in Iraq."[151] Immediately after throwing his shoes at President Bush, Mr. Al-Zaidi- a twenty-nine-year-old journalist for private Iraqi television channel Al-Baghdadia- was then quickly overpowered by Iraqi security forces because his 'shoe gesture' was described by *Agence France Presse* as "the supreme mark of disrespect in the Muslim world." According to the Associated Press, some regional television channels in the Middle East aired the infamous shoe-throwing footage from the press conference "more than a dozen times in [the first] several hours [alone]" after the incident.

In response to the shoe hear around the world, I wrote a front-page column for CNN.com two days after the Iraqi shoe incident in December 2008 stating quite clearly that it should be "made clear that no shoes should have been thrown at President Bush...Aside from being patently childish (and simply bad Muslim manners), notwithstanding the global public's distaste for President Bush's policies, the job of a journalist is to be a purveyor of truth and information to his or her audience." I further wrote in my CNN column that, "Mr. Al-Zaidi's job as a journalist is to report the news to his citizens, who otherwise would have little or no access to information...Thus, as a journalist, Al-Zaidi failed miserably in his profession by not keeping his shoes firmly on his feet...Although many people are applauding the '15 minutes of fame' achieved by the shoe incident, there is simply little excuse for such childish and silly behavior by Mr. Al-Zaidi."

Everyone knows that throwing a shoe at someone in the Muslim world (or anywhere else in the world) is a patently insulting gesture on its face. The context of the 'shoe' incident may have been different had it been a 'cream-filled pie' (a la Bill Gates or Ann Coulter) as the projectile in question. Within this cultural context, simply even <u>showing the soles of your shoes</u> to someone- let alone tossing your shoes at them- is a sign of brazen contempt for that person in that part of the world. For example, as Saddam Hussein's statue was famously toppled in April 2003, Iraqi protesters on the streets of Baghdad pelted the toppled statue with their "shoes and sandals". To highlight this point even further, a CNN news story on the April 2003 statue toppling called the throwing of shoes a "grave insult in the Arab world."[152]

Thus, for numerous reasons, this notorious Iraqi shoe incident actually took away the real focus from the actual humanitarian suffering of the Iraqi people and was wrongfully applauded by many people in certain parts of the world. According to ABC News, a wealthy Saudi Arabian citizen named Hasan Muhammad Makhafa had apparently offered $10 million for one of the famous shoes thrown by the Iraqi TV journalist towards President Bush shortly after the incident. Mr. Makhafa, described as a landowner and retired teacher, told Dubai-based Arabic satellite TV station Al-Arabiya that Al-Zaidi's shoes were "a symbol of freedom, not just footwear." He continued to say that "they represent a victory for those who have disgraced the Arabs by occupying their lands and killing innocent people."

Are you kidding me, Mr. Makhafa?

As I further wrote in my December 2008 CNN column as a direct response to Mr. Makhafa, "[Sir]; why don't you instead take your $10 million and donate it directly to the Iraqi people to help build more water wells, educate Iraqi women or help resettle Iraqi refugees in Syria and Jordan?" Why would anyone settle on a pair of worthless leather shoes when you can actually help the starving women and children of Iraq with that sizable $10 million donation? How could it ever help the plight of an impoverished nation when you are willing to spend millions of dollars on eBay auction fees for these infamous leather shoes rather than figuring out real tangible ways to help the nation of Iraq rebuild into a functional and prosperous society again?

Truthfully, the answer is that the 'shoe' story did not help the plight of the Iraqi people in any tangible way whatsoever. Instead of perpetuating tired stereotypical tropes that Arabs and Muslims are less-than-civilized-shoe-throwers, perhaps we Muslims should instead be more self-critical and help propagate the more accurate stereotypes of Muslim/Arab 'hospitality' and 'warmth' around the world. As our global community thankfully transitioned from the ill-fated presidency of George W. Bush to the much-anticipated presidency of U.S. President Barack Obama, we could all finally take a little comfort knowing that the gigantic (and embarrassing) imprint of 'History's Shoe' will leave a much more humiliating mark on the entire Bush administration legacy than a simple pair of misguided Size-10 Iraqi shoes thrown in his general direction.

CHAPTER SEVEN: WAR AND/OR PEACE

"Peace is the only battle worth waging..."
-Albert Camus

To be completely honest with you, these bloodshot eyes of mine have not had one peaceful night of sleep since September 11, 2001 and they have also calmly been resigned to the utterly humbling mortal conclusion that they may never truly peacefully sleep again until the glorious day when I hit my grave and the time has come for me to "meet my Maker and to repay him in kind for all that he has done."[1] In other words, for the remainder of my own living days, in the timeless words of Paul Hewson (better known by his *nom de guerre*, Bono): "I'm wide awake...I'm not sleeping."[1] Thus, with these perpetually-bloodshot eyes, my last few remaining days left upon our wonderful earth shall only be dedicated to the quixotic pursuit of peaceful coexistence within the global marketplace of ideas. However, because of both extremist terrorists and racist neoconservative polemicists alike on both sides of the current geopolitical spectrum, many global observers have spent much of their professional lives scratching their graying heads and perilously pondering whether our global human civilization is actually *en route* towards some morbidly nihilistic violent 'crash' course pathway between two of our major human 'civilizations' in existence.

The 'Clash of Knuckleheads' Theory: Samuel Huntington's Final Interview Ever

First coined within a 1993 magazine article for *Foreign Affairs*, in its modest two decades of existence, the basis of three simple words have dominated our current geopolitical discourse on cultural, socio-religious, and international affairs as they relate to the foreign policy *realpolitik* of our modern times. The 'Clash of Civilizations' theory (as originally coined by Harvard Professor Samuel Huntington within this aforementioned[2] 1993 *Foreign Affairs* article) has stirred heated debate across the globe, but particularly among many in non-Western Muslim nations because of its seemingly simplistic proclamation of "an inherent and fundamental incompatibility between the 'Christian West' and the 'Muslim World'." Especially because of its central civilizational collision premise, the full-scale impact of Professor Huntington's theory on modern international affairs is sometimes difficult to quantify in objective empirical terms.

For example, an April 2011 Google search[3] of "clash of civilizations" yielded over 775,000 search results alone; and to this very day, this famous political catch-phrase is often quoted within newspapers, books, academic journals and media articles around the world. After this initial 1993 *Foreign Affairs* magazine article introducing his controversial concept to our modern *realpolitik*, Professor Huntington later expanded on this thesis into a book entitled *The Clash of Civilizations and the Remaking ofWorld Order;* which was published in 1996 and has since been translated into over 39 languages.[4]

In terms of its overall effect on our global political stage, one of the more recent acknowledgements (and direct political refutations) of Professor Samuel Huntington's theory came from the United Nations- which under the patronage of former Secretary General Kofi Annan- launched a global public diplomacy initiative called 'The Alliance of Civilizations' in 2005, presumably as a means of countering this 'clash' theory put forward by Professor Huntington many years ago. For this and many other reasons, the widespread political influence of Professor Huntington's ideas are readily apparent and this circuitous geopolitical debate will most likely continue to remain towards the forefront of international relations for much of the foreseeable future.

In one of his rare (and final) on-the-record public interviews before his death in December 2008, Professor Samuel P. Huntington sat down for an exclusive and extensive formal interview with our *Islamica* Magazine in the summer of 2006 in what would be the "only Muslim [publication] to whom Huntington [ever] granted a formal interview during his lifetime."[5] Ironically enough, our magazine's exclusive on-the-record interview with Professor Huntington in the summer of 2006 also "happened to be his last [interview ever]; several weeks later, he suffered a stroke and retired to Cape Cod [before he ultimately passed away on December 24, 2008]."[6]

"I think it is a mistake, let me just repeat, to think in terms of two homogenous sides starkly confronting each other," began Professor Samuel Huntington during his wide-ranging 2006 final sit-down interview with our *Islamica* Magazine on the 'clash of civilizations' theory. "Global politics remains extremely complex and countries have different interests, which will also lead them to make what might seem as rather bizarre friends and allies."

"Again, I think it's hard to talk about the Muslim world and Christian world as [distinctly separate] 'blocks'," continued Professor Huntington during his 2006 *Islamica* interview. "There will be association and partnerships between some Muslim countries and some Christian countries. Those already exist. And they may shift as different regimes come and go and interests change. I do not think it is all that useful [for the world] to think in terms of those two 'solid blocks' [like the Muslim world and the West]."[7] According to the *Harvard Gazette* newspaper shortly after his death, Professor Huntington "said in a 2006 interview with *Islamica* Magazine that 'cultural identities, antagonisms and affiliations will not only play a role, but play a major role, in relations between states'" in the future.

During his long tenure as the Albert J. Weatherhead III University Professor at Harvard University in Boston, Dr. Huntington ultimately identified these major reductive 'civilizations' as including the: "Western (including the United States and Europe), Latin American, Islamic, African, Orthodox (with Russia as a core state), Hindu, Japanese, and 'Sinic' (including China, Korea, and Vietnam)" civilizations around the world.[8]

Directly refuting the 'clash of civilizations' theory, his fellow Harvard colleague (and winner of the 1998 Nobel Prize for Economics) Professor Amartya Sen published a book as a challenge to Huntington entitled *Identity and Violence: The Illusion of Destiny* where he directly challenged Professor Huntington's central civilizational thesis on the basis that "identity is not destiny" and that each individual human being can construct and reconstruct their own respective chosen identities. Nobel laureate Dr. Amartya Sen further continued to argue that the clash of civilizations theory comes from the "miniaturization of human beings", meaning that each and every living human being is simplistically reduced to "unique and choice-less identity made to fit into the [compartmentalized and reductive] boxes of 'civilization'."[9]

Getting back to Professor Huntington's final 2006 on-the-record interview with *Islamica* magazine, in speaking about political 'fundamentalist' movements around the world, Professor Huntington said this during his final interview with our magazine: "I think fundamentalism is what you said: this radical attitude toward one's own identity and civilization as compared to other people's identities and cultures."

"Certainly here in the United States, we have [definitely] had [our own] fundamentalist movements," conceded Professor Huntington towards the end of his final interview of his lifetime. In speaking about minority rights within Western societies, Dr. Huntington further stated that, "The larger society has to recognize some degree of autonomy for the minority: the right to practice their own religion and way of life and to some extent their language." When asked directly about whether he believed if his 'clash of civilizations' theory had been duplicitously and disingenuously used by certain people for their own myopic right-wing political agendas, Professor Huntington immediately responded: "Oh absolutely, all the time...There isn't much I can do about that...In the past, some of my other writings have also set forth ideas and arguments that people have found controversial and have criticized." He continued his answer by stating, "Initially, with respect to these past writings, I would try to respond to them, but by doing so, I would call attention to their [inaccurate] arguments. Instead of having one article in one magazine, we would have two or three articles in separate magazines and the whole thing would be blown out of proportion. So, except under rare circumstances, I do not write responses to criticism."

"I am not an expert on Islam," Professor Huntington finally conceded during this interview; which would probably come as a surprise to many of his neoconservative political cheerleaders around the world. Furthermore, during the end of his 2006 interview with *Islamica*- which again happened to be the last interview of his lifetime- when asked directly about the one single thing that most people around the world would be surprised to learn about him; Professor Samuel Huntington smiled and simply replied:

"A lot of people tend to think [that] I am a dogmatic ideologue; which I am not."[10]

Professor Samuel Phillips Huntington passed away on December 24, 2008 at his home on the island of Martha's Vineyard, Massachusetts at the age of 81. Although a lifelong dedicated neoconservative political scientist, along with his passing, billions of people around the world sincerely prayed that his silly and reductive 'clash of civilizations' theory would be buried alongside with him never to wreak intellectual havoc upon our global marketplace of ideas ever again. Personally speaking, as someone who has dedicated his entire life to being a 'Clash Dispeller' (according to a 9/11 anniversary profile of my work in a 2008 *Christian Science Monitor* article) and as a contributing member of the human race whose mission it is "to dispel the theory of a clash of civilizations in American and global venues and to play a part in making a better world for all";[11] I would be monumentally remiss if I did not tweak Professor Huntington's myopic worldview by offering an opposing millennial counter-narrative entitled 'The Clash of Knuckleheads Theory'.

Under this theory, mainstream Muslims worldwide will continue to spend the rest of our waking days condemning terrorist knuckleheads like Al-Qaeda Inc. as long as they continue to commit acts of ungodly murder in the name of our beautiful religion. Again, notwithstanding the categorical prohibition of <u>both</u> suicide <u>and</u> civilian murder within Islam, these treacherous murderous knuckleheads like Osama bin Laden have done nothing but add madness to the already existing madness in the world today. From Bali to Madrid to London to Mumbai, my seething disgust increases exponentially each time one of their irreligious and ungodly attacks occurs during our global watch. For instance, whenever an innocent 9-year old child (anywhere in the world) is considered to be a 'legitimate target' for acts of murder and terrorism, you should know full well that these godless maniacs have lost their bloody minds when they commit these ungodly acts of mass murder. As well as being an arch-nemesis for the late Osama bin Laden and his extremist cronies worldwide, we shall also continue to rhetorically spit in the face of every racist neoconservative around the world by completely and categorically condemning Islamophobia, Anti-Semitism and all other forms of racial and religious intolerance in existence today.

All racism is wrong; period.

Out of the nearly seven billion human beings[12] that currently share our universe today, it would be objectively safe for any reasonable global observer to say that the vast numerical majority of the human race at this moment today would obviously prefer peace over war on any given day of the week. Following suit, this would necessarily (and mathematically) make the warmongering knucklehead dinosaurs (on both sides of the global political velvet rope) among the infinitesimal minority of the world's total combined numerical population. Thus, since many of our global political problems today revolve around extremist 'knuckleheads' on both sides who are not even close to representing the numerical majority of any given reductive 'civilization' around the world; this global political hypothesis should probably tweak Huntington's and be renamed 'The Clash of Knuckleheads Theory'.

Sorry, Professor Huntington.

An Evening With Nobel Peace Prize Winner Dr. Shirin Ebadi

When TIME Magazine rightfully named 2003 Nobel Peace Prize Winner Dr. Shirin Ebadi as one of their "*TIME 100: The One Hundred Most Influential People in the World*" in 2004, the super-magazine's editors cogently noted that Dr. Ebadi was indeed "a woman of steel" and a human rights champion with "a heart of gold".[13] She had made history the previous year on October 10, 2003 when Dr. Shrin Ebadi became the first Muslim woman ever (and the first Iranian citizen) to be awarded the 2003 Nobel Peace Prize in Oslo, Norway. In awarding her the 2003 Nobel Peace Prize, the prestigious five-member panel of the Norwegian Nobel Committee in Oslo noted Dr. Ebadi's lifelong dedication for "the rights of women and children" around the world and especially within her home country of Iran. Furthermore, the Nobel Peace Prize committee also noted that Dr. Ebadi has "consistently supported non-violence" and also publicly favors "enlightenment and dialogue as the best path to changing attitudes and resolving conflict"[14] around the world. With that brilliant enlightened legacy of promoting Muslim nonviolence, it sure sounds like Dr. Shirin Ebadi is another one of us proud global Islamic pacifists as well.

To the pleasure of us Washingtonians, Nobel Peace Prize laureate Dr. Shrin Ebadi was here in Washington DC in October 2009 to receive the 3rd annual 'Human Security Award' sponsored by the Muslim Public Affairs Council Foundation. At an exclusive private dinner reception of nearly 40 journalists, congressional members, ambassadors and other dignitaries at the suburban Washington DC uber-mansion of Pakistani Ambassador-At-Large Rafat Mahmood;[15] Dr. Shirin Ebadi graciously accepted her prestigious award that evening and gave us her current thoughts on Islam, democracy, human rights and the aforementioned 'clash of civilizations' theory. Although a physically tiny adorable little woman, our multi-cultural interfaith audience of nearly fifty dignitaries that evening were listening with pleasant awe at this Muslim political lioness who was also the first-ever female to ever serve as a judge in the hard-core theocratic state of Iran. In speaking to our small private audience of journalists and global diplomats, Dr. Ebadi began her remarks to us that evening (through her Farsi translator) by saying: *"For a few years now, the question has constantly been raised as to whether Islam can indeed be compatible with human rights standards and democracy…This question came as a result of the theory developed by Samuel Huntington and the 'clash of civilizations' which basically questioned the compatibility between mainly Muslim civilizations and Western civilizations based on the flawed argument that because human rights and democracy were 'born' in the West, that this is not possible at all in the Muslim world."*[16]

"This [clash of civilizations] theory is incorrect both historically and if you look at it logically," she continued to tell us that evening. After eloquently dismantling the central thesis of the 'clash of civilizations theory', Dr. Ebadi then shifted the focus of her talk on the responsibility of over 1.57 billion global Muslims[17] living within the millennial age today. *"We must educate the true teachings of Islam to the world, especially the West,"* she continued during her talk at our private dinner in Washington in October 2009. *"We must provide a cure for the wounds that were created in the West by the Taliban and the tragic events of September 11…And to embark on that process we must review the true compassionate teachings of Islam…And we can begin to do that by looking within ourselves,"* she told our captivated audience that evening. As she spoke to our diverse Washington audience of Muslim, Christian and Jewish citizens of all religions and backgrounds, Dr. Ebadi continued to highlight our shared humanistic commonalities as members of one single global family and human race.

She highlighted the fact that it was imperative on global Muslims *"to extend a hand of friendship to all non-Muslims"* and that we must *"extend our communities to include others"* of all other religions and races around the world today. *"The Abrahamic religions, meaning Christianity, Judaism and Islam, all have [the same] common roots…Now, how come it is that no one ever approaches us to ask whether Judaism or Christianity are compatible with human rights or not? But Islam is always brought up in this [pejorative] way,"* she said during her October 2009 acceptance speech that evening. Since the three major Abrahamic religions again all share the same monotheistic religious foundations of the Ten Commandments, Dr. Ebadi believed that we should *"always start from those [shared] commonalities and leave the [minutiae of theological] differences aside."*

"Let us be giving like the skies," she said in her concluding remarks that evening. *"Let us spread friendship as the wind…Let us rage like fire against ignorance and against prejudice…Let us sow the seeds of cooperation like the earth."* Dr. Shirin Ebadi, the legendary Muslim women human rights lawyer and more-than-deserving winner of the 2003 Nobel Peace Prize ended her moving address to us that evening in October 2009 with one simple sentence:

"Let us be kind to one another…Kind…"[18]

Dear Muslim Youth of the World: Welcome to the 'Love Jihad'

As a rising young member of the next generation of millennial Islam, my simple overall message to my fellow generation members of the Muslim world will always be to show the rest of humanity the true essence of Islam by embracing non-violence and implementing the central 'love and compassion' ethical teachings of our religion towards every other living creature within every aspect of your daily respective lives. As cartoonish terrorists like Osama bin Laden and the Bali, 3/11 Madrid and 7/7 London bombers have tragically taught our global village, we must also band together help re-establish a global human *détente* where we will jointly condemn any future armed or violent response to <u>any</u> modern-day geopolitical grievance where the taking of even one innocent woman, child or man's life may even potentially occur during our global watch.

We can call it a 'millennial farewell to arms'; if you will.

Our millennial 'farewell to arms' (or 'love *jihad*') will be a very simple global pacifist philosophy based on the ethical thesis that every single geopolitical issue in existence today (and from this day onwards) will only be resolved through diplomatic, peaceful, and nonviolent means. As millennial pacifists of all colors, we must help to elevate and enlighten our next generation by finding innovative and productive humanitarian ways to help positively contribute to our respective societies. To the youth of the Muslim world, this process can easily be started by refocusing your educational and professional goals to focus on helping the human race by either becoming a second-grade public school teacher or water purification civil engineer in your wonderful countries around the world. As the future representatives of millennial Islam, each one of you can help to reclaim the humanitarian central ethos of our faith by using the overall positive 'love and compassion' ethical teachings of our Islamic faith as the major driving force in helping you to become the best at each one of your respective life callings.

For instance, imagine for one moment that there was some hypothetical (and futuristic) Muslim female doctor somewhere in Jakarta, Paris or Islamabad who would one day discover the cure for cancer sometime in the not-so-distant future. In addition to this hypothetical female Muslim doctor helping to save the lives of billions of her fellow human beings around the world, this major global societal contribution of curing cancer by one lone female Muslim doctor would go miles in helping to convey the true humanitarian message of Islam to the rest of the world in one fell scientific swoop; simultaneously besting the venomous ideology of Osama bin Laden in one fell humanitarian swoop as well. Being a mischievous global pacifist vagabond jumping from the rooftops of the world, it becomes a moral sociopolitical imperative to tell our next generation of Muslim youth to also self-reflect and self-criticize your own respective so-called 'Muslim' governments (like in the Arab Spring) so that we may collectively recalibrate our spiritual equilibrium towards the loving center which we all know rapidly beats at the living heart of our beloved Islam.

Politics be damned; in order for us to progress forward as a vibrant contributing religious demographic community, we must continue to teach our Muslim children of today how to be loving members of our global village for tomorrow. As keepers of our own shared human destiny, we must also proudly embrace our positions as 'Millenial Muslims' to help show our global sisters and brothers of all colors the true meaning of 21st century millennial Islam which is lovingly practiced by one-in-five people across the globe. In order to successfully re-awaken from our shared geopolitical 'Muslim *Malaise*', we must continue to reclaim the overall essence of 21st-century millennial Islam from the sharp claws of our own internal dinosaur extremists by wholeheartedly embarking upon this non-violent antidote of a 'Love *Jihad*'.

A complete sociopolitical counter-ideology (and peaceful non-violent Islamic antidote) to our current scourge of fringe internal extremism; by together embarking upon a 'love *jihad*', we can help refocus our collective Islamic gaze inwards upon our religion's central ethical teachings of 'love and compassion' by reawakening the slumbering giant of 'gentle Islam'. Regardless of which corner of the world where you may currently live, we can together embark upon this journey of a 'love *jihad*' in many simple ways within our own local communities. As Muslims, we can begin these sweeping sociopolitical and legal reforms within our countries by collectively (and publicly) calling for the following major reforms around the Islamic world:

1) ***Improve women's rights*** *within your countries within every legal and sociopolitical arena;*
2) ***Abolish the death penalty*** *within our 56 Muslim-majority nations worldwide;*
3) *Protect the* ***religious freedom of every human being*** *around the whole world;*
4) *Call for a comprehensive* ***global Muslim moratorium on sectarianism*** *within Islam to finally end the global Sunni / Shia conflict; and*
5) ***Call-out your own autocratic political regimes*** *within our so-called 'Muslim' nations for any continued international human rights violations of any of its people.*

Further, we must also better educate our young orphaned 'Kite Runner' generations to help them succeed within a rapidly-growing modern super-industrialized 21st-century global economy. By addressing some of these major sweeping universal reforms and sociopolitical solutions for the greater Muslim world on some of these major hot-button issues, the future Muslim youth of tomorrow can help recalibrate our Islamic equilibrium for the betterment of every baby around the world; especially for our wonderful daughters.

Memo to Muslim Men: Treat Your Women Better!

Any honest and knowledgeable observer of the Muslim world knows that the politics of 'gender equity' are beyond abysmal within most of our Muslim nations today. Notwithstanding the empirical (and historical) facts that four (4) different Muslim countries have already elected female heads-of-state (Pakistan, Bangladesh, Turkey and Indonesia); it is still a sad truth that the political and legal status of the average Muslim woman (and sister) on the streets of Khartoum or Jeddah is most certainly in need of major legal and sociopolitical repair around the Muslim world today. Notwithstanding the Western media's obsession and fixated lens on global Islamic feminist issues like the *hijab* (head scarf) and other compelling (albeit fringe) media stories of (dis)honor killings, female genital mutilation (FGM) and/or the absurdity of 'morality police' anywhere around the globe; any knowledgeable observer would also have to unflinchingly concede that Muslim women around the world today have suffered the vast majority of these disparate sociopolitical impacts primarily because of anachronistic medieval cultural tribalism and ridiculous un-Islamic legal edicts (*a la* 'women are not allowed to drive' laws) aimed at continuing patriarchal hegemonic societies clinging onto their dinosaur mentality from their own tortured historical pasts.

For that reason, even casual readers should also know that many (if not most) of these uncivilized anachronistic policies are in complete contradiction to the actual mainstream teachings of Islam on the honored, esteemed and equal status of women and how females in general are to be treated as equally-integral contributing members of our respective modern societies. Sadly, to the contrary, our Muslim countries around the world today would probably score an overall 'F-minus' in their overall miserable human rights failures within this global 'gender equity' arena of their current human social experiment thus far. Thus, on behalf of every living (and intellectually honest) Muslim man worldwide who is alive today, I feel implored to quietly take a moment of silence to lower my head and humbly apologize to any and all Muslim women around the globe who has ever had to unjustly face societal suffering or oppression simply because of the fact that you are a woman, a mother, a daughter, a niece, a sister or a wife.

"Heaven lies at the feet of mothers" is probably one of the most well-known (and often-repeated) sayings of the Prophet Muhammad on the overall esteemed status of women within Islam. Similarly, most Muslims alive also know of the famous story of a traveler who once came to the Prophet and asked him which person within our human lives has the greatest claim to our love, devotion, honor and respect.

Without hesitation, the Prophet replied, "Your mother." Understanding his first answer, the traveler then asked him a second time as to who would rank next behind his mother in terms of love, devotion and reverence.

"Your mother," the Prophet replied a second time. When asked the same question a third time, the Prophet once again replied with the answer "Your mother" and only after the fourth round of questioning did the Prophet respond:

"Your father."

Although Muslim men worldwide may actually fulfill this loving obligation towards our Muslim mothers on a regular daily basis, we as Muslim men have failed miserably in our other societal roles protecting the rights of our Muslim wives, nieces, granddaughters and sisters all around the world. For instance, we have illiterate bearded idiots like the Taliban (Arabic or Pashto for 'students') in Afghanistan who have 'legislated' that women are now allowed to work or get a job. This is in complete and absurd contradiction to Islamic historical traditions which shows that the Prophet Muhammad's wife, Khadijah, was historically known to have been one of the most successful (and richest) business merchants in all of Arabia as early as the 7th century. Furthermore, in relation to women's economic rights within Islam, it should also be noted that Muslim women were granted major economic legal rights from the moment of Islam's birth in the 7th century (like property ownership, inheritance and divorce rights) which were not granted to many white Christian European women until after the beginning of the 19th century over 1200 years later.[19]

Even so, a mere cursory glance at the 56 so-called 'Muslim' nations today clearly shows that it is high time for our next generation of Muslim writers, thinkers, intellectuals and political leaders worldwide to dedicate ourselves towards drastically improving the overall empowerment of our mothers, sisters, daughters and wives within our respective homes, villages and metropolitan cities everywhere. To be sure, it is indeed a heartening sociopolitical trend to witness that global Muslim women are taking the lead (within their respective nations) at the forefront of this revival of their own versions of Islamic feminism. Interestingly enough, many of these Muslim feminist thinkers and leaders are also finding that their millennial sociopolitical ethos of Islamic feminism can be firmly supported by their own scared text: the Holy Quran.

Many modern-day Islamic feminist academics and scholars have found that an objective and holistic reading of the Quran shows the holy book to actually be a "very liberating document which holds before us a sublime version of our human potential, our destiny, and our relationship with God and God's creatures."[20] Like every other world religion in existence today, however, the status of women (or any other minority group) must be re-examined within a 21st century millennial human-rights context in order to create a distinctive normative mainstream understanding of what role the sociopolitical status of women should play in the future.

Since time immemorial, we have always known that every single human society and religious tradition on earth has inherited certain 'patriarchal' gender inequity issues from their previous (and utterly fallible) generational predecessors. That being the case, Muslims throughout history have absolutely been no exception to this sad truth of our inherently shared human fallibility as mere mortals. The current global political *zeitgeist* on the status of women in Islam was nicely summed up by Professor Anne Sofie Roald who once wrote that, "In the last decade, there has been an increasing concern with women's rights in Islam. Not only have Muslim feminists highlighted the status of women in Muslim societies, but [even political] Islamists, [both] male and female have also joined the debate, stressing the liberating potential Islam has for women."[21] Professor Roald further noted that even: "[Political] Islamists' attitudes towards gender and gender relations [have] changed character. Muslim women's reinterpretation of Islamic women's sources is...not only an intellectual discussion within a feminist sphere, but has [also] entered the contemporary [political] debate."

Sadly though, most people in the world will still only hear about Muslim gender issues through ridiculous media stories of female Sudanese journalists being threatened with lashes simply because she (God forbid) wears pants or the continued unlawfully atrocious *panchayat* (tribal council) systems which sanction random 'honor killings' (aka blatant murder) of innocent female rape victims in the forgotten village hinterlands of Pakistan. As proud Muslims, we should simply be collectively ashamed of ourselves that these barbaric human atrocities continue to occur during our global watch. Understanding the importance and need to address such pressing sociopolitical challenges, many academics and scholars of Islam believe that we are at an important civilizational crossroads between 'tradition' and 'modernity'. As such, the Islamic feminism debate is one crucial sociopolitical facet surfacing at this challenging (yet manageable) intersection between 'Islam' and 'modernity' for the hearts and minds of the next generations of our future Muslim youth.

Particularly in relation to gender issues, in understanding certain frameworks dealing with the intersection of Islam and modernity, Professor Barbara

Stowasser of Georgetown University once identified three (3) basic socio-political frameworks which can help distill certain underlying foundations of current-day Islamic thought and their simultaneous intersectional relationship with the concepts of modernity. These three basic major sociopolitical frameworks within current global Muslim intellectual thought can broadly be identified through the following primary lenses: A) **Modernists**, B) **Conservatives** and C) **Traditionalists**.

Within their overall general worldview, the framework of Muslim 'modernists' would generally hold that "specific legal rules of the Qur'an are conditioned by the socio-historical background of their enactment; what are eternal therein are the social principles explicitly stated or strongly implied in that legislation"[22] for that specific historical time period in question. According to this basic Muslim 'modernist' sociopolitical framework, they would tend to chronologically distinguish the Islam practiced by the Prophet and the first community in the 7th century of sandy Arabia from the later expressions of Islam under the same name over more subsequently-modern centuries. Professor Stowasser further noted that these later sociopolitical expressions of Islam eventually became less ideal for women over time and devolved rapidly during the subsequent "acculturation processes" of newer generations of Muslims living during the (aptly named) Medieval era of the Middle Ages within our human historical timeline.

Thus, many Muslim 'modernists' usually advocate for a figuratively moral 'rebirth' (or return) to the original essence of Islam by using *ijtihad* (Arabic for "interpretation") by deductive logical reasoning and other modern legal reforms to reflect the true holistic and egalitarian essence of the Quran; not the corrupted puritanical (and culturally patriarchal) interpretations practiced by our fallible previous Muslim human generations from the historical medieval eras of our recent political past. For example, a Muslim 'modernist' might want to rework women's current legal and political status to ensure that they are consistent with a holistic reading of the Quran. In other words, millions of Muslim modernists around the world see the true holistic message of Islam as being completely consistent with most of our modern-day sociopolitical values of our global community; namely, gender equity towards all human beings.

Slightly different from Muslim modernists, the second major sociopolitical framework presented includes Muslim 'conservatives' who seem to tend to take more of a "defensive stance against modernity; which it perceives to be exemplified by Westernization and, hence, cultural contamination."[23] Usually, many Muslim religious 'conservatives' usually desire to preserve tradition and generally understand Islam to be "a balanced system of faith and action based on...scripture and its interpretation through...community consensus." Until very recently, Muslim conservatives had mainly advocated for very traditional gender 'roles' as well advocating women's general "innate physical and mental" insufficiencies. According to Professor Stowasser, the recent silver lining for the Muslim conservative movement is that there has been a slow international political shift towards a more egalitarian emphasis on women's "equality with men in the spiritual and cultural sense."[24] This recent positive political trend from within the Muslim conservative movement is most likely in response to rightful political pressure from within the leadership of the current Islamic feminist global debate towards Muslim conservative thought leaders around the world.

The third and final Muslim sociopolitical framework presented is generally categorized as 'traditionalists' (also known pejoratively as 'fundamentalists') who are political "activists who see themselves as the [self-proclaimed] 'conscience' of the Islamic way of life."[25] Quite a few current-day political Islamist movements would probably align themselves most closely to this 'traditionalist' sociopolitical framework and have been analogously likened by American and European academic historians to versions of their own past Western religious 'fundamentalists' easily found in the stories of the American Puritans or Europe's Radical Reformers of the 16th century. In general, Muslim 'traditionalists' tend to translate the letter of the Quran 'literally' (more like 'puritanically') and insist on implementing centuries-old religious parables into modern-day contemporary legal or millennial political action. As a sociopolitical framework within modern-day Islam itself, Muslim 'traditionalists' would mainly differ from 'modernists' or 'conservatives' in that they tend to neglect or overlook most of the interpretative scholastic traditions of established mainstream Muslim legal and religious scholars; thus avoiding any modern-day adaptation to their puritanical (and sometimes medieval) interpretations of Islamic legal doctrine. On the status of women and gender equity, Muslim traditionalists usually "recognize women as 'soldiers' in [their] battle...In her traditional role as loving wife and nurturing mother, the woman fights a 'holy war' for the sake of Islamic values where conduct, domesticity and dress are vital for the survival of the Islamic way of life."[26]

In summarizing the three basic frameworks, at least within the parameters of the modern Islamic debate on gender equity issues involving the legal and political status of women, most Muslim 'modernists' want to rightfully adapt Islam to conform to the pressing questions of modernity within a 21st-century millennial context. Second, the basic sociopolitical framework of Muslim 'conservatives' seek to preserve traditional Islam by being wary of 'modernity' based on modern-day universal corrupting influences of our societies' perceived narcissistic materialism. The major point that sets apart Muslim 'conservatives' from 'traditionalists' is that the conservative Islamic movement has shown a more recent political willingness to shift certain emphases of Islamic discourse in response to some (albeit an insufficient number of) modern-day gender equity concerns. Finally, to the complete sociopolitical contrary, the 'traditionalist' (or pejoratively 'fundamentalist') framework within modern-day Islamic thought staunchly rejects all forms of 'modernity' or any compromise with it as being antithetical to their strongly-held beliefs.

Like any other religious tradition in existence, many people worldwide have asked the question: If the message of Islam and the Quran is one of an egalitarian nature; why are there so many so-called 'Muslim' nations who happen to be the tragic bastions of egregious gender inequality today? Since the Quran has been interpreted and reinterpreted by us fallible human beings for countless generations for nearly 1500 years of our beautiful religion's existence, many historians and academics of Islam accurately show from the historical record what is deemed to be a mainstream academic global consensus and "prevalent notion that it was the Muslim scholars…from the 3rd to 9th centuries [of Islamic history who severely] downgraded the legal and sociopolitical position of women in Islam."[27] For these reasons, much of what we are witnessing around the world today in terms of the overall mistreatment of women, such as it exists among Muslim (or Christian or Jewish or Hindu or Buddhist) societies, is based primarily on cultural and tribalism phenomena and should not be a reflection of adherence or devoutness to any basic 'Golden Rule' religious principle inherently taught by Islam, Christianity, Judaism, Hinduism, Buddhism and every other major world religion in existence.

Nonetheless, there will always be perpetual naysayers who will always automatically equate Islam with 'oppression' without ever actually bothering to truly learn a bloody thing about the religion. In fact, any truly holistic reading of the Quran (or any other religious holy book) actually reinforces the divine idea that males and females are all created by God as equal human beings meant to be inseparable and complementary to one another - to coexist with mutual love and recognition.

For instance, in many passages of the Quran pertaining to the creation of men and women, the Quran does not present the male as the main subject and the female as an unimportant sidekick without any human significance. To that point, as contrary to Christian theology, there is a stark absence of hierarchy and gender differentiation within the 'creation narrative' of the Quran. For example, the Quran never singles out the woman (Eve) as the initiator of evil nor does it apportion blame upon the 'temptress doctrine' within the Islamic story of Adam and Eve's 'fall' from heavenly grace to the actual mortal hardship of life upon earth. This concept of inherent human gender equality is actually further proved by the fact that since there is again no 'temptress doctrine' of Eve within the Quran; similarly, there is also no Muslim concept of 'original sin' stemming from the same Adam and Eve parable of the 'Fall of Man' story within our Islamic tradition:

> ***"The believing men and women are 'mutually supporting friends' of each other; they enjoin what is just, and forbid what is evil; they observe regular prayers, practice regular charity, and obey God and God's Apostle. On them will God send down His Mercy: For God is exalted in power, Wise...***
>
> ***God has promised to believers, men and women, Gardens under which rivers flow, to dwell therein, and beautiful mansions, in Gardens of everlasting bliss, But the greatest bliss is the Good pleasure of God: That is the supreme felicity..." (Quran 9:71-72)***

From these basic Quranic verses above, it is clear that the oft-forgotten universal egalitarian message of Islam shows that men and women are not portrayed as adversaries; to the contrary, rather that we as men and women are all seen as complimentary halves of one single human whole. Furthermore, this Islamic ideal of the complimentary nature of all men and women can only become a reality once we truly remember the Quranic teachings of us being each other's 'mutually supporting friends' and helping our sisters eradicate gender inequality within our respective nations and countries once and for all.

As a another political silver lining for the greater Muslim world and our own internal Islamic feminism debate, one blatantly evident (and highly-overlooked) aspect of the current political status of Muslim women within contemporary Islam blindly (and casually) overlooks the historical fact that there have already been four (4) out of our 56 Muslim-majority nations on earth who have already successfully elected a female to be their president, prime minister and/or political head-of-state. Politically succeeding in something that we Americans have yet to master, the countries of Pakistan (Benazir Bhutto), Bangladesh (twice with Khaleda Zia and Sheikh Hasina Wazed), Turkey (Tansu Penbe Çiller) and Indonesia (Megawati Sukarnoputri) have all broken the political 'gender ceiling' within their respective densely-populated Muslim countries by showing the true political status of Muslim women by electing these four visionary females to lead their nations as their presidents and/or prime ministers.

Most people worldwide are completely unaware that the Islamic Republic of Pakistan is the sixth most-populated country on earth with a total population of over 176.2 million people.[28] Pakistan was politically created (by founder Muhammad Ali Jinnah) when it became independent from British viceroy colonial rule on August 14, 1947 (one day before neighboring India's independence day of August 15, 1947). Since that time, the second-largest Muslim country in the world had successfully elected a prominent female politician named Benazir Bhutto to serve two (2) terms as the post of Prime Minister of Pakistan. Tragically, former prime minister Benzair Bhutto was assassinated in late December 2007 on the upcoming eve of national general elections in Pakistan and Mrs. Bhutto was widely speculated to again win a massive majority of the popular vote before her untimely death during the December 27, 2007 assassination attack on her political caravan in the garrison city of Rawalpindi (which also killed over 19 other people during the assassination).[29]

On highlighting the devastating societal impact of Benazir Bhutto's assassination on the nearly 200 million people of Pakistan, I once said during a December 2007 live evening broadcast of *The O'Reilly Factor* on FOX News Channel immediately following her assassination that, "I believe that it [the Benazir Bhutto assassination] will have the same sort of societal impact that November 22, 1963 did with the JFK assassination here in America and I think that the Pakistani public is going to be reeling from it for quite a while."[30] Neighboring their South Asian compatriots of India and Pakistan, Bangladesh (formerly known as East Pakistan before 1971) is currently the fourth-largest Muslim populated country on earth and has already successfully elected two (2) different women to be their political head-of-state. A Bangladeshi Muslim woman named Mrs. Begum Khaleda Zia served as Prime Minister of Bangladesh for three (3) consecutive terms beginning in 1991. Another Bangladeshi Muslim woman, Sheikh Hasina Wajed won the December 2008 Bangladeshi elections in a landslide victory and was serving in her second term as Prime Minister of Bangladesh at the time of the writing of this book.

In Indonesia, the most populous Muslim country in the world, Megawati Sukarnoputri, an Indonesian Muslim woman, made history by being elected to serve as President of Indonesia from 2001 to 2004. Although she was ultimately defeated in the 2004 presidential elections, this prominent Indonesian Muslim woman was still listed at #8 on *Forbes* magazine's list of the '100 Most Powerful Women' in the world later that same year.[31] Next, the Eurasian Muslim-majority gateway nation of Turkey has a population of 72 million people and between 1993-1995; a Muslim woman named Tansu Ciller served as her country's Prime Minister. Furthermore, it would also probably come as an additional surprise to even the most astute western global observers to learn that even the Islamic Republic of Iran has <u>twice</u> elected women to be their vice-presidents - Dr. Masoumek Ebtekar (1997-2005) and Fatemeh Javadi (2005-2009).

Although nearly ten percent of Muslim nations on earth have already elected a female head-of-state, the current human rights legal struggle on far-reaching global issues like gender equity, religious freedom and free speech issues are still plaguing the deteriorating legal human rights framework of many of our 56 Muslim-majority countries to this very day. Thus, it again becomes another personal moral imperative to generate even more irreverent controversy by calling for further major sweeping human rights legal reforms within our Muslim world by telling our millennial global Muslim youth of today to peacefully rally your friends and neighbors together to call for the complete abolition of the death penalty in every single one of our 56 Muslim countries around the world.

Dear Muslim Nations: Time to Abolish the Death Penalty

For anyone who cherishes the sanctity of human life, the mere thought of cutting off the hand of a bread thief or beheading a veiled woman in a public square or lining up a firing squad in a ramshackle soccer stadium should be completely and utterly repugnant to any civilized human being living within the millennial age today. Because of this and many other reasons, there should be a complete moratorium (with the eventual goal towards the complete abolition) on the 'death penalty' within each one of our 56 Muslim-majority countries around the globe.

By following the brave political lead of the European Union and every other major industrialized nation in the world (with my United States being the tragic lone exception), the diverse spectrum of 56 Muslim nations can finally start to show to the rest of the world that our millennial global Muslim community are helping to improve our respective legal, political and human rights frameworks to comfortably fit within our global village's accepted standards of current international humanitarian law. As a proud Muslim death penalty abolitionist, aside from our own disastrous death penalty experiment here in the United States, it is important for every reader to again remember that every single other country in the entire global community of modern-day industrialized nations has already outlawed the death penalty from their respective legal and judicial systems. As long ago as 1962, it was reported to the Council of Europe that "the facts clearly show that the death penalty is regarded in Europe as something of an anachronism." Today, either by law or in practice, all of Western Europe has abolished the death penalty. In Great Britain, the death penalty was abolished (except for cases of treason) in 1971; France abolished it in 1981. Canada abolished the death penalty in 1976. Furthermore, the United Nations General Assembly once officially affirmed in a formal resolution that anywhere in the world, it is desirable to "progressively restrict the number of offenses for which the death penalty might be imposed, with a view to the desirability of abolishing this punishment."[32]

By mid-1995, eighteen (18) major countries around the world had ratified the Sixth Protocol to the European Convention on Human Rights; an international treaty which outlaws the death penalty during peacetime. Emphasizing the overwhelming worldwide support for death penalty abolition was the action of the South African constitutional court; which banned the death penalty as an "inhumane" punishment in 1995. Between 1989 and 1995, two dozen other countries around the world had also abolished the death penalty for all crimes.

As of the writing of this book, more than half (50%) of all the nations around the planet have completely abolished the death penalty either by law or in practice.[33]

For these reasons, it now becomes high time for us to help put some of our 56 Muslim countries around the world on this honorable list of nations who have abolished the 'death penalty' from within our legal and judicial systems. To the millions of Muslim boys and girls who are reading this book in your bedrooms in Cairo, Islamabad, Gaza or Jakarta; we can all agree that the overall concepts of 'human rights', 'due process' and 'rule of law' are pretty laughable in most of our Muslim countries today. From the constitution of Pakistan not being worth the piece of paper that it is printed upon to Egypt's not-so-democratic former leader Muhammad Hosni Mubarak regularly imprisoning innocent Egyptian bloggers for merely exercising their free speech; our respective legal and justice systems within the Muslim world are astonishingly flawed and are in dire need of sweeping global legal reforms like re-visiting constitutional conventions (Hint: Pakistan) or other major grass-roots sociopolitical legal measures undertaken peacefully like global campaigns to abolish the death penalty.

Our world saw a small political silver lining when Pakistani lawyers and judges boldly took to the streets of Lahore and Islamabad in December 2007 wearing their black-and-white-suited protest version of the saffron monks of Burma to challenge the dictatorship of a two-star (and two-bit) general named Pervez Musharraf. It was during this peaceful lawyers' uprising that the world began to see (for the first time) the formation of a critical mass of a viable (and nonviolent) Pakistani middle-class who were simply fed up with Musharraf's two-bit dictatorship and decided wisely to *peacefully* protest for constitutional democracy in Pakistan for all of its people. Sadly for the nearly 200 million people of Pakistan, expecting a tin-pot military dictator like Pervez Musharraf to live up to his democratic promises was like waiting for a Hershey's chocolate bar to belt out a Shakespearean sonnet.

Notwithstanding many of our overly-corrupt Muslim governments worldwide, we must still nonetheless persevere and help our respective countries reclaim their honorable legal traditions by calling *en masse* for our 56 Muslim countries around the world to abolish the death penalty. Again, with our United States as the lone sad exception, the entireties of the European Union and the rest of the industrialized world have already abolished the death penalty and our Muslim nations worldwide would be severely remiss if we failed to promptly follow legal suit in joining this global 'death penalty' abolitionist movement. We can begin these sweeping sociopolitical changes and reforms by simply reaffirming the fact that only God should be in the business of taking any human life.

As such, young girls and boys walking on the streets of Amman, Jeddah or Tehran can peacefully rise up and continue to call upon our elected governments to join the community of civilized nations who loudly say that our mortal concept of the 'death penalty' is completely antithetical to modern human civilization and should be completely abolished everywhere; now and forever more.

Religious Freedom: A Church, Mosque and Synagogue in Every City

As a self-proclaimed religious freedom freak, the first thing that I would ever construct in my own modern-day utopian daydream city would be an official 'Religious District' on the shores of my fictitious river banks. Within this fantasy city's official 'Religious District', we would house every place of worship, including our diverse citizens' National Cathedral, Great Synagogue and Grand Mosque (and every other primary house of worship) that would be built there and which would share the same earthly space together. The symbolic reasoning and clear strategic purpose behind my building every single house of worship next to one another on my city's river banks within our official 'Religious District' would be to show all of our diverse citizens that an attack on any house of worship shall always be considered an attack on every house of worship on my watch.

Article 18 of the Universal Declaration of Human Rights states clearly that, "Everyone has the right to freedom of thought, conscience and religion; this right includes the freedom to change his religion or belief, and freedom, either alone or in community with others and in public or private, to manifest his religion or belief in teaching, practice, worship and observance."[34] In terms of religious freedom for every living human being today, our revived gentle giant of 'global pacifism' shall welcome all people, regardless of any race, religion or socioeconomic status. Whether you are white, black, brown, green or purple, whether you are Christian, Jewish, Hindu, Buddhist or celebrate Festivus; our next generation of youthful global pacifists of all colors and religions will help reclaim our 'culture of humanity' from sinister racist warmongering dinosaurs with names like Osama, Coulter, Hamas and Cheney.

Being a stalwart for religious freedom for everyone; I want to live in a 21st century global village where a Muslim woman can proudly wear her *hijab*, a Jewish man can proudly wear his *yarmulke* and a Sikh man can proudly keep his turban as they walk together peacefully within the 'Coexistence Plaza' of my fictitious Religious District without any fear of harm or violence whatsoever. We must all simply learn to peacefully live in a futuristic world where every church, synagogue, temple, mosque, or other house of worship is completely safe from any ungodly attack on the religious freedom of <u>any</u> of the inhabitants of our lovely planet. Before we can improve outward interfaith relations between over-a-billion Muslims and people of other faiths, we have the internal Islamic self-reflective obligation to first 'clean our own house' by calling for better intra-faith harmony within our own religion by officially calling for a complete end to the Sunni/Shia sectarian violence which has plagued much of our Islamic history for over the last one thousand years.

No More Sectarianism: A Sunni and Shia walk into a Hookah Café Together

As stated earlier in this book, we know that there has empirically been no greater internal *fitna* (Arabic for "division" or "strife") within our global Muslim *ummah* (Arabic for "community") more tragically absurd than the Sunni-Shia sectarian divide which historically began bearing its tragically-ugly fruits during the caliphate of Muawiyah I around the calendar year 661 CE. Since that time, the checkered human history of Muslim communities has been ravaged by this intra-religious ideological sectarian venom which was passed between our two major sects of Islam (and amongst some of its respective followers) throughout the world over the duration of our modern times.

"First, I don't believe that there is a conflict between Shia and Sunnis. It seems that there is a [current] conflict between Shia and Sunnis, but indeed the conflict is between a minority of Shia and a minority of Sunnis, the extremists, the fanatics," said Imam Sayid Hassan Qazwini, an Iraqi-American Shia imam of the largest mosque in America (in Dearborn, Michigan) during his opening statements for the April 2008 television episode of *The Doha Debates* on BBC World News Television. He continued: "The majority of Shia and Sunnis get along [perfectly well] and they are peaceful [to each other]...I believe that these are extremists, these are the *takfiris* [apostates], the fanatics, people who basically disagree, who launch war against anyone disagrees with them, and this is not between Shia and Sunnis only."

On the long-standing peaceful history between global Sunnis and Shias around the world, Professor Juan Cole of the University of Michigan (and author of *Engaging the Muslim World*) noted during the same April 2008 episode of *The Doha Debates* that historians and academics have always found that "traditionally Sunnis and Shias...have not been at each other's throats... [I]n fact there were relatively good relations between them for most of the 20th century."[35] Professor Cole continued to say that, "[Sadly], in the past five years, Sunnis and Shias in Iraq have been mobilized for political purposes against one another and they have engaged in the most horrific violence against one another on the TV screens, and they have ethnically cleansed one another, they have killed one another...Why don't the Sunnis, the Shias and the Kurdish Iraqis sit together and come to a solution that's not violent? Why do they keep invading each other's territory?"[36]

Additionally, there have been many other modern high-profile Sunni and Shia Muslim leaders around the world who are beginning to band together to re-patch the sociopolitical swatches of our diverse fabric of global Islam. On the issue of Sunni/Shia sectarianism, many leaders have stated that we should embrace a new collective Islamic sociopolitical ethos where anyone who simply states (and sincerely believes) the Islamic declaration of faith ("There is no God but God and Muhammad is his final messenger"); that person (regardless of sect) should then simply be considered a Muslim; no questions asked. They highlight that we should rededicate ourselves to the divine Islamic teaching that any and all religious judgment on the inherent 'Muslim-ness' of another human being shall rest only in the eyes of God alone.

Although this global reconciliation effort between leading Sunni and Shia sociopolitical leaders has been hard at work trying to promote this universalism message of Islam by condemning the practice of *takfir* (declaring another Muslim to be an 'apostate'); nonetheless, this global reconciliation process between Sunnis and Shias has not been making many airwaves within our current global media stratosphere. "If a group of distinguished leaders who are speaking the voice of sanity and moderation, calling for peace, and calling for reconciliation between Shia and Sunnis, between Muslims and non-Muslims, there aren't many media outlets that are interested in their voice, so I believe that the media and the West; it is part of the [Sunni-Shia] problem as well," Imam Hassan Qazwini reiterated on this subject.[37] In his book *American Crescent*, Imam Qazwini rightfully points out that "Shia and Sunnis are not as different as some believe. Westerners sometimes compare the two groups to Catholics and Protestants, but our differences do not reach even that level and are more historical than theological."[38]

The political differences between Sunnis and Shias over the centuries grew as both branches have their own collections of supplemental traditions and texts that they recognize as being Islamically valid. Sunni Muslims' legal rulings "rely heavily on the work of four esteemed eighth- and ninth-century scholars" while Shia Muslims have modern-day scholars who have "more flexibility to interpret existing law". Today, most Sunni Muslims generally recognize Al-Azhar University in Cairo as the highest seat of Sunni scholarship and most Shia Muslims scholarship resides in many different cities with the highest seat of Shia scholarship residing with "Ayatollah [Ali] Sistani in Najaf, Iraq." Similarly, Imam Qazwini wrote that it should also be noted that both Sunni and Shia Muslims "agree on 90 percent of Islamic practices...Both Shia and Sunni pray five times a day... Shia and Sunni frequently worship at each others' mosques, a practice one would rarely see among Catholics and Protestants." He also noted that many Muslims are "reluctant to distinguish themselves as one or the other...Rather, they prefer, as I do, simply to be called a Muslim."[39]

During a joint September 2008 interview for National Public Radio (NPR), both Imam Qazwini and I spoke to NPR host Michel Martin about the challenges facing American Muslims in the United States today. During the interview, Imam Qazwini said that, "For Muslims, to be still viewed as suspects- and as my friend Arsalan mentioned- to have added scrutiny simply because they are Muslims, it is really a main source of concern for us. It's very disappointing to see that Muslims are being singled out simply because they are Muslims, simply because of their origins, and I really hope that the new [Obama] administration...can help in dispelling some of these grievances."[40]

Since nobody gives a bloody damn whether we are a Sunni or Shia; then why should we as global Muslims care?

Whether we like it or not, we as the next generation of young millennial Muslims will continue to face many of our geopolitical challenges through the global lens of being one monolithic 'Muslim global community' (or *ummah*). Since much of the world will only see us as one monolithic 'Muslim' community, we would be remiss if we did not protect the future safety of all of our children by also completely 'killing' all of this Sunni and Shia sectarian poisonous nonsense; once and for all.

Again, we are all Muslims; pure and simple.

We should end all Sunni/Shia sectarianism around the world by simply remembering these visionary words of our Prophet Muhammad: "Do not become disbelievers after me by cutting the necks of one another."[41] Since many people already see us through a monolithic lens and do not differentiate between Sunni and Shia, then we might as well pray that God also grants us the tranquil serenity and enlightened Zen-like grace to finally see this honest simple truth of unity as well. Having said that, for the love of Islam, go become friends with a Sunni human rights lawyer or a wonderful Shia imam which will help us all enrich and strengthen the diverse social fabric of our Muslim community worldwide.

A Millenial Farewell to Arms

Mahatma Gandhi once said that, "I have nothing new to teach the world...Truth and nonviolence are as old as the hills." Since time immemorial, our human experiment has revolved around the enlightened advancement of our collective human thought. Within the current ungodly global mix of perpetual war, everlasting human poverty, extremist terrorism and global racism; it has become quite clear that our human race has completely and utterly lost its bloody mind. Since our world has already gone completely bonkers, the unquenchable thirst for universal social justice of this young American Muslim lefty human rights lawyer must positively be channeled at this juncture of infinite global sadness towards a purpose-driven life guided down an untaken road called *Islamic Pacifism*.

Malcolm X once said that, "It is a time for martyrs now, and if I am to be one, it will be for the cause of brotherhood. That is the only thing that can save this country." With the infamous likes of Osama, Cheney and every other global 'pimp-of-war' maniacally bent on the ungodly destruction of our planet; this bleeding heart Muslim pacifist shall continue to offer himself as their adversarial rhetorical 'peace assassin' in the quixotic quest to cure the toxic venom of all racists and warmongers worldwide. As everyone scurries to kill each other over dollars, euros, riyals and Halliburton stocks, this Islamic pacifist shall playfully use his trusty black IBM ThinkPad laptop, white iPod earbuds and red *Swingline* stapler to help shape and officially introduce this evolved millennial version of Islamic Pacifism to our global community today. With the genteel kindness of Mahatma Gandhi (a former lawyer himself) and the righteous ferocity of post-Hajj Malcolm X (aka post-racial 'El Hajj'), this sociopolitical ethos of Islamic Pacifism will be redefined for this new millennium and shall trade the loincloths of the former and the spectacles of the latter for a wool herringbone suit and ruthless black leather gloves to serve as the modern-day global pacifist uniform.

Again, this revived gentle giant of global pacifism shall welcome all people, regardless of any race, religion or socioeconomic status around the world. Whether you are white, black, brown, green or purple, whether you are Christian, Jewish, Buddhist or celebrate Festivus; our next generation of youthful global pacifists can help reclaim our culture of humanity from sinister warmongering dinosaurs with names like Osama, Coulter, Hamas and Cheney.

Dr. Martin Luther King Jr. once said that, "Peace is not merely a distant goal that we seek, but a means by which we arrive at that goal." By giving global pacifism a Generation X makeover, we can use the witty humor of Jon Stewart, the humanistic nuance of Noam Chomsky and the fearless determination of Nelson Mandela to help quench our collective thirst for social justice everywhere. With the hipster slyness of Danny Ocean to the groovy idealism of John Lennon, we rhetorical 'peace assassins' shall never physically harm another human being with our silent Bourne-like precision as we continue to leave warmongering racist dinosaurs scratching their brainless heads within shadowy caves or frigid television studios around the globe using only our words as our righteous weapons. For any person in the world who has ever earnestly prayed for a Muslim Gandhi, you can sleep peacefully at night now knowing that the life memoirs of this young American Muslim pacifist shall one day be playfully entitled *The Autobiography of Gandhi X*. Finally proving that the razor-sharp pacifist pen is indeed mightier than any rusty terrorist sword, everyone can rest easy knowing that

Barack Obama is not the only brown civil rights lawyer from Chicago with the audacity of hope running through his every vein.

As we come towards the end of our journey together, with a tip of my proverbial hat to the rest of humanity, I again welcome one and all to the wonderful world of *Islamic Pacifism*. First, it should be noted that I absolutely love reading the Quran and I also love listening to Nirvana. As a Muslim political troubadour and interpreter of global maladies, my life as a young public intellectual since the tragedy of 9/11 has now become one big absurd game of television musical chairs and YouTube video clips. From CNN to Al-Jazeera English to BBC World News, I have spent a dizzying chunk of the last several years on the proverbial 'hot seat,' as a young global Muslim public voice for over a billion peaceful mainstream Muslims who never want to be represented by the bobble-headed terrorist named Osama bin Laden.

Secondly, I have also performed the Hajj pilgrimage to Mecca and have also been a ball-boy for my hometown NBA team, the Chicago Bulls. Additionally, from the warm microphones of National Public Radio (NPR) to the literally-frigid FOX News television studios of *The O'Reilly Factor*, I have had to explain to the world countless times that the godless maniacs who murder civilians in places like Bali, Madrid, London and Mumbai have lost their bloody minds and are simply committing irreligious acts of mass murder that have nothing to do with the true religion of Islam. Do not worry, ladies and gentlemen; over a billion Muslim pacifist sisters and brothers will continue to challenge those who hijacked Islam on that fateful day and we will spend the rest of our own living days serenely hijacking it back; by any <u>peaceful</u> means necessary.

Honoring the amazing fact that two different Nobel Peace Prize winners and an American president (Bill Clinton) have also previously graced that same esteemed stage, please remember the fact that this young Muslim pacifist again used the global television stage of *The Doha Debates* on BBC World News television to go in front of 300 million people worldwide to <u>publicly</u> call for the complete eradication of <u>every</u> form of global racism in the world; including Islamophobia and Anti-Semitism. Whether it is Islamophobia, Anti-Semitism or any other form of global racism in existence, these are all categorically wrong and despicably antithetical to any religious tradition or human civilization.

Nonetheless, I still get called a 'terrorist' by knucklehead racists because of my unabashed love of Islam and am still also called the Muslim 'hippy' by knucklehead extremists for my unabashed platform of peace. Well, since Islam means 'peace' anyway, I shall proudly wear the 'Islamic Peacenik' label as a badge of honor for the rest of my insignificant life mission as a global diplomatic peace mercenary.

Because with such seething hatred in the world today, the only thing that anyone can condemn me for is my seething love.

Similarly, as an international human rights lawyer, I will also always continue to be a stoic stalwart for the religious freedom for all of humanity; with zero exceptions whatsoever. Until the day that I die, my heart will continue to always smile every time that I see a Muslim woman proudly wearing her *hijab*, a Jewish man proudly wearing his *yarmulke* or a Sikh man proudly keeping his turban within any corner of our universe. Because of all of this, you can probably imagine that I have literally been called every single name in the book over the years. From time to time, global haters and lovers worldwide have rubbed their brain cells together to create *ad hominem* monikers to try to reductively compartmentalize 'The Muslim Guy'. Over the years, people have called me everything from the Islamic Hippy to The Muslim Dark Knight. In honesty, out of all of the names that I have ever been called in my life, my personal favorite will always be 'The Anti-Osama'.

Either way, as the Religious Lefty or whatever other silly names that haters can conjure up inside of their puny little brains; this pacifist vagabond will continue to reclusively perch atop the shadowy rooftops of our global Gotham somberly awaiting the next global light-beacon from the Muslim Bat-Signal in the sky; whether in the form of silly Danish cartoons, ungodly acts of terrorism and/or diplomatic calls for interfaith global reconciliation. Simply put; If 'A' is for Ann Coulter and 'O' is for Osama bin Laden, you may simply consider this Muslim Pacifist their collective 'V' for Vendetta for the rest of my living days.

Sadly, if I also had a dollar for every death threat or piece of hate-mail that I have ever received where I have been called either a 'camel jockey', 'slumdog millionaire', 'towel-head' or 'sand nigger', I would also happily be able to buy the entire world a Coke and we would all be well on our way towards the reality of world peace. Even sadder though, although Muslims have won 3 out of the last 10 Nobel Peace Prizes, all because of one terrorist cave-dweller; nearly 1500 years of Pan-Islamic cultural and societal progress has gone down the drain.

Thanks a lot, Osama.

In explaining the utter human simplicity of my global pacifism, I am reminded of these words of Albert Einstein: "My pacifism is an instinctive feeling; a feeling that possesses me because the murder of men is disgusting...My attitude is not derived from any intellectual theory but is based on my deepest antipathy to every kind of cruelty and hatred."[42] It should be no secret to anyone that our world is in darkness tonight. As pacifist Mozarts to every racist Salieri out there, we millennial global pacifists of all colors and religions have as our life missions the opportunity to make Samuel Huntington's dinosaur civilizational theory completely and utterly obsolete; once and for all. By successfully turning the world into a United Colors of Benetton advertisement, we can ensure that the only thing that all the beautiful babies of the world will ever need to worry about is filling their cute tummies with food, pooping inside of their smelly diapers and deciding on which color Nerf ball to play with today. Simply put, if you hurt any innocent woman or child anywhere around the world today, the life mission of this ruthless pacifist will be to haunt your sinister sleep and wag my very large foam finger in your face until you beg for God's forgiveness for your ungodly acts.

Again, let it be shouted from the rooftops and minarets of the world that this renewed message of global pacifism is about the message of world peace and not the silly messenger. For if Mahatma Gandhi and Dr. Martin Luther King had nothing new to teach the world, then surely it is essential to remember that the life of this insignificant Muslim pacifist is merely one single teardrop on a massive fire. However, if every member of our human race would help embrace a 'culture of humanity' for every other living human being; our nearly seven billion collective teardrops would obliterate any earthly trace of this sinister racist fire set by arsonist knuckleheads like Osama and Cheney. To my sisters and brothers of every color and religion around the world today, let us begin to aspire for a world where there are no sticks, stones, guns or bombs. As Muslim pacifists, we welcome our siblings of all colors and religions to advance these very simple humanitarian and godly ideals:

1) ***All human beings are God's beautiful creations;***
2) ***All murder is ungodly;***
3) ***All racism is devilish; and***
4) ***All wars are crimes.***

Since our world has clearly gone completely bananas, everyone on all sides of the world should take a very deep breath and lay down their guns, bombs and/or water-boards for one moment and contemplate a 'millennial farewell to arms'. Just imagine for one moment if Abraham, Moses, Jesus and Muhammad (peace be upon them all) were all alive today; our entire human race would not have the collective audacity to look them directly into their watering eyes because of the ungodly horrors that we have committed upon each other.

Myself included, as a human race, we are all simply broken. Jimi Hendrix once said that "when the power of love overcomes the love of power, the world will know peace." Whether we decide as a human race to take a path towards perpetual ungodly war or coexistent loving peace will directly dictate whether we align ourselves with devilish racist warmongers or choose to be on the side of loving warrior angels. Among my personal dream of joining the esteemed literary ranks of historical pacifist authors like Albert Camus, Leo Tolstoy and Henry David Thoreau, some of my own silly little personal life-dreams include sharing a dumpling with the Dalai, a cup of coffee with Kofi, a stage with Bono and a movie frame with Clooney. In addition to hopefully seeing a Democrat being perpetually sworn into The White House; this proud American Muslim pacifist human rights lawyer's uber-dream would be to perhaps simply one day receive a nomination piece of paper for a silly little medallion trinket given by the Nobel girls and boys in Oslo every year.

As such, our next generation of global pacifists shall continue to spend our lives throwing our arms around the world towards all of our sisters and brothers of every color, religion and nationality around the globe in our quixotic quest for that elusive gazelle within our global jungle known as 'world peace'. Regardless of whether this book lines the floor of a public bathroom or hangs next to the Mona Lisa in the Louvre Museum in Paris, this brown dude from Chicago can one day finally lay penniless on his deathbed in Islamic Zen-like tranquility taking his last breaths knowing that he sincerely dedicated his entire life as a proud millennial Muslim simply trying to be one of God's peacemakers.

Until that glorious day, this Islamic Pacifist welcomes one and all to our globally-warmed Sherwood Forest as our merry band of billion believers continue to gently comfort the afflicted and ruthlessly afflict the comfortable as our next generation of young global pacifists of all colors, races and religions humbly kneel ourselves down within our homes, churches, synagogues, temples and mosques around the world for the remainder of our living days praying for peace and also wondering if God will ever truly forgive us for what we have done to each other.

NOTES

Chapter 1: We Condemn This Act

1 Arsalan Iftikhar, "Muslims share USA's sorrow in attacks" *USA Today*, September 13, 2001 *available at* http://www.scribd.com/doc/46821134/USA-Today-Arsalan-911-Condemnation and Arsalan Iftikhar, "We Condemn This Act" *New York Times*, September 14, 2001 *availableat*http://www.nytimes.com/2001/09/14/opinion/l-stories-of-a-stricken-city-and-a-grieving-land-we-condemn-this-act-180645.html?n=Top%2FReference%2FTimes%20Topics%2FSubjects%2FI%2FIslam (Accessed January 13, 2011).

2 Ibid.

3 Ibid.

4 "Mohammad Salman Hamdani: An All-American Jedi" The New York Times, March 9, 2003 available at http://events.nytimes.com/2003/03/09/national/portraits/POG-09HAMDANI.html?ex=1238731200&en=4b693420eca48eee&ei=5070 (Accessed April 1, 2009).

5 Full text of HR 3126 available at http://epic.org/privacy/terrorism/hr3162.html (Accessed April 1, 2009).

6 Ibid.

7 "Islamic world deplores U.S. losses" British Broadcasting Corporation (BBC), September 14, 2001 available at http://news.bbc.co.uk/2/hi/americas/1544955.stm (Accessed April 1, 2009).

8 Harry Kawilarang, Quotations on Terrorism, Trafford Publishing, Victoria (Canada), July 2006 at 225.

9 Associated Press, "Official: 15 of 19 Sept. 11 hijackers were Saudi", February 6, 2002 available at http://www.usatoday.com/news/world/2002/02/06/saudi.htm (Accessed April 2, 2009).

10 Reshma Memon Yaqub, "I'm Not the Enemy" The Washington Post, September 13, 2001 available at http://www.washingtonpost.com/ac2/wp-dyn?pagename=article&node=&contentId=A21488-2001Sep12 (Accessed April 1, 2009).

11 http://www.ammanmessage.com/ (Accessed January 12, 2011)

12 See http://ammanmessage.com/index.php?option=com_content&task=view&id=21&Itemid=34 (Accessed January 12, 2011)

13 See Fareed Zakaria, "How We Can Prevail" Newsweek, July 18, 2005 available at http://www.fareedzakaria.com/articles/newsweek/071805.html (Accessed April 15, 2009)

14 H.M. King Abdullah II bin al-Hussein, "Foreward: The Amman Message" July 26, 2006 available at http://ammanmessage.com/index.php?option=com_content&task=view&id=13&Itemid=27 (Accessed April 15, 2009)

15 Press Release, "Secretary-General Announces Composition of High-Level Group for Alliance of Civilizations", United Nations (UN) Department of Public Information, February 9, 2005 available at http://www.un.org/News/Press/docs/2005/sgsm10073.doc.htm (Accessed April 15, 2009)

16 See Leadership Group on US-Muslim Engagement, Changing Course: A New Direction for U.S. Relations with the Muslim World, February 2009 at 78. Full text of report available at http://www.usmuslimengagement.org/index.php?option=com_content&task=view&id=21&Itemid=50 (Accessed April 15, 2009)

17 Jorge Sampaio, "How to achieve sustainable peace?" Common Ground News Service, November 2, 2008 available at http://www.haaretz.com/hasen/spages/1033078.html (Accessed April 15, 2009)

18 http://www.silatech.com/ (Accessed April 15, 2009)

19 http://money.cnn.com/magazines/fortune/fortune500/2007/snapshots/307.html (Accessed June 23, 2009)

20 Press Release, "Silatech and Cisco Accelerate Strategic Collaboration To Develop Technology Platforms in Support of Youth Enterprise and Employment in the Arab World" Silatech, June 1, 2008 available at http://www.silatech.com/sub.news8.aspx (Accessed April 15, 2009)

21 Leadership Group on US-Muslim Engagement, Changing Course at 78.

22 Ibid.

23 http://www1.jp.dk/info/about_jyllands-posten.htm (Accessed April 3, 2009)

24 Martin Asser, "What the Muhammad cartoons portray" British Broadcasting Corporation (BBC), February 9, 2006 available at http://news.bbc.co.uk/1/hi/world/middle_east/4693292.stm (Accessed April 3, 2009)

25 The Times (London), "Timeline: the Muhammad cartoons" February 6, 2006 available at http://www.timesonline.co.uk/tol/news/world/article725158.ece (Accessed April 3, 2009)

26 CNN, "Protestors burn consulate over cartoons" February 5, 2006 available at http://www.cnn.com/2006/WORLD/asiapcf/02/05/cartoon.protests/index.html (Accessed April 3, 2009)

27 Kevin Sullivan, "E-mail, Blogs, Text Messages Propel Anger Over Images" The Washington Post, February 9, 2006 available at http://www.washingtonpost.com/wp-dyn/content/article/2006/02/08/AR2006020802293.html (Accessed April 3, 2009)

28 Deborah Howell, "Why not publish these cartoons?" Washington Post, February 12 2006, B6 available at http://www.washingtonpost.com/wp-dyn/content/article/2006/02/10/AR2006021001504.html (Accessed April 3, 2009)

29 Ibid.

30 Gwladys Fouché, Danish paper rejected Jesus cartoons, The Guardian (UK), February 6 2006 available at http://www.guardian.co.uk/cartoonprotests/story/0,,1703552,00.html (Accessed April 3, 2009)

31 Ibid.

32 British Broadcasting Corporation (BBC), "Pope sorry for offending Muslims" September 17, 2006 available at http://news.bbc.co.uk/2/hi/europe/5353208.stm (Accessed April 3, 2009)

33 Ibid.

34 See ibid.

35 "Pope John Paul II Enters Mosque; Pleads Peace" ABC News, May 6, 1991 available at http://abcnews.go.com/International/story?id=81117&page=1 (Accessed January 12, 2011)

36 BBC, "Pope sorry for offending Muslims" Sep. 17, 2006.

37 Ibid.

38 Karen Hughes, "Encouraging Interfaith Dialogues" Yemen Observer, December 4, 2007 available at http://www.yobserver.com/opinions/10013380.html (Accessed April 3, 2009)

39 Dinesh, D'Souza, "Muslims Who Renounce Violence", America Online (AOL) News, February 20, 2008 available at http://news.aol.com/newsbloggers/2008/02/20/muslims-who-renounce-violence/ (Accessed April 3, 2009)

40 "Rowan Williams: An Interview with the Archbishop of Canterbury" Islamica magazine, Volume 21, February 2009 at 50-52.

41 Ibid.

42 See http://www.thedohadebates.com/ (Accessed April 8, 2009)

43 "Doha Debates Focus on US-Israel Relations" Tell Me More with Michel Martin, National Public Radio (NPR) April 2, 2009 available at http://www.npr.org/templates/transcript/transcript.php?storyId=102637817 (Accessed April 8, 2009)

44 Ibid.

45 See http://www.thedohadebates.com/page.asp?p=3259 (Accessed January 13, 2011)

46 Video of March 2008 Doha Debates available at http://www.thedohadebates.com/debates/player.asp?d=4&res=hi (Accessed April 8, 2009)

47 Transcript of March 2008 Doha Debates available at http://www.thedohadebates.com/debates/debate.asp?d=4&s=4&mode=transcript (Accessed April 8, 2009)

48 "Muslim Leaders Debate Extremism"Tell Me More with Michel Martin, National Public Radio (NPR), March 7, 2008 available at http://www.npr.org/templates/story/story.php?storyId=87979472 (Accessed April 8, 2009)

49 NPR, "Doha Debates Focus on US-Israeli Relations" Apr. 2, 2009.

50 Transcript, Interview with Tim Sebastian. Chairman and Host of The Doha Debates, May 5, 2009.

51 Text of the 2006 Mecca Declaration available at http://www.islamicity.com/Articles/articles.asp?ref=IC0611-3172 (Accessed January 13, 2011)

52 See also Press Release, "The Makkah Appeal for Interfaith Dialogue" Royal Embassy of Saudi Arabia, June 1, 2008 available at http://www.saudiembassy.net/announcement/announcement09260806.aspx (Accessed June 23, 2009)

53 Usra Ghazi, "Saudi Interfaith Intiative" Islamica magazine, Volume 21, February 2009 at 78.

54 Ibid.

55 Text of 2008 Madrid Declaration available at http://www.saudiembassy.net/announcement/announcement07180801.aspx (Accessed January 13, 2011)

56 Ghazi, "Saudi Interfaith Initiative" Islamica, Feb. 2009 at 78.

57 Ibid.

58 http://www.usmuslimengagement.org/ (Accessed April 15, 2009)

59 See Rahul Mahajan, "We Think the Price is Worth it" Fairness & Accuracy in Reporting (FAIR), November/December 2001 available at http://www.fair.org/index.php?page=1084 (Accessed January 13, 2011)

60 See Arsalan Iftikhar, "Madeleine Albright on Future of Human Rights" April 2008 available at http://www.themuslimguy.com/madeleine-albright-on-future-of-human-rights.html (Accessed April 15, 2009)

61 Leadership Group on US-Muslim Engagement, Changing Course at 4-5.

62 Ibid at 28. See also Public Agenda and Foreign Affairs, "Confidence in U.S. Foreign Policy Index," Spring 2008 at 19 available at http://www.foreignaffairs.com/features/collections/the-confidence-in-us-foreign-policy-index-2005 (Accessed April 15, 2009)

63 Leadership Group on US-Muslim Engagement, Changing Course at 3.

64 Arsalan Iftikhar, "What would Muhammad Do?" Newsweek/Washington Post On-Faith, May 19, 2010 available at http://newsweek.washingtonpost.com/onfaith/patheos/2010/05/what_would_muhammad_do.html (Accessed January 12, 2011)

65 See Huntington, Samuel P. The Clash of Civilizations and the Remaking of World Order. New York, NY: Simon and Schuster, 1996.

Chapter 2: The Midwives of Islamophobia

5 Public Broadcasting Service (PBS) NewsHour, "Bin Laden Statement" available at http://www.pbs.org/newshour/terrorism/international/binladen_10-7.html (Accessed May 30, 2009)

6 Ann Coulter, "This is War" National Review Oniline, September 13, 2001 available at http://www.nationalreview.com/coulter/coulter.shtml (Accessed April 3, 2009)

7 Runnymede Trust, "Commission on British Muslims" available at http://www.runnymedetrust.org/projects/commissionOnBritishMuslims.html (Accessed May 30, 2009)

8 PBS NewsHour, "Bin Laden Statement".

9 Public Broadcasting Service (PBS) Frontline, "Osama bin Laden vs. The U.S.: Edicts and Statements" available at http://www.pbs.org/wgbh/pages/frontline/shows/binladen/who/edicts.html (Accessed May 31, 2009)

10 Ibid.

11 World Islamic Front statement, "Jihad against Jews and Crusaders" February 28, 1998 available at http://www.library.cornell.edu/colldev/mideast/wif.htm (Accessed June 11, 2009)

12 Peter Bergen, The Osama bin Laden I Know, (New York: Free Press, 2008), 183.

13 Rahimullah Yusufzai, "Conversations with Terror" TIME Magazine, January 11, 1999 available at http://www.time.com/time/magazine/article/0,9171,17676-2,00.html (Accessed March 15, 2011)

14 Bruce Hoffman, "Scarier than bin Laden" Washington Post, September 9, 2007 at B01 available at http://www.washingtonpost.com/wp-dyn/content/article/2007/09/07/AR2007090702056.html (Accessed May 30, 2009)

15 Ibid.

16 Ibid.

17 Coulter, "This is War", National Review Online, September 13, 2001.

18 Media Matters for America "Coulter: 'Isn't it great to see Muslims celebrating something other than the slaughter of Americans?'" February 3, 2005 available at http://mediamatters.org/items/200502030008 (Accessed May 30, 2009)

19 Jonah Goldberg, "L'Affaire Coulter" National Review Online, October 3 2001 available at http://www.nationalreview.com/nr_comment/nr_comment100301.shtml (Accessed May 30, 2009)

20 Ann Coulter, "Detainment isn't Enough" Townhall.com, October 4, 2001 available at http://townhall.com/columnists/AnnCoulter/2001/10/04/detainment_isnt_enough (Accessed May 30, 2009)

21 Ann Coulter, "Murder for Fun and Prophet." FrontPageMag.com, September 5, 2002 available at http://www.frontpagemagazine.com/articles/ReadArticle.asp?ID=2757 (May 30, 2009)

22 Ann Coulter, "Arab Hijackers Now Available for Pre-Boarding," HumanEvents.com, April 29 2004 available at http://www.humanevents.com/article.php?id=3748 (Accessed May 30, 2009)

23 Ann Coulter, "Coulter gets results," HumanEvents.com, November 30 2006 available at http://www.townhall.com/columnists/column.aspx?UrlTitle=coulter_gets_results&ns=AnnCoulter&dt=11/30/2006&page=2 (Accessed May 30, 2009)

24 Media Matters for America, "Coulter: Islam is 'a car-burning cult'" February 10, 2006 available at http://mediamatters.org/items/200602100003 (Accessed May 30, 2009)

25 Sherrie Gossett, "Ann Coulter 'Raghead' Comments Spark Blogger Backlash", CNS News, July 7, 2008 available at http://www.cnsnews.com/node/30499 (Accessed March 15, 2011)

26 Ibid.

27 Ibid.

28 Media Matters for America, "700 Club website scrubbed Robertson's controversial comments calling Muslims 'satanic'" March 14, 2006 available at http://mediamatters.org/items/200603140008 (Accessed May 30, 2009)

29 Ibid.

30 Joel Connelly and Ed Offley, "McCain and Bush clash over Revs. Robertson, Falwell," Seattle Post-Intelligencer, February 29 2000 available at http://seattlepi.nwsource.com/national/gops29.shtml (Accessed May 30, 2009)

31 Dan Harris, "Evangelical Christians Take Aim at Islam" ABC News, November 18, 2002 availableathttp://abcnews.go.com/WNT/Beliefs/story?id=130008&page=1(Accessed March 15, 2011)

32 Media Matters for America, "Robertson labeled Islam a 'bloody, brutal type of religion" May 1, 2006 available at http://mediamatters.org/items/200605010007 (Accessed May 30, 2009)

33 People for the American Way (PFAW) Newsletter, "September: The Right's Demonization of Muslims," September 14 2002 available at http://www.pfaw.org/pfaw/general/default.aspx?oid=5005 (Accessed May 30, 2009)

34 The Official Site of Pat Robertson, "Prevent the Tyranny of Oligarchy" May 4, 2005 available at http://www.patrobertson.com/PressReleases/thisweekgs.asp (Accessed May 30, 2009)

35 Media Matters for America, "Pat Robertson claimed that Islam 'at its core teaches violence'" July 18, 2005 available at http://mediamatters.org/items/200507180003 (Accessed May 30, 2009)

36 Media Matters for America, "Robertson: The West is ignoring from 'Islam in general,' just as it ignored 'what Adolf Hitler said in Mein Kampf'" April 24, 2006 available at http://mediamatters.org/items/200604240007 (Accessed May 30, 2009)

37 Ibid.

38 Media Matters for America, "Robertson: Islam is a 'Christian heresy', Jews are 'very thrifty, extraordinarily good business people" May 24, 2006 available at http://mediamatters.org/items/200605240010 (Accessed May 30, 2009)

39 Ibid.

40 CNN.com, "Sen. John McCain Attacks Pat Robertson, Jerry Falwell, Republican Establishment as Harming GOP Ideals," February 28 2000 available at http://transcripts.cnn.com/TRANSCRIPTS/0002/28/se.01.html (Accessed May 30, 2009)

41 CBS '60 Minutes', "Zion's Christian Soldiers" June 8 2003 available at http://www.cbsnews.com/stories/2002/10/03/60minutes/main524268.shtml (Accessed May 30, 2009)

42 CBS '60 Minutes', "Falwell Sorry for Bashing Muhammad," October 14 2002 available at http://www.cbsnews.com/stories/2002/10/11/60minutes/main525316.shtml (Accessed May 30, 2009)

43 National Council of Churchs (NCC) Press Release, "National Council of Churches Board Repudiates Jerry Falwell's "60 Minutes" Comments on Islam, Asks President Bush To Condemn Falwell's Remarks," October 7, 2002 available at http://www.ncccusa.org/news/02news86.html (Accessed March 15, 2011)

44 Kim Lawton "Franklin Graham on Islam," PBS Religion & Ethics NewsWeekly, Episode 549, August 9, 2002 available at http://www.pbs.org/wnet/religionandethics/week549/news.html (Accessed May 30, 2009)

45 Jon Meacham, "Pilgrim's Progress" Newsweek, August 13, 2006 available at http://www.newsweek.com/2006/08/13/pilgrim-s-progress.html (Accessed March 15, 2011)

46 People for the American Way E-Newsletter, "September: The Right's Demonization of Muslims," September 14 2002.

47 See Arsalan Iftikhar, "No-name radicals vs. 'South Park' just a distraction" CNN.com, April 26, 2010 available at http://www.cnn.com/2010/OPINION/04/26/iftikhar.south.park/index.html?hpt=C2 (Accessed March 15, 2011)

48 Jeffrey McMurray, "U.S. Congressman Says He Regrets Joke bout Arresting Muslims" Associated Press, November 20, 2001.

49 Counterpunch Wire, "Rep. Saxby Chambliss: Arrest Ever Muslim that Enters Georgia", November 21, 2001 available at http://www.counterpunch.org/chambliss1.html (Accessed May 30, 2009)

50 Houston Chronicle, "Lawmaker regrets 'diaper' comment," September 20, 2001 available at http://www.chron.com/cs/CDA/story.hts/special/terror/aftermath/1056615 (Accessed May 30, 2009)

51 Official Website of Wil Wheaton, "Change that diaper, Mr. Cooksey" September 2001 available at http://www.wilwheaton.net/2001/09/change_that_diaper_mr_cooksey_1.php (Accessed May 30, 2009)

52 Cal Thoms, "Men of Faith in Washington D.C. Need Our Prayers" Crosswalk.com, November 2001 available at http://www.crosswalk.com/news/1108858.html (Accessed May 30, 2009)

53 Tribune Media Services, "Biography: Cal Thomas" available at http://www.tmsfeatures.com/bio/cal-thomas/ (Accessed May 30, 2009)

54 Richard T. Cooper, "General casts war in religious terms," Los Angeles Times, October 16, 2003 available at http://www.commondreams.org/headlines03/1016-01.htm (Accessed May 30, 2009)

55 Ibid.

56 Johanna Neuman, "Bush's Inaction Over General's Islam Remarks Riles Two Faiths," Los Angeles Times, November 23, 2003 available at http://www.commondreams.org/headlines03/1123-06.htm (Accessed May 30, 2009)

57 Ibid.

58 Media Matters for America, "CNN's Beck to first-ever Muslim congressman: "[W]hat I feel like saying is, 'Sir, prove to me that you are not working with our enemies'", November 15, 2006 available at http://mediamatters.org/mmtv/200611150004 (Accessed March 15, 2011)

59 Julian Borger, "September 11 revenge killer to die for shooting Sikh"The Guardian (UK) newspaper, October 11, 2003 available at http://www.guardian.co.uk/world/2003/oct/11/usa.julianborger (Accessed March 15, 2011)

60 BBC World News, "Victim of 'hate crime' buried," September 20, 2001 available at http://news.bbc.co.uk/1/hi/world/americas/1553796.stm (Accessed June 2, 2009)

61 Emil Guillermo, "The war has already started in America," Asian Week, September 21, 2001 available at http://www.asianweek.com/2001_09_21/opinion_emil.html (Accessed June 5, 2007)

62 Southern Poverty Law Center (SPLC), "The Forgotten", Spring 2002 available at http://www.splcenter.org/intel/intelreport/article.jsp?pid=248 (Accessed June 2, 2009)

63 Jeff Coen, "Hate-crime reports reach record level," Chicago Tribune, October 9, 2001 available at http://www.mcall.com/entertainment/movies/sns-worldtrade-hate-crimes-ct,0,5277962.story?page=2 (Accessed June 2, 2009)

64 "Irving Mosque target of shooting," DALLAS BUSINESS JOURNAL, September 12, 2001 available at http://dallas.bizjournals.com/dallas/stories/2001/09/10/daily31.html (Accessed June 2, 2009)

65 Ibid.

66 Associated Press, "Mosque Vandalized in Columbus, Ohio" January 3, 2002 available at http://pluralism.org/news/view/2903 (Accessed March 15, 2011)

67 Seattle Post-Intelligencer, "News from around the nation" January 10, 2002 available at http://www.seattlepi.com/national/53922_natn10.shtml (Accessed March 15, 2011)

68 Ibid.

69 Tanya Schevitz, "FBI sees leaps in anti-Muslim hate crimes" San Francisco Chronicle, November 26, 2002 available at http://www.sfgate.com/cgi-bin/article.cgi?f=/c/a/2002/11/26/MN224441.DTL (Accessed June 2, 2009)

70 See Arsalan Iftikhar, "What the President should say in Cairo" CNN Anderson Cooper 360, June 3, 2009 available at http://ac360.blogs.cnn.com/2009/06/03/obama-in-the-middle-east-draft/ (Accessed March 15, 2011)

71 David Morris, "Unease over Islam" ABC News, September 11, 2003 available at http://abcnews.go.com/sections/us/World/sept11_islampoll_030911.html (Accessed May 31, 2009)

72 Jennifer Hoar, "Poll: Sinking Perceptions of Islam" CBS News, April 12, 2006 available at http://www.cbsnews.com/stories/2006/04/12/national/main1494697.shtml (Accessed March 15, 2011)

73 Cornell University Press Release, "Fear factor: 44 percent of Americans queried in Cornell national poll favor curtailing some liberties for Muslim Americans" December 17, 2004 available at http://news.cornell.edu/releases/Dec04/Muslim.Poll.bpf.html (Accessed May 31, 2009)

74 Suzanne Goldenberg, "Islamophobia Worse in America Now Than after 9/11, Survey Finds" The Guardian (UK), March 10, 2006 available at http://www.commondreams.org/headlines06/0310-07.htm (Accessed May 31, 2009)

75 Jon Cohen, "Poll: Americans skeptical about Islam and Arabs" ABC News, March 8, 2006 available at http://abcnews.go.com/US/story?id=1700599 (Accessed May 31, 2009)

76 Arsalan Iftikhar, "What the President SHOULD Say in Cairo" CNN Anderson Cooper 360, June 3, 2009.

77 Susan Page, "On security, public draws blurred lines" USA TODAY, August 3, 2005 available at http://www.usatoday.com/news/nation/2005-08-03-security-lines-public-opinion_x.htm (Accessed May 31, 2009)

78 Paul Steinhauser, "Poll: Few Americans have good view of Muslim world" CNN.com, June 2, 2009 available at http://us.cnn.com/2009/POLITICS/06/02/us.muslims.poll/index.html (Accessed June 2, 2009)

79 Arsalan Iftikhar, "Letter to Obama on the Muslim World" CNN.com, November 14, 2008 available at http://www.cnn.com/2008/POLITICS/11/12/iftikhar.obama/index.html?imw=Y&iref=mpstoryemail (Accessed June 1, 2009)

80 Arsalan Iftikhar, "Amen, Mr. President" CNN.com, June 4, 2009 available at http://www.cnn.com/2009/POLITICS/06/04/iftikhar.obama.cairo/index.html (Accessed June 7, 2009)

81 Arsalan Iftikhar, "Mr. Obama goes to Al-Arabiya" CNN Anderson Cooper 360, January 27, 2009 available at http://ac360.blogs.cnn.com/2009/01/27/mr-obama-goes-to-al-arabiya/ (Accessed June 1, 2009)

82 See also John Wright, The Obama Haters: Behind the Right-Wing Campaign of Lies, Innuendo & Racism (Potomac Books, Inc., 2011.)

83 NBC 'Meet The Press', "Transcript for October 19, 2008" available at http://www.msnbc.msn.com/id/27266223/page/2/ (Accessed June 1, 2009)

84 Ibid.

85 Transcript of interview with Daisy Khan, February 1, 2011.

86 Michael Honda, "Hearings on Muslim-Americans are un-American" San Francisco Chronicle, February 28, 2011 available at http://www.sfgate.com/cgi-bin/blogs/opinionshop/detail?entry_id=84016 (Accessed March 15, 2011)

87 Brian Bennett, "Rep. Peter King's hearing on American Muslims a 'very person' quest', Los Angeles Times, March 9, 2011 available at http://articles.latimes.com/2011/mar/09/nation/la-na-king-hearings-20110310/3 (Accessed March 15, 2011)

88 Eugene Robinson, "Peter King's modern-day witch hunt" Washington Post, March 10, 2011 available at http://www.washingtonpost.com/wp-dyn/content/article/2011/03/10/AR2011031004680.html (Accessed March 15, 2011)

89 Bob Herbert, "Flailing after Muslims" The New York Times, March 7, 2011 available at http://www.nytimes.com/2011/03/08/opinion/08herbert.html (Accessed March 15, 2011)

90 Richard Cohen, "Rep. Peter King's hearings on Islamic radicalization: Fuel for the bigots" Washington Post, March 8, 2011 available at http://www.washingtonpost.com/wp-dyn/content/article/2011/03/07/AR2011030703896.html (Accessed March 15, 2011)

91 Sheryl Gay Stolberg, "White House Seeks to Allay Muslims' Fear on Terror Hearings" The New York Times, March 6, 2011 available at http://www.nytimes.com/2011/03/07/us/politics/07muslim.html (Accessed March 15, 2011)

92 See http://www.africawithin.com/malcolmx/letter_from_mecca.htm (Accessed June 2, 2009)

93 Fordham University, "Internet Medieval Sourcebook". Text of sermon available at http://www.fordham.edu/halsall/source/muhm-sermon.html (Accessed March 15, 2011)

94 See Robert S. Wistrich, Who's Who in Nazi Germany, (New York: Routledge, 1995).

Chapter 3: The Ghosts of John Ashcroft Past

1 William Temple Franklin, Memoirs of the Life and Writings of Benjamin Franklin, (London: British and Foreign Public Library), 1818 available at http://books.google.com/books?id=W2MFAAAAQAAJ&pg=PA270&lpg=PA270t#PPA270,M1 (Accessed June 15, 2009)

2 Public Law 107-56, 115 Stat. 272 Full text available at http://frwebgate.access.gpo.gov/cgi-bin/getdoc.cgi?dbname=107_cong_public_laws&docid=f:publ056.107 (Accessed June 19, 2009)

3 From Arsalan Iftikhar, "Presumption of Guilt: September 11 and the American Muslim Community" from Keeping Out the Other: A Critical Introduction to Immigrations Enforcement Today, edited by David C. Brotherton, and Philip Kretsedemas. Copyright © 2008 Columbia University Press. Reprinted with permission of the publisher.

4 See TIME Magazine, "The 2004 'TIME 100'" available at http://www.time.com/time/subscriber/2004/time100/scientists/100ramadan.html (Accessed June 17, 2009)

5 Memorandum, Office of the Deputy Attorney General, "Guidance for Absconder Apprehension Initiative" January 25 2002. See also http://news.findlaw.com/hdocs/docs/doj/abscndr012502mem.pdf *(Accessed June 19, 2009)*

6 Ibid.

7 See Arsalan Iftikhar, The Status of Muslim Civil Rights in the United States, 2005: Unequal Protection (Washington D.C.: Council on American-Islamic Relations, 2005). See also supra note 3 at 131.

8 Ibid.

9 See Dan Eggen and Cheryl W. Thompson, "United States seeks thousands of fugitive deportees; Middle Eastern men are focus of search," Washington Post, January 8 2002: A01.

10 Scott Shane, "Glare of Publicity Finds an Inspector General" March 26, 2007 available at http://www.nytimes.com/2007/03/26/washington/26inspector.html?_r=2 (Accessed June 17, 2009)

11 Supra note 3.

12 Ibid.

13 Press Release, "U.S. Supreme Court Should Review and Reject Secret Detentions," Human Rights Watch, September 30, 2003 available at http://www.hrw.org/en/news/2003/09/29/us-supreme-court-should-review-and-reject-secret-detentions (Accessed June 19, 2009)

14 Kelli Arena and Terry Frieden, "U.S. report critical of 9/11 detainee treatment," CNN, June 3, 2003 available at http://edition.cnn.com/2003/LAW/06/02/detainees/ (Accessed June 19, 2009)

15 Supra note 3 at 110.

16 Ibid.

17 Ibid.

18 Arsalan Iftikhar, "Losing Liberties" TomPaine.com, May 19, 2005 available at http://www.tompaine.com/articles/2005/05/19/losing_liberties.php (Accessed June 17, 2009)

19 American Civil Liberties Union (ACLU), Sanctioned Bias: Racial Profiling Since 9/11, February 2004 available at http://www.aclu.org/SafeandFree/SafeandFree.cfm?ID=15102&c=207 (Accessed June 19, 2009)

20 Ibid.

21 Ibid.

22 Supra note 3 at 110-11.

23 Ibid at 111.

24 Fact Sheet: National Security Entry Exit Registration System, U.S. Department of State, June 5, 2002 available at http://www.fas.org/irp/news/2002/06/doj060502b.html (Accessed June 19, 2009)

25 In addition to Iran, Iraq, Libya, Sudan and Syria, the 25 "Special Registration" countries include Afghanistan, Algeria, Bahrain, Eritrea, Lebanon, Morocco, North Korea, Oman, Qatar, Somalia, Tunisia, United Arab Emirates, Yemen, Pakistan, Saudi Arabia, Bangladesh, Egypt, Indonesia, Jordan and Kuwait.

26 Supra note 24.

27 Press Release, "Deadlines Approach for Ashcroft Immigrant Fingerprinting Program; ACLU Says Plan is Full of Holes, Advises Immigrants to Seek Counsel" American Civil Liberties Union (ACLU), December 13, 2001 available at http://www.aclu.org/immigrants/gen/11705prs20021213.html (Accessed June 19, 2009)

28 See http://news.corporate.findlaw.com/legalnews/us/terrorism/cases/civil.html (Accessed June 19, 2009)

29 Cam Simpson, "Aspiring politician at center of policy," Chicago Tribune, November 16, 2003 available at http://www.chicagotribune.com/news/specials/chi-111603tossed-sidebar-story,1,3565717.story?coll=chi-site-nav (Accessed June 19, 2009)

30 "ACLU Says New Border Fingerprinting System Likely To Sow Confusion, Tracking of Arab and Muslims Based on National Origin Will Continue," American Civil Liberties Union (ACLU) press release, January 5, 2004 available at http://www.aclu.org/SafeandFree/SafeandFree.cfm?ID=14649&c=206 (Accessed June 18, 2009)

31 Ibid.

32 Supra note 30.

33 See http://www.usatoday.com/news/washington/2009-01-25-civillibertiesinside_N.htm (Accessed June 17, 2009)

34 Esquire's The Rules: A Man's Guide to Life, Hearst Books, 2003, New York at 77. See also http://www.commondreams.org/views04/1116-35.htm (Accessed June 17, 2009)

35 Full text of USA PATRIOT Act available at http://epic.org/privacy/terrorism/hr3162.html (Accessed June 19, 2009)

36 See United States Senate Roll Call Votes, 107th Congress (Session 1) available at http://www.senate.gov/legislative/LIS/roll_call_lists/roll_call_vote_cfm.cfm?congress=107&session=1&vote=00313 (Accessed June 17, 2009)

37 See United States Senate Roll Call Votes, 107th Congress (Session 1) available at http://www.senate.gov/legislative/LIS/roll_call_lists/roll_call_vote_cfm.cfm?congress=107&session=1&vote=00313#position (Accessed June 17, 2009)

38 Arsalan Iftikhar, "Patriots Against USA PATRIOT" Counterpunch.org, June 22, 2005 available at http://www.counterpunch.org/iftikhar06222005.html (Accessed June 18, 2009)

39 Sara Gamay and Diane Lee, "Patriot Act Encourages National Insecurity," The (Georgetown) Hoya, November 7, 2003 available at http://www.thehoya.com/viewpoint/110703/view3.cfm

40 Supra note 38.

41 Press Release, "Largest City to Date Passes Pro-Civil Liberties Resolution; Los Angeles Rejects Bush's Call to Continue Civil Liberties Curtailment," American Civil Liberties Union (ACLU), January 21, 2004 available at http://www.aclu.org/news/NewsPrint.cfm?ID=14765&c=206 (Accessed June 18, 2009)

42 Michelle Garcia, "N.Y. City Council Passes Anti-Patriot Act Measure" The Washington Post, February 5, 2004, A11 available at http://www.washingtonpost.com/wp-dyn/articles/A13970-2004Feb4.html (Accessed June 19, 2009)

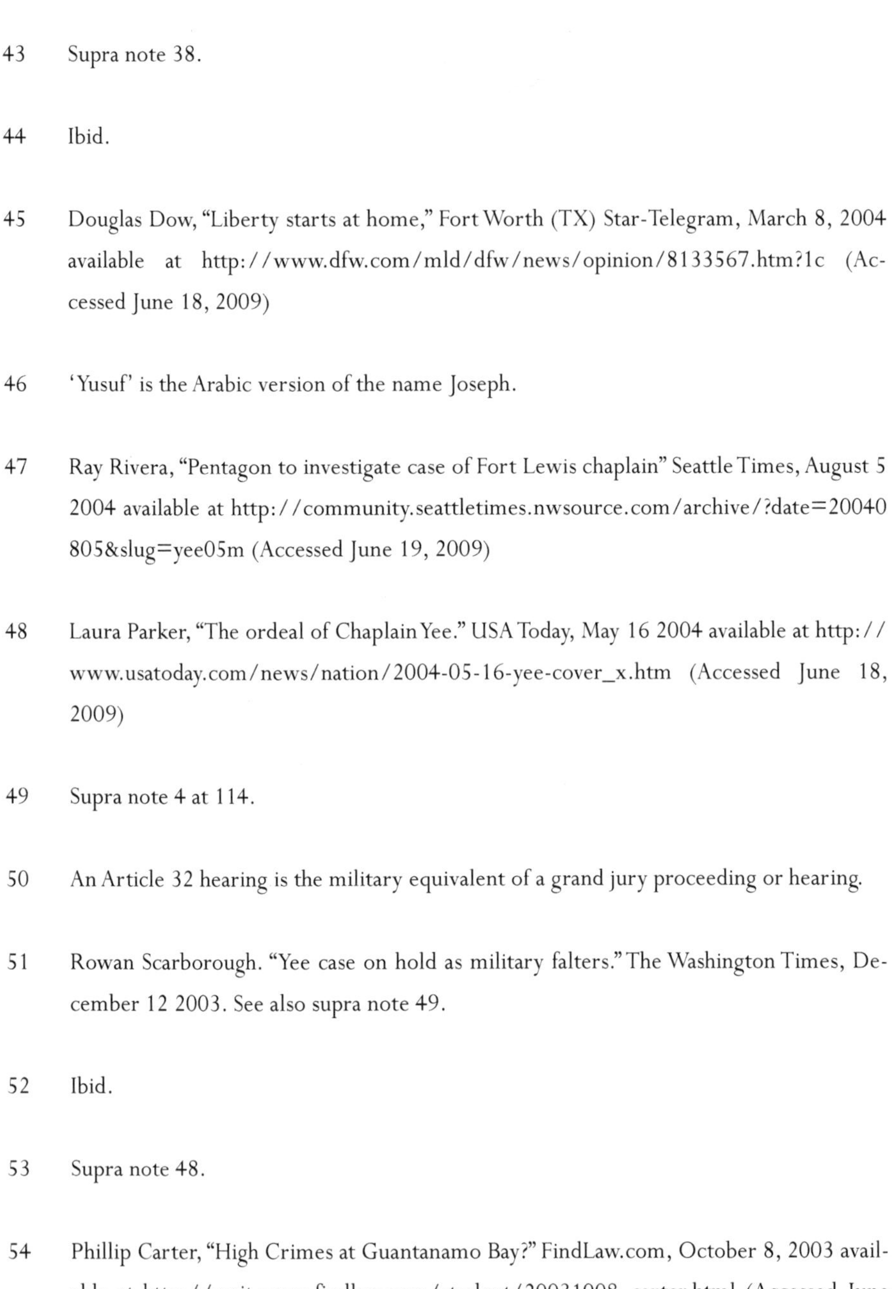

43 Supra note 38.

44 Ibid.

45 Douglas Dow, "Liberty starts at home," Fort Worth (TX) Star-Telegram, March 8, 2004 available at http://www.dfw.com/mld/dfw/news/opinion/8133567.htm?1c (Accessed June 18, 2009)

46 'Yusuf' is the Arabic version of the name Joseph.

47 Ray Rivera, "Pentagon to investigate case of Fort Lewis chaplain" Seattle Times, August 5 2004 available at http://community.seattletimes.nwsource.com/archive/?date=20040805&slug=yee05m (Accessed June 19, 2009)

48 Laura Parker, "The ordeal of Chaplain Yee." USA Today, May 16 2004 available at http://www.usatoday.com/news/nation/2004-05-16-yee-cover_x.htm (Accessed June 18, 2009)

49 Supra note 4 at 114.

50 An Article 32 hearing is the military equivalent of a grand jury proceeding or hearing.

51 Rowan Scarborough. "Yee case on hold as military falters." The Washington Times, December 12 2003. See also supra note 49.

52 Ibid.

53 Supra note 48.

54 Phillip Carter, "High Crimes at Guantanamo Bay?" FindLaw.com, October 8, 2003 available at http://writ.news.findlaw.com/student/20031008_carter.html (Accessed June 18, 2009)

55 Rowan Scarborough, "Islamic chaplain is charged as a spy," Washington Times, September 20, 2003. See also supra note 49 at 115.

56 Supra note 48.

57 Joel Arak "Gitmo Chaplain Charged." CBS News, October 10 2003 available at http://www.cbsnews.com/stories/2003/10/24/attack/main579836.shtml (Accessed June 19, 2009)

58 Guy Taylor, "Muslim Chaplain Charged by Army." The Washington Times, October 10 2003. See also supra note 4 at 115.

59 See id. See also "Guantanamo Muslim chaplain charged." Al-Jazeera, October 11 2003.

60 Mike Barber, "Yee reunited with family." Seattle Post-Intelligencer, April 6 2004 available at http://www.seattlepi.com/local/167868_yee06.html (Accessed June 19, 2009)

61 Supra note 4 at 115-16. See also "Chaplain's prosecutors focus on porn, sex charges" CNN.com, December 8 2003 available at http://www.cnn.com/2003/LAW/12/08/yee.hearing.ap/ (Accessed June 18, 2009)

62 Ray Rivera, "Painful Secrets" The Seattle Times, October 2003 available at http://seattletimes.nwsource.com/html/nationworld/2002150414_yeechapter7.html (Accessed June 18, 2009)

63 Supra note 48.

64 Ray Rivera and Janet Tu, "Muslim chaplain out of prison, faces new charges" Seattle Times, November 26, 2003 available at http://community.seattletimes.nwsource.com/archive/?date=20031126&slug=yee26m (Accessed June 18, 2009)

65 Supra note 56.

66 Supra note 4 at 116. See also "Yousef Yee Charged With Adultery, Storing Porn on Gov't Computer." FOX News, November 26, 2003.

67 Ibid.

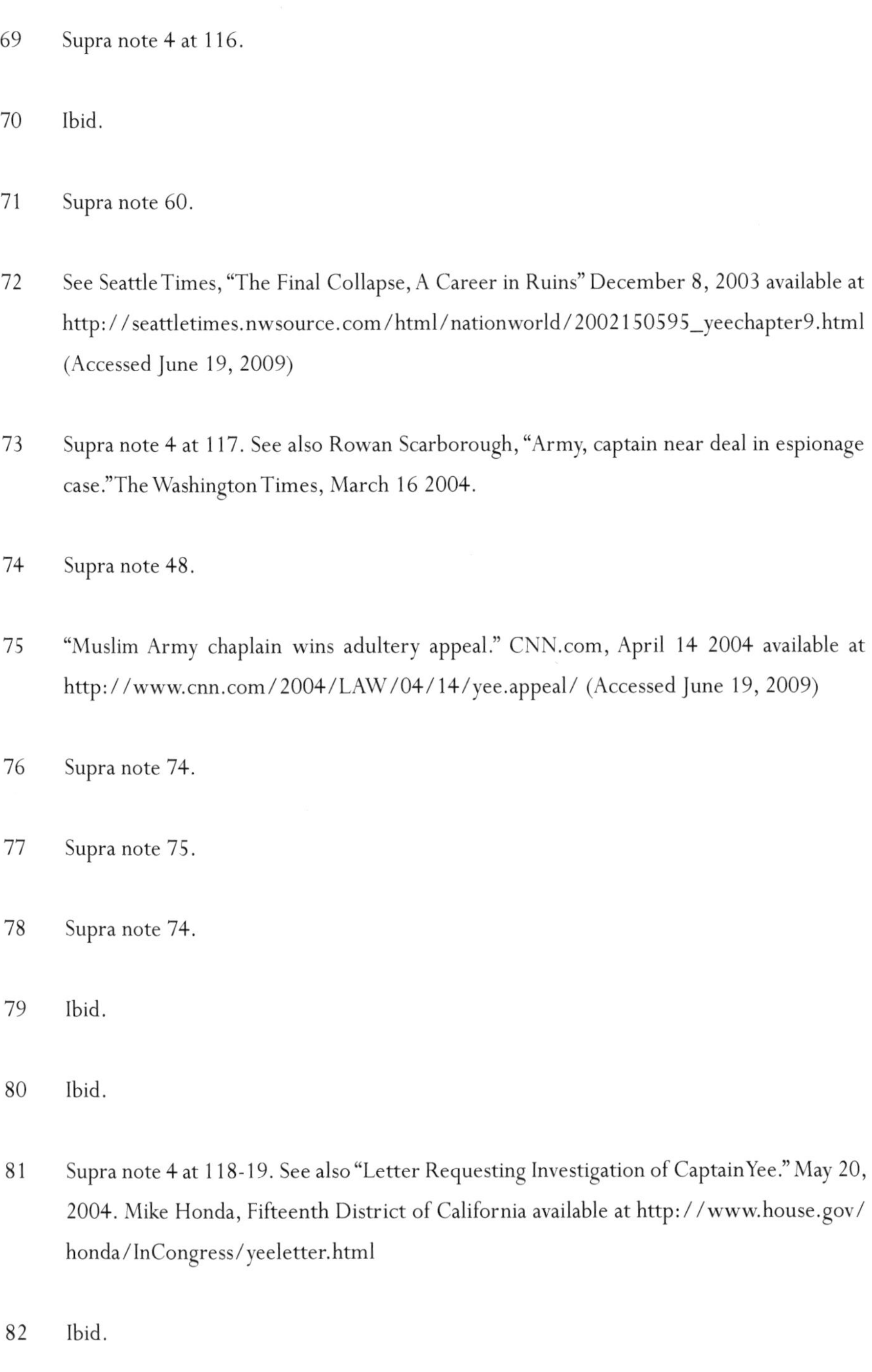

68 Ibid.

69 Supra note 4 at 116.

70 Ibid.

71 Supra note 60.

72 See Seattle Times, "The Final Collapse, A Career in Ruins" December 8, 2003 available at http://seattletimes.nwsource.com/html/nationworld/2002150595_yeechapter9.html (Accessed June 19, 2009)

73 Supra note 4 at 117. See also Rowan Scarborough, "Army, captain near deal in espionage case." The Washington Times, March 16 2004.

74 Supra note 48.

75 "Muslim Army chaplain wins adultery appeal." CNN.com, April 14 2004 available at http://www.cnn.com/2004/LAW/04/14/yee.appeal/ (Accessed June 19, 2009)

76 Supra note 74.

77 Supra note 75.

78 Supra note 74.

79 Ibid.

80 Ibid.

81 Supra note 4 at 118-19. See also "Letter Requesting Investigation of Captain Yee." May 20, 2004. Mike Honda, Fifteenth District of California available at http://www.house.gov/honda/InCongress/yeeletter.html

82 Ibid.

83 Supra note 4 at 119.

84 Ibid.

85 Ibid.

86 Mike Barber, "Army chaplain Yee to resign," Seattle Post-Intelligencer, August 3 2004 available at http://seattlepi.nwsource.com/local/184640_yee03.html (Accessed June 19, 2009)

87 Ibid.

88 Supra note 4 at 120. See also "Timeline: Madrid Investigation." British Broadcasting Corporation (BBC), August 11 2004.

89 Affidavit of Special Agent Richard K. Werder, FBI. May 6, 2004. United States District Court for District of Oregon at 3 available at http://www.bordc.org/threats/court/mayfieldmww.pdf (Accessed June 19, 2009)

90 "Statement on Brandon Mayfield Case." U.S. Department of Justice, May 24 2004 available at http://www.fbi.gov/pressrel/pressrel04/mayfield052404.htm (Accessed June 19, 2009)

91 "Family: Oregon lawyer has no connection to Madrid attacks." USA Today, May 8 2004 available at http://www.usatoday.com/news/nation/2004-05-08-mayfield-profile_x.htm (Accessed June 19, 2009)

92 Supra note 90.

93 Supra note 4 at 120. See also Kevin Johnson, "Bomb case against U.S. lawyer dropped." USA Today, May 24 2004

94 Supra note 90.

95 Ibid.

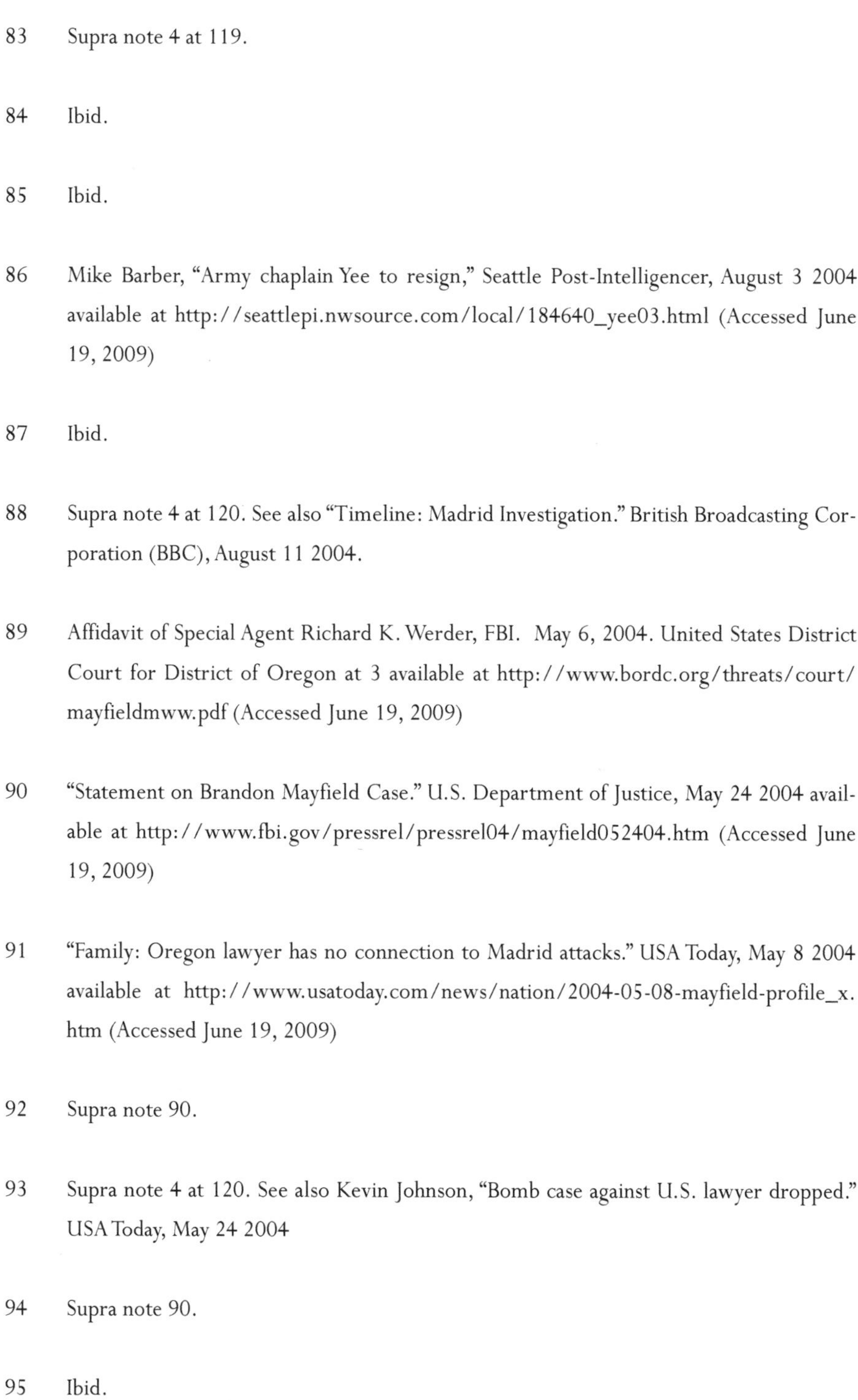

96 Ben Jacklet and Todd Murphy. "Now Free, Attorney Brandon Mayfield Turns Furious." Washington Report on Middle East Affairs July/August 2004 available at http://www.wrmea.com/archives/July_Aug_2004/0407068.html (Accessed June 19, 2009)

97 Supra note 4 at 121. See also Daniel Wools, "Fingerprint Evidence Cited."Topeka Capital-Journal, May 8 2004.

98 Ibid.

99 Robyn Blumner, "All the fear that's fit to print." St. Petersburg Times June 6 2004 available at http://www.sptimes.com/2004/06/06/Columns/All_the_fear_that_s_f.shtml (Accessed June 19, 2009) According to the affidavit by FBI Special Agent Werder, the prints were on file from his service as an army officer and because of an arrest for burglary in 1984.

100 Supra note 94.

101 Supra note 98.

102 Supra note 94.

103 Supra note 4 at 122. See also David Sarasohn "In Mayfield case, fingers are pointing"The Oregonian, June 9, 2004.

104 Ibid.

105 Supra note 4 at 122. See also Michael Isikoff, "An American conncetion?" Newsweek, May 7 2004.

106 Sarah Kershaw, "Spain and U.S. at Odds on Mistaken Terror Arrest"The New York Times, June 5, 2004 available at http://www.nytimes.com/2004/06/05/national/05LAWY.html?pagewanted=1 (Accessed June 19, 2009)

107 Christopher Brauchli, "The Federal Bureau of Errors" Counterpunch.org, June 12-13, 2004 available at http://www.counterpunch.org/brauchli06132004.html (Accessed June 19, 2009)

108 Ibid.

109 Supra note 4 at 122.

110 Ibid.

111 Official report, Human Rights Watch and American Civil Liberties Union, "Witness to Abuse" June 2005 available at http://www.hrw.org/reports/2005/us0605/11.htm (Accessed June 19, 2009)

112 Supra note 90.

113 Ibid.

114 Editorial, "The FBI messes up," The New York Times, May 26, 2004 at A22 available at http://www.nytimes.com/2004/05/26/opinion/the-fbi-messes-up.html (Accessed June 19, 2009)

115 Kevin Johnson, "Bomb case against U.S. lawyer dismissed," USA Today, May 24, 2004 available at http://www.usatoday.com/news/nation/2004-05-24-ore-lawyer_x.htm (Accessed June 19, 2009)

116 "Apology is not enough" Washington Post, May 27 2004 at A30 available at http://www.washingtonpost.com/wp-dyn/articles/A59014-2004May26.html (Accessed June 19, 2009)

117 Ibid.

118 18 U.S.C. 3144

119 See Ibid. The text of the Material Witness Statute says that a person may be arrested and detained as a "material witness" only "…if it is shown that it may become impracticable to secure the presence of the person by subpoena."

120 Supra note 4 at 124. See also Brett Zongker "Secret legal process misused, American-Islamic group says," Associated Press, August 30 2004.

121 Ibid.

122 Supra note 4 at 124.

123 Ibid. See also Larry Neumeister, "Judge declares imprisonment of material witnesses unconstitutional," Associated Press, May 1 2004

124 Ibid.

125 Ibid.

126 Supra note 4 at 125. See also Rukmini Callimachi, "'Smoking Gun' author to represent Brandon Mayfield," Associated Press, August 26 2004

127 Ben Jacklet, "Mayfield calls in heavy hitter," Portland Tribune, September 28 2004 available at http://www.portlandtribune.com/archview.cgi?id=26394 (Accessed June 19, 2009)

128 Supra note 4 at 125. See also "Judge quits wrongly accused lawyer's suit" Associated Press, November 9 2004.

129 Ben Jacklet, "Mayfield calls in heavy hitter" Portland (OR) Tribune, September 28, 2004 available at http://www.portlandtribune.com/news/story.php?story_id=26394 (Accessed June 19, 2009)

130 Supra note 4 at 125. See also Arsalan Iftikhar "Worst since J. Edgar Hoover Era" South Florida Sun-Sentinel, November 16 2004.

131 Ryan Geddes, "Mayfield settles case against feds for $2 million" Beaverton (OR) Valley Times, November 29, 2006 available at http://www.beavertonvalleytimes.com/news/story.php?story_id=116482687291016800 (Accessed June 19, 2009)

132 Public Law 107-71 available at http://www.tsa.gov/assets/pdf/Aviation_and_Transportation_Security_Act_ATSA_Public_Law_107_1771.pdf (Accessed June 19, 2009)

133 Airline Watchlists: Overview, Human Rights First available at http://www.humanrightsfirst.org/us_law/privacy/airwatch_overview.htm (Accessed June 19, 2009)

134 Green et al. v. Transportation Security Administration et al. available at http://news.findlaw.com/cnn/docs/aclu/greenvtsa40604cmp.pdf *(Accessed June 19, 2009)*

135 Supra note 4 at 126. See also Stella Richardson "ACLU Challenges 'No-Fly' Lists: Citizens targeted as terrorists" ACLU News of ACLU of Northern California, Spring 2004.

136 Ibid.

137 TIME Magazine, "2004 'TIME 100'" available at http://www.time.com/time/innovators/spirituality/profile_ramadan.html (Accessed June 19, 2009)

138 Jay Tolson, "Should this man come to the U.S.?" U.S. News and World Report, December 6 2004 available at http://www.usnews.com/usnews/culture/articles/041206/6islam.htm (Accessed June 19, 2009)

139 Interview with Tariq Ramadan and Scott Appleby "Leading Muslim Scholar Tariq Ramadan Denied U.S. Visa to Teach at Notre Dame" Democracy Now! September 13 2004 available at http://www.democracynow.org/article.pl?sid=04/09/13/1428249 (Accessed June 19, 2009)

140 Ibid.

141 See supra note 2.

142 Supra note 4 at 127. See also Genieve Abdo "Muslim scholar has visa revoked" Chicago Tribune, August 24 2004.

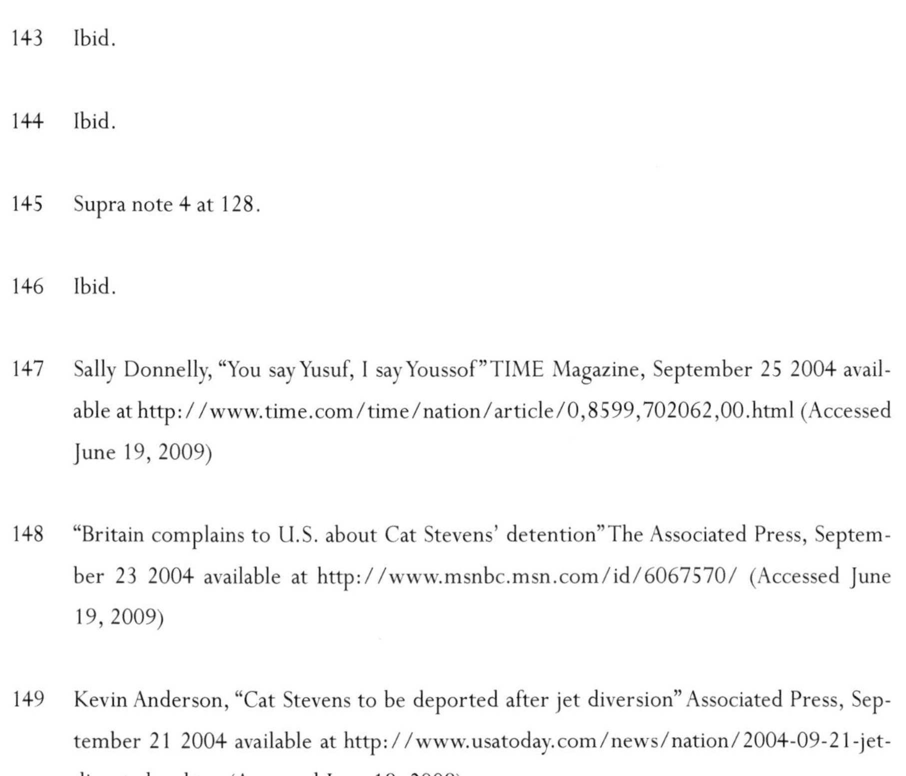

143 Ibid.

144 Ibid.

145 Supra note 4 at 128.

146 Ibid.

147 Sally Donnelly, "You say Yusuf, I say Youssof" TIME Magazine, September 25 2004 available at http://www.time.com/time/nation/article/0,8599,702062,00.html (Accessed June 19, 2009)

148 "Britain complains to U.S. about Cat Stevens' detention" The Associated Press, September 23 2004 available at http://www.msnbc.msn.com/id/6067570/ (Accessed June 19, 2009)

149 Kevin Anderson, "Cat Stevens to be deported after jet diversion" Associated Press, September 21 2004 available at http://www.usatoday.com/news/nation/2004-09-21-jet-diverted_x.htm (Accessed June 19, 2009)

150 Ibid.

151 Transcript, "New Drug Could Help Women's Sexual Desire; Cat Stevens Denied Entry Into U.S; Elections Heats Up, Kerry, Bush Remain On Offensive" CNN Anderson Cooper 360, September 22, 2004 available at http://transcripts.cnn.com/TRANSCRIPTS/0409/22/acd.00.html (Accessed June 23, 2009)

152 Jeanne Meserve, "Detained Cat Stevens heading home" CNN.com, September 22 2004 available at http://www.cnn.com/2004/US/09/22/plane.diverted.stevens/ (Accessed June 19, 2009)

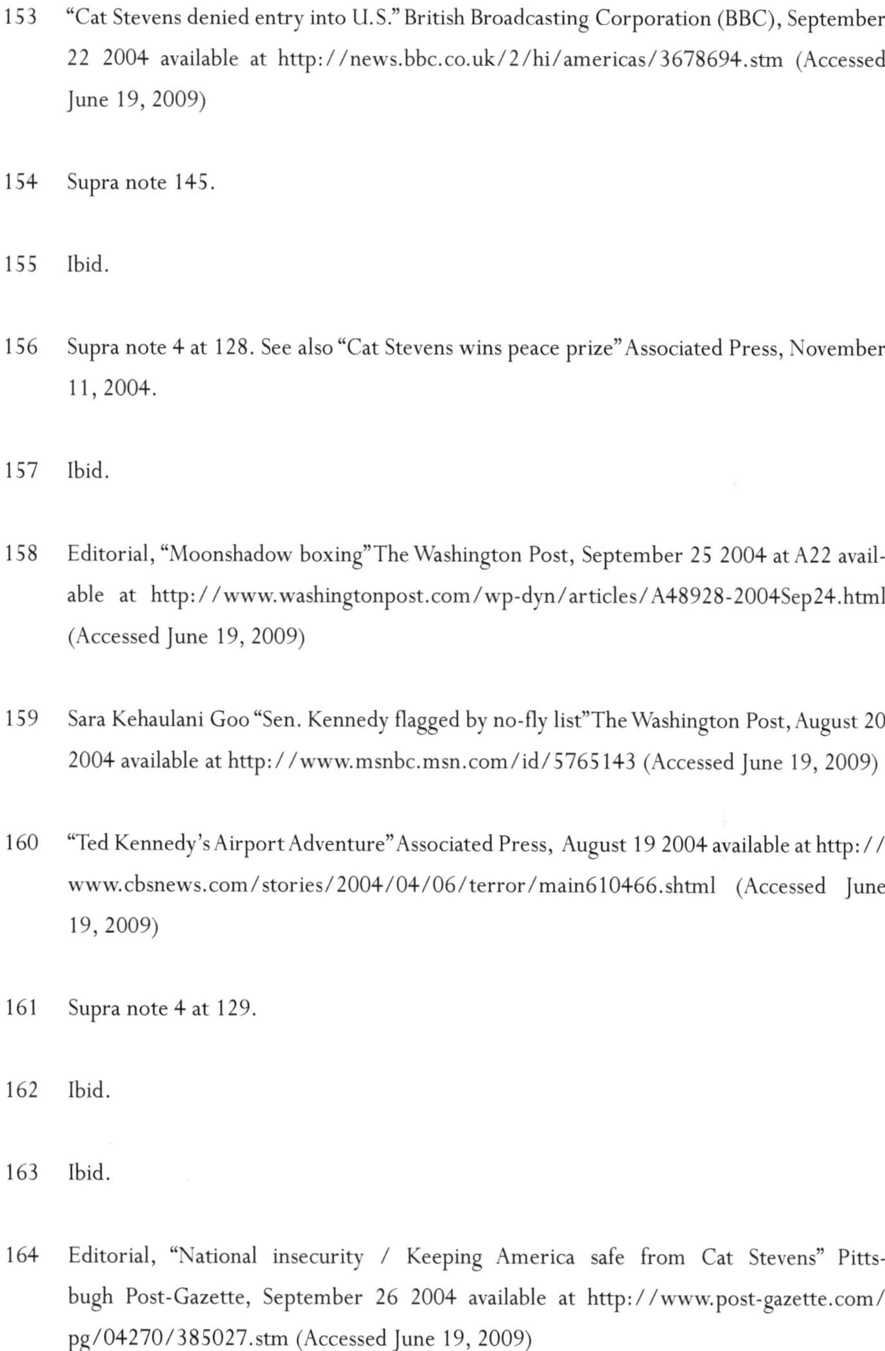

153 "Cat Stevens denied entry into U.S." British Broadcasting Corporation (BBC), September 22 2004 available at http://news.bbc.co.uk/2/hi/americas/3678694.stm (Accessed June 19, 2009)

154 Supra note 145.

155 Ibid.

156 Supra note 4 at 128. See also "Cat Stevens wins peace prize" Associated Press, November 11, 2004.

157 Ibid.

158 Editorial, "Moonshadow boxing" The Washington Post, September 25 2004 at A22 available at http://www.washingtonpost.com/wp-dyn/articles/A48928-2004Sep24.html (Accessed June 19, 2009)

159 Sara Kehaulani Goo "Sen. Kennedy flagged by no-fly list" The Washington Post, August 20 2004 available at http://www.msnbc.msn.com/id/5765143 (Accessed June 19, 2009)

160 "Ted Kennedy's Airport Adventure" Associated Press, August 19 2004 available at http://www.cbsnews.com/stories/2004/04/06/terror/main610466.shtml (Accessed June 19, 2009)

161 Supra note 4 at 129.

162 Ibid.

163 Ibid.

164 Editorial, "National insecurity / Keeping America safe from Cat Stevens" Pittsbugh Post-Gazette, September 26 2004 available at http://www.post-gazette.com/pg/04270/385027.stm (Accessed June 19, 2009)

165 Ibid.

166 "Cat Stevens 'shock' at US refusal" British Broadcasting Corporation (BBC), September 23 2004 available at http://news.bbc.co.uk/2/hi/uk_news/3682434.stm (Accessed June 19, 2009)

167 "Cat Stevens honoured by Gorbachev" British Broadcasting Corporation (BBC), November 9 2004 available at http://news.bbc.co.uk/1/hi/entertainment/music/3994905.stm (Accessed June 19, 2009)

168 Ibid.

169 Supra note 4 at 130.

170 "Cat Stevens named 'Man of Peace'" Associated Press, November 10 2004 available at http://www.msnbc.msn.com/id/6444741/ (Accessed June 19, 2009)

171 Supra note 167. See also "Sweet vindication" Miami Herald, November 10, 2004.

Chapter 4: Historical Roots of Muslim Pacifism

1 Hadith Sahih Bukhari, *Vol. 8, Book 73, No. 42,* trans. M. Muhsin Khan. Shaykh al-Amin 'Ali Mazrui, The Content of Character: Ethical Sayings of the Prophet Muhammad, trans. Hamza Yusuf (London: Sandala LLC, 2005), 28.

2 James S. Robbins, "More of the Same on Al-Arabiya," National Review Online, January 28, 2009, http://article.nationalreview.com/?q=YTJiM2U0MDIwYzgwYzVhMWViMDRlMDY4Mjc4NzMyOWU=&w=MQ (Accessed July 14, 2009).

3 See D. G. Tendulkar, Abdul Ghaffar Khan: Faith is a Battle, (Bombay: Popular Prakashan, 1967), 235.

4 Dr. Umar Faruq Abd-Allah, "One God, Many Names," Zaytuna Institute Seasons Journal, Spring/Summer 2004. Full text available at http://muslimpresence.com/?p=3080 (Accessed March 27, 2011)

5 Id.at 47.

6 Surat an-Nahl, Qur'an, Ch. 16, v. 123.

7 D. G. Tendulkar, Abdul Ghaffar Khan: Faith is a Battle, 46.

8 Id at 53.

9 Coleman Barks, "Rumi's Poetry: 'All Religions, All This Singing, One Song'" The Huffington Post, November 2, 2010 available at http://www.huffingtonpost.com/coleman-barks/rumi-and-some-new-ways-to_b_777382.html (Accessed March 26, 2011)

10 Scott Alexander, "We Should Deconstruct Our Supremacist Master Narratives," Islamophobia and Anti-Americanism: Causes and Remedies, (Beltsville, MD: Amana Publications, 2007), 41.

11 John F. Kennedy, Radio and Television Report to the American People on Civil Rights, June 11, 1963, http://www.jfklibrary.org/Historical+Resources/Archives/Reference+Desk/Speeches/JFK/003POF03CivilRights06111963.htm (Accessed August 14, 2009).

12 See Harry Gensler, "The Golden Rule," http://www.jcu.edu/philosophy/gensler/goldrule.htm (Accessed July 20, 2009).

13 Shaykh al-Amin 'Ali Mazrui, The Content of Character: Ethical Sayings of the Prophet Muhammad, trans. Hamza Yusuf, 14.

14 See also B.A. Robinson, "Shared Belief in the 'Golden Rule,'" ReligiousTolerance.org, http://www.religioustolerance.org/reciproc.htm (Accessed July 20, 2009).

15 Amjad Jaimoukha, The Chechens: A Handbook, (New York: Routledge, 2005), 119.

16 See also Robert Schaefer, Insurgency and Chechnya, (Washington: Potomac Books, 2008).

17 Amjad Jaimoukha, The Chechens: A Handbook, 2005.

18 Karl Meyer, "The Peacemaker of the Pashtun Past," New York Times, December 7, 2001, http://www.nytimes.com/2001/12/07/opinion/07MEYE.html (Accessed November 5, 2009)

19 See id.

20 Rajmohan Gandhi, Ghaffar Khan: Nonviolent Badshah of the Pakhtuns, (New Delhi: Penguin Books India, 2004), 3.

21 Ibid at 91.

22 Ibid at 98.

23 Rajmohan Gandhi, Ghaffar Khan: Nonviolent Badshah of the Pakhtuns, 140.

24 D.G. Tendulkar, Abdul Ghaffar Khan: Faith is a Battle, 267-68.

25 Eknath Easwaran, Nonviolent Soldier of Islam: Badshah Khan, A Man to Match His Mountains, (Tomales [CA]: Nilgiri Press, 1999), 233.

26 Rajmohan Gandhi, Ghaffar Khan: Nonviolent Badshah of the Pakhtuns, 264.

27 Ibid at 273.

28 Ibid at 276.

29 Eknath Easwaran, Nonviolent Soldier of Islam, 1999.

30 See Official Website of Al-Azhar University, http://www.azhar.edu.eg/ (Accessed November 7, 2009).

31 Bashar Humeid, "Jawdat Said: Islam as a Violence-free Religion," Qantara (Germany), December 19, 2006, http://www.qantara.de/webcom/show_article.php/_c-575/_nr-17/i.html (Accessed November 7, 2009)

32 Ibid.

33 Ibid.

34 See John J. Donohoe, S.J. "Muslim-Christian Relations: Dialogue in Lebanon." Occasional Papers Series, Washington, DC: Center for Muslim-Christian Understanding, 1996, 9.

35 John L. Esposito, "Pluralism in Muslim-Christian Relations" Occasional Papers Series, Washington DC: Center for Muslim-Christian Understanding, April 2008, 7.

36 Ibid at 6.

37 Ibid at 27.

38 Ibid at 23.

39 See Mohamed Fathi Osman, "The Children of Adam: An Islamic Perspective on Pluralism," Occasional Paper Series, Washington DC: Center for Muslim-Christian Understanding, 1997, 13-21.

40 John L. Esposito, "Pluralism in Muslim-Christian Relations", 33.

41 See John Esposito, Unholy War: Terror in the Name of Islam, (New York: Oxford University Press, 2002), 28.

42 Hadith Sahih Bukhari, *Vol. 2, Book 23, No. 446,* trans. M. Muhsin Khan.

43 Hadith Sahih Bukhari, *Vol. 8, Book 73, No. 135,* trans. M. Muhsin Khan.

44 John Esposito, What Everyone Needs to Know About Islam, (New York: Oxford University Press, 2002), 125.

45 Ibid.

46 Ahmad ibn Naqib al-Misri, Reliance of the Traveler, (Beltsville, MD: 1999), 670 available at http://www.usc.edu/schools/college/crcc/engagement/resources/texts/muslim/hadith/bukhari/023.sbt.html#002.023.445 (Accessed August 25, 2009).

47 Ibid.

48 Dr. Umar Faruq Abd-Allah, "One God, Many Names", 2004.

49 Edward Burman, The Assassins: Holy Killers of Islam, (London: Inner Traditions International), 1988.

50 Asma Afsaruddin, "Jihad and Its Multiple Meanings in the Early Period," in Understanding Jihad: Deconstructing Jihadism, John Esposito and Brian Glenn, Eds., Edmund A. Walsh School of Foreign Service, (Washington DC: Georgetown University, 2007).

51 See Ibn Abi al-Dunya, Al-Sabr wa-'l-thawab 'alayhi (Beirut, 1997) at 85.

52 See Mishkat, Book of Rulership and Judgment, ch. 1, sec. 2

53 See Mahmoud Khalaf Jarad al-Issawi, Fiqh al-ghazw (Islamic Jurisprudence of Battle), (Amman: Dar Ammar Printing Press, 2000), 151-209.

54 Michael Young, "The Islamic Rules of Warfare," Islam For Today, September 16, 2001, http://www.islamfortoday.com/war.htm (Accessed August 28, 2009)

55 Hadith Sahih Bukhari, *Vol. 6, Book 60, No. 362,* trans. M. Muhsin Khan.

56 See also, Mohamad Baianonie, "Jihad in Islam, I," December 2, 1994, sermon, Islamic Association of Raleigh, http://islam1.org/khutub/Jihad%20in%20Islam%201.htm (Accessed August 30, 2009).

57 Hadith Sahih Bukhari, *Vol. 8, Book 75, No. 135,* trans. M. Muhsin Khan.

58 Population Reference Bureau (PRB), "Secondary School Enrollment, Female, 2002/2004," available at http://www.prb.org/Datafinder/Topic/Bar.aspx?sort=v&order=d&variable=28 (Accessed August 3, 2009).

Chapter 5: Ungodly Terror: Bali, Madrid and London

1 Al Goodman, "Madrid train bomb suspect moved to Spain," CNN.com, August 12, 2009 available at http://www.cnn.com/2009/WORLD/europe/08/12/spain.bomb.suspect/ (Accessed September 15, 2009).

2 Francie Grace, "Madrid Massacre Probe Widens," CBS News, March 11, 2004 available at http://www.cbsnews.com/stories/2004/03/12/world/main605547.shtml (Accessed September 15, 2009).

3 Ibid.

4 British Broadcasting Corporation (BBC), "Madrid Attacks Timeline," March 12, 2004 available at http://news.bbc.co.uk/2/hi/europe/3504912.stm (Accessed September 15, 2009).

5 Ibid.

6 Ibid.

7 Supra note 4.

8 Ibid.

9 Ibid.

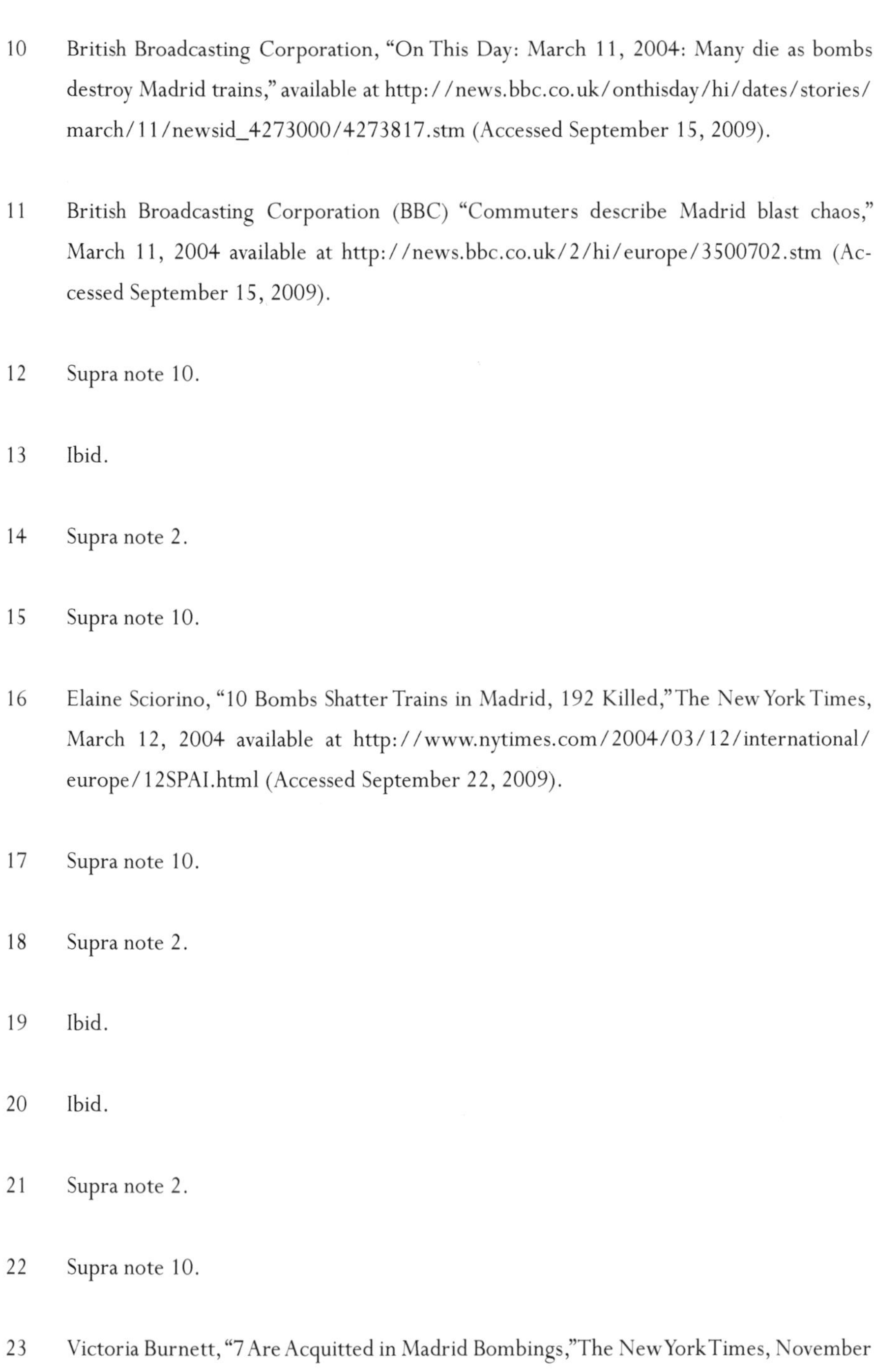

10 British Broadcasting Corporation, "On This Day: March 11, 2004: Many die as bombs destroy Madrid trains," available at http://news.bbc.co.uk/onthisday/hi/dates/stories/march/11/newsid_4273000/4273817.stm (Accessed September 15, 2009).

11 British Broadcasting Corporation (BBC) "Commuters describe Madrid blast chaos," March 11, 2004 available at http://news.bbc.co.uk/2/hi/europe/3500702.stm (Accessed September 15, 2009).

12 Supra note 10.

13 Ibid.

14 Supra note 2.

15 Supra note 10.

16 Elaine Sciorino, "10 Bombs Shatter Trains in Madrid, 192 Killed," The New York Times, March 12, 2004 available at http://www.nytimes.com/2004/03/12/international/europe/12SPAI.html (Accessed September 22, 2009).

17 Supra note 10.

18 Supra note 2.

19 Ibid.

20 Ibid.

21 Supra note 2.

22 Supra note 10.

23 Victoria Burnett, "7 Are Acquitted in Madrid Bombings," The New York Times, November 1, 2007 available at http://www.nytimes.com/2007/11/01/world/europe/01spain.html (Accessed September 22, 2009).

24 Ibid.

25 Supra note 10.

26 British Broadcasting Corporation, "Madrid bombing suspects," March 10, 2005 available at http://news.bbc.co.uk/2/hi/europe/3560603.stm (Accessed September 15, 2009).

27 Britsh Broadcasting Corporation, "Madrid Bombings: Defendants"..July 17, 2008, http://news.bbc.co.uk/2/hi/europe/4899544.stm (Accessed April 18, 2011)

28 Ibid.

29 Agence France Press (AFP), "Muslims issue bin Laden fatwa," March 11, 2005 available at http://wwrn.org/articles/15860/?&place=spain-portugal (Accessed April 5, 2011).

30 "Pain Still Raw as Spain Remembers Victims," Deutsche Welle, November 3, 2005, available at http://www.dw-world.de/dw/article/0,,1515442,00.html (Accessed April 18, 2011).

31 "American Muslims Should Speak Up,"The News-Times (CT), March 18, 2005, http://www.newstimes.com/news/article/American-Muslims-should-speak-up-238423.php (Accessed April 18, 2011).

32 "Report of the Official Account of the Bombings in London on 7th July 2005,"The British House of Commons, May 11, 2006. Full text of report available at http://news.bbc.co.uk/2/shared/bsp/hi/pdfs/11_05_06_narrative.pdf (Accessed September 15, 2009).

33 Ibid at pg. 4.

34 British Broadcasting Corporation, "In Depth: 7 July Bombings," available at http://news.bbc.co.uk/2/shared/spl/hi/uk/05/london_blasts/what_happened/html/ (Accessed September 15, 2009)

35 Ibid.

36 See id.

37 British Broadcasting Corporation, "In Depth: Russell Square," available at http://news.bbc.co.uk/2/shared/spl/hi/uk/05/london_blasts/what_happened/html/russell_sq.stm (Accessed September 15, 2009).

38 British Broadcasting Corporation, "In Depth: Aldgate," available at http://news.bbc.co.uk/2/shared/spl/hi/uk/05/london_blasts/what_happened/html/aldgate.stm (Accessed September 15, 2009).

39 British Broadcasting Corporation, "In Depth: Edgeware Road," available at http://news.bbc.co.uk/2/shared/spl/hi/uk/05/london_blasts/what_happened/html/edgware_rd.stm (Accessed September 15, 2009).

40 British Broadcasting Corporation, "In Depth: Tavistock Square," available at http://news.bbc.co.uk/2/shared/spl/hi/uk/05/london_blasts/what_happened/html/tavistock.stm (Accessed September 15, 2009).

41 British Broadcasting Corporation, "In Depth: London Attacks" available at http://news.bbc.co.uk/2/shared/spl/hi/uk/05/london_blasts/victims/ (Accessed September 22, 2009).

42 Supra note 32.

43 Ibid.

44 Supra note 32 at 19.

45 Ibid.

46 See ibid.

47 Associated Press, "Al-Qaeda Claims Responsibility for London Bombings," September 1, 2005 available at http://www.foxnews.com/story/0,2933,168207,00.html (Accessed September 15, 2009).

48 Ibid.

49 See ibid.

50 Supra note 32 at 21.

51 "Report of the 7 July Review Committee," London Assembly, June 2006. Full text available at http://news.bbc.co.uk/2/shared/bsp/hi/pdfs/05_06_06_london_bombing.pdf (Accessed September 15, 2009)

52 British Broadcasting Corporation, "Full text: Fatwa issued after London bombs," July 19, 2005 available at http://news.bbc.co.uk/1/hi/uk/4697365.stm (Accessed April 2, 2009).

53 Ibid.

54 CNN, "Bali terrorist attacks kill at least 26," October 2, 2005, available at http://edition.cnn.com/2005/WORLD/asiapcf/10/01/bali.blasts/index.html (Accessed September 15, 2009).

55 Ibid.

56 Ibid.

57 Ibid.

58 British Broadcasting Corporation, "Bali bombs were suicide attacks," October 2, 2005, available at http://news.bbc.co.uk/2/hi/asia-pacific/4301630.stm (Accessed September 15, 2009).

59 British Broadcasting Corporation, "Bali bomb attacks claim 26 lives," October 2, 2005 available at http://news.bbc.co.uk/2/hi/asia-pacific/4300274.stm (Accessed September 15, 2009).

60 Supra note 54.

61 Australian Broadcasting Corporation, "Bali bombings: Eyewitness accounts," October 3, 2005 available at http://www.abc.net.au/news/indepth/featureitems/s1472756.htm (Accessed September 15, 2009).

62 Supra note 54.

63 Supra note 54.

64 Associated Press (AP), "Police: Bali bombing suspect narrowly escaped raid," USA TODAY, October 7, 2005 available at http://www.usatoday.com/news/world/2005-10-07-balisuspect_x.htm (Accessed September 15, 2009).

65 Ibid.

66 Ibid.

67 Ibid.

68 Ibid.

69 James Sturcke, "Bali bombing suspect 'blows himself up,'" The Guardian (UK) Newspaper, November 9, 2005 available at http://www.guardian.co.uk/world/2005/nov/09/terrorism.indonesia (Accessed September 15, 2009).

70 British Broadcasting Corporation, "Indonesian jailed for Bali bomb," September 14, 2006 available at http://news.bbc.co.uk/2/hi/asia-pacific/5344396.stm (Accessed September 15, 2009).

71 Ibid.

72 British Broadcasting Corporation, "Profile: Noordin Mohamed Top," August 12, 2009, available at http://news.bbc.co.uk/2/hi/asia-pacific/4302368.stm (Accessed September 15, 2009).

73 Ibid.

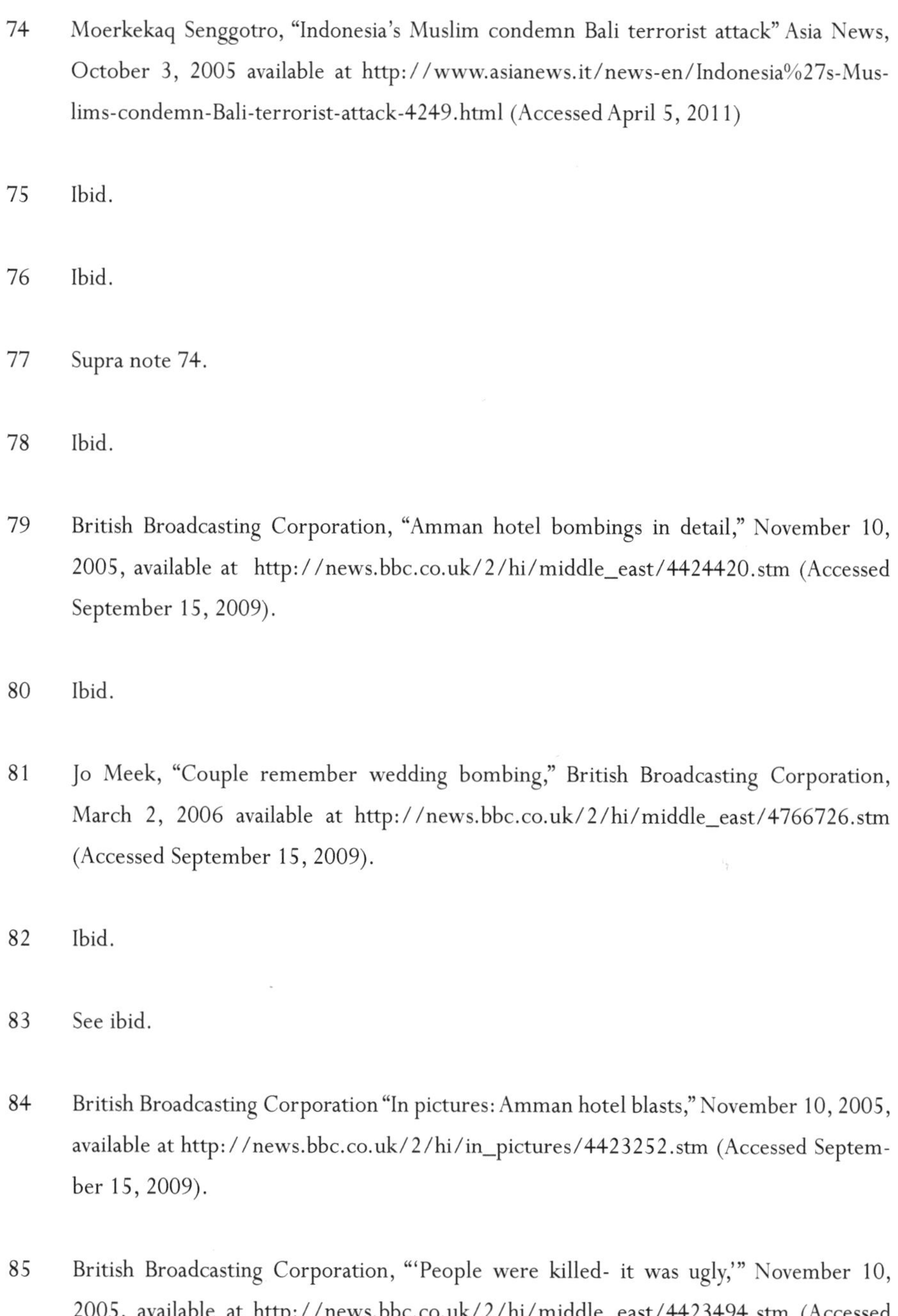

74 Moerkekaq Senggotro, "Indonesia's Muslim condemn Bali terrorist attack" Asia News, October 3, 2005 available at http://www.asianews.it/news-en/Indonesia%27s-Muslims-condemn-Bali-terrorist-attack-4249.html (Accessed April 5, 2011)

75 Ibid.

76 Ibid.

77 Supra note 74.

78 Ibid.

79 British Broadcasting Corporation, "Amman hotel bombings in detail," November 10, 2005, available at http://news.bbc.co.uk/2/hi/middle_east/4424420.stm (Accessed September 15, 2009).

80 Ibid.

81 Jo Meek, "Couple remember wedding bombing," British Broadcasting Corporation, March 2, 2006 available at http://news.bbc.co.uk/2/hi/middle_east/4766726.stm (Accessed September 15, 2009).

82 Ibid.

83 See ibid.

84 British Broadcasting Corporation "In pictures: Amman hotel blasts," November 10, 2005, available at http://news.bbc.co.uk/2/hi/in_pictures/4423252.stm (Accessed September 15, 2009).

85 British Broadcasting Corporation, "'People were killed- it was ugly,'" November 10, 2005, available at http://news.bbc.co.uk/2/hi/middle_east/4423494.stm (Accessed September 15, 2009).

86 Supra note 81.

87 Ibid.

88 Supra note 85.

89 Ibid.

90 British Broadcasting Corporation, "Failed Amman hotel bomber to hang," September 21, 2006, available at http://news.bbc.co.uk/2/hi/middle_east/5366438.stm (Accessed September 15, 2009).

91 Associated Press, "Hollywood producer, daughter died in bombing," November 11, 2005 available at http://www.msnbc.msn.com/id/10002363/a (Accessed September 27, 2009).

92 See also http://www.aaiusa.org/press-room/2165/mustread111205 (Accessed September 23, 2009).

93 Merissa Khurma, "This is Our 9-11," National Public Radio (NPR), November 11, 2005 available at http://www.npr.org/templates/story/story.php?storyId=5010212 (Accessed September 23, 2009).

94 Hassan Fattah, "Angry Jordanians protest bombings,"The New York Times, November 10, 2005 available at http://www.nytimes.com/2005/11/10/world/africa/10iht-jordan.html (Accessed September 15, 2009).

95 Ibid.

96 Ed O'Loughlin, "Al-Qaeda in Iraq claims Amman bombings," Sydney Morning Herald, November 11, 2005, available at http://www.smh.com.au/news/world/alqaeda-in-iraq-claims-amman-bombings/2005/11/10/1131578177741.html (Accessed September 15, 2009).

97 AFX News Limited, "Top Jordanian official says Zarqawi likely suspect in Amman bombing," November 9, 2005 available at http://www.forbes.com/feeds/afx/2005/11/09/afx2328543.html (Accessed September 15, 2009).

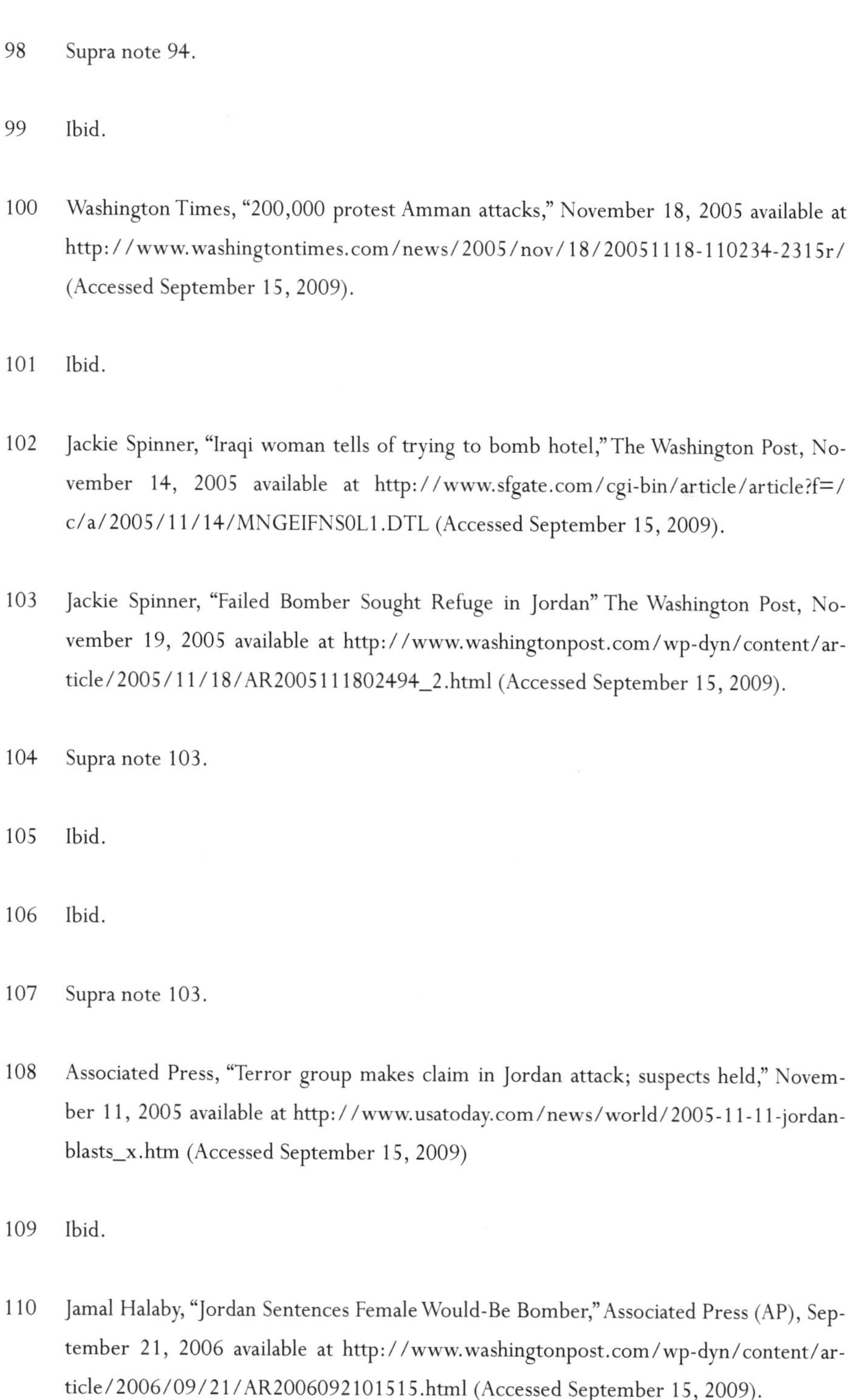

98 Supra note 94.

99 Ibid.

100 Washington Times, “200,000 protest Amman attacks,” November 18, 2005 available at http://www.washingtontimes.com/news/2005/nov/18/20051118-110234-2315r/ (Accessed September 15, 2009).

101 Ibid.

102 Jackie Spinner, “Iraqi woman tells of trying to bomb hotel,” The Washington Post, November 14, 2005 available at http://www.sfgate.com/cgi-bin/article/article?f=/c/a/2005/11/14/MNGEIFNS0L1.DTL (Accessed September 15, 2009).

103 Jackie Spinner, “Failed Bomber Sought Refuge in Jordan” The Washington Post, November 19, 2005 available at http://www.washingtonpost.com/wp-dyn/content/article/2005/11/18/AR2005111802494_2.html (Accessed September 15, 2009).

104 Supra note 103.

105 Ibid.

106 Ibid.

107 Supra note 103.

108 Associated Press, “Terror group makes claim in Jordan attack; suspects held,” November 11, 2005 available at http://www.usatoday.com/news/world/2005-11-11-jordan-blasts_x.htm (Accessed September 15, 2009)

109 Ibid.

110 Jamal Halaby, “Jordan Sentences Female Would-Be Bomber,” Associated Press (AP), September 21, 2006 available at http://www.washingtonpost.com/wp-dyn/content/article/2006/09/21/AR2006092101515.html (Accessed September 15, 2009).

111 Ibid.

112 Ibid.

113 Supra note 110.

114 Ibid.

115 Ibid..

116 Asharq Alawsat (UK) Newspaper, "Jordan: Iraqi Woman's Death Sentence Upheld," January 27, 2007 available at http://aawsat.com/english/news.asp?section=1&id=7807 (Accessed September 15, 2009).

117 Ellen Knickmeyer and Jonathan Finer, "Insurgent Leader Al-Zarqawi Killed in Iraq," Washington Post Foreign Service, June 8, 2006 available at http://www.washingtonpost.com/wp-dyn/content/article/2006/06/08/AR2006060800114.html (Accessed September 23, 2009).

118 British Broadcasting Corporation (BBC), "Obituary: Benazir Bhutto," December 27, 2007 available at http://news.bbc.co.uk/2/hi/south_asia/2228796.stm (Accessed September 15, 2009).

119 Ibid.

120 John F. Burns, "Pakistan's Premier Bhutto is Put Under House Arrest," The New York Times, November 5, 1996, available at http://query.nytimes.com/gst/fullpage.html?res=980CE2D61238F936A35752C1A960958260&pagewanted=1 (Accessed April 18, 2011). See also "Pakistan Ex-Premier's Spouse Indicted for Murder", The New York Times, July 6, 1997 available at http://select.nytimes.com/gst/abstract.html?res=FA0B12FB35540C758CDDAE0894DF494D81 (Accessed April 18, 2011).

121 Ibid.

122 Supra note 118.

123 Ibid.

124 Supra note 118.

125 Ibid.

126 MSNBC, "2 Blasts Strike Crowd Celebrating Bhutto's Return," December 29, 2007 available at http://www.msnbc.msn.com/id/21344367/ (Accessed September 27, 2009).

127 British Broadcasting Corporation (BBC) "UN opens Bhutto probe in Pakistan," July 16, 2009 available at http://news.bbc.co.uk/2/hi/south_asia/8153182.stm (Accessed September 15, 2009).

128 Ibid.

129 Supra note 126.

130 Isambard Wilkinson, "Benazir Bhutto killed in gun and bomb attack" The Telegraph (UK) Newspaper, December 27, 2007 available at http://www.telegraph.co.uk/news/worldnews/1573794/Benazir-Bhutto-killed-in-gun-and-bomb-attack.html (Accessed September 15, 2009).

131 Simon Robinson, "Bhutto Conspiracy Theories Fill the Air," TIME Magazine, December 28, 2007 available at http://www.time.com/time/world/article/0,8599,1698828,00.html?cnn=yes (Accessed September 15, 2009)

132 Supra note 126.

133 Supra note 130.

134 Ibid.

135 Ibid.

136 Arsalan Iftikhar, "Good night, Benazir," DiversityInc Magazine, December 28, 2007 available at http://diversityinc.com/content/1757/article/2883/ (Accessed September 24, 2009).

137 Arsalan Iftikhar, "The Madness of King Musharraf," Providence Journal, November 13, 2007 available at http://www.projo.com/opinion/contributors/content/CT_pakistan12_11-12-07_H67OOJ1_v16.359549e.html (Accessed September 24, 2009).

138 Mark Thompson, Brian Bennett, "Where Bhutto's Death Leaves the U.S." Time Magazine, December 27, 2007, available at http://www.time.com/time/world/article/0,8599,1698562,00.html (accessed April 18, 2011).

139 British Broadcasting Corporation, "Bhutto suspects 'confess to role,'" February 13, 2008 available at http://news.bbc.co.uk/2/hi/south_asia/7243892.stm (Accessed September 15, 2009). See also British Broadcasating Corporation, "UN opens Bhutto probe in Pakistan," July 16, 2009, available at http://news.bbc.co.uk/2/hi/south_asia/8153182.stm (Accessed April 18, 2011).

140 British Broadcasting Corporation, "UN opens Bhutto probe in Pakistan," July 16, 2009, available at http://news.bbc.co.uk/2/hi/south_asia/8153182.stm (Accessed April 18, 2011).

141 Supra note 138.

142 Supra note 139.

143 Ibid.

144 Ibid.

145 Andre de Nesnera, "World Leaders Condemn Bhutto Assassination," Voice of America (VOA) News, December 27, 2007 available at http://www.voanews.com/english/archive/2007-12/2007-12-27-voa50.cfm?CFID=271953321&CFTOKEN=20386289&jsessionid=00301da95f21042782083b6e55b377c2e703 (Accessed September 15, 2009).

146 Arsalan Iftikhar, "The madness in Pakistan,"The Providence (RI) Journal, January 5, 2008 available at http://www.projo.com/opinion/contributors/content/CT_ars5_01-05-08_E58DRNQ_v9.2b10476.html (Accessed October 1, 2009).

147 "Marriott Islamabad Reopens," Pakistan Travel & Culture Blog, December 28, 2008, available at http://blog.travel-culture.com/2008/12/marriott-islamabad-reopens/ (Accessed September 15, 2009).

148 Isambard Wilkerson, "Islamabad Marriott hotel bomb killed Czech ambassador and 51 others, says Pakistan,"The Telegraph (UK) Newspaper, September 21, 2008 available at http://www.telegraph.co.uk/news/worldnews/asia/pakistan/3041376/Islamabad-Marriott-hotel-bomb-killed-Czech-ambassador-and-51-others-says-Pakistan.html (Accessed September 15, 2009).

149 Omar Waraich, "Blast Leaves Pakistan Shaken," TIME Magazine, September 21, 2008 available at http://www.time.com/time/world/article/0,8599,1843169,00.html (Accessed September 15, 2009).

150 Ibid.

151 Supra note 148.

152 Supra note 149.

153 Ibid.

154 Ibid.

155 Supra note 148.

156 Supra note 149.

157 Ibid.

158 Ibid.

159 Canadian Broadcasting Corporation (CBC) "4 Pakistanis arrested in Islamabad Marriott Hotel bombing," October 24, 2008 available at http://www.cbc.ca/world/story/2008/10/24/marriott-arrests.html (Accessed September 15, 2009).

160 Reuters, "Pakistan arrests suspect in Marriott bombing," August 1, 2009 available at http://www.reuters.com/article/latestCrisis/idUSISL468374 (Accessed September 15, 2009)

161 Laura King, "Islamabad Marriott reopens three months after truck bombing," Los Angeles Times, December 29, 2008 available at http://articles.latimes.com/2008/dec/29/world/fg-pakistan-hotel29 (Accessed September 15, 2009).

162 Supra note 147.

163 Supra note 161.

164 British Broadcasting Corporation "Excerpts from Mumbai Suspect's Confession," July 20, 2009 available at http://news.bbc.co.uk/2/hi/south_asia/8160243.stm (Accessed September 15, 2009).

165 British Broadcasting Corporation (BBC), "Mumbai Attacks: Key Sites" December 2, 2008 available at http://news.bbc.co.uk/2/hi/south_asia/7751876.stm (Accessed September 15, 2009).

166 Ibid.

167 British Broadcasting Corporation, "Officials quit over India attack," November 27, 2008 available at http://news.bbc.co.uk/2/hi/south_asia/7751707.stm (Accessed September 15, 2009).

168 Supra note 165.

169 Ibid.

170 Ibid.

171 Supra note 165.

172 Prachi Pinglay, "Bereaved Mother at Mumbai Trial," British Broadcasting Corporation (BBC), June 11, 2009 available at http://news.bbc.co.uk/2/hi/south_asia/8095753.stm (Accessed September 15, 2009).

173 Prachi Pinglay, "Girl 'identifies Mumbai gunman'" British Broadcasting Corporation (BBC), June 10, 2009 available at http://news.bbc.co.uk/2/hi/south_asia/8093749.stm (Accessed September 15, 2009).

174 Aryn Baker, "Pakistan in Denial Over Alleged Links to Mumbai Attack," TIME Magazine, February 4, 2009 available at http://www.time.com/time/world/article/0,8599,1877048,00.html?iid=fb_share (Accessed September 15, 2009).

175 Rajesh Shah, "Gunman in Mumbai attacks says he is guilty," Associated Press (AP), July 21, 2009 available at http://www.boston.com/news/world/asia/articles/2009/07/21/gunman_in_mumbai_attacks_says_he_is_guilty_links_plot_to_pakistani_group/ (Accessed September 15, 2009).

176 Matthew Taylor, "Mumbai terror suspect admits role in shootings," The Guardian (UK) Newspaper, July 20, 2009 available at http://www.guardian.co.uk/world/2009/jul/20/mumbai-terror-attacks-india-gunman (Accessed September 15, 2009).

177 Supra note 164.

178 Prachi Pinglay, "Shock and surprise in Mumbai court," British Broadcasting Corporation (BBC), July 20, 2009 available at http://news.bbc.co.uk/2/hi/south_asia/8159788.stm (Accessed September 15, 2009).

179 "Main Mumbai suspect pleads guilty" British Broadcasting Corporation (BBC), July 20, 2009 available at http://news.bbc.co.uk/2/hi/south_asia/8158741.stm (Accessed September 15, 2009).

180 Safiya Boucaud, "Pakistan authorities place Mumbai terror attack suspect under house arrest," University of Pittsburgh School of Law 'Jurist', September 21, 2009 available

at http://jurist.law.pitt.edu/paperchase/2009/09/pakistan-authorities-place-mumbai.php (Accessed September 25, 2009).

181 "India," CIA World Factbook, available at https://www.cia.gov/library/publications/the-world-factbook/rankorder/2119rank.html (Accessed September 28, 2009).

182 Zubair Ahmed, "Muslims refuse to bury militants," British Broadcasting Corporation (BBC), December 1, 2008 available at http://news.bbc.co.uk/2/hi/south_asia/7758651.stm (Accessed September 25, 2009).

183 "Bali and Indonesia," Indo.Com, available at http://www.indo.com/indonesia/archipelago.html (Accessed September 25, 2009).

184 British Broadcasting Corporation, "Fatal blasts hit Jakarta hotels," July 17, 2009 available at http://news.bbc.co.uk/2/hi/asia-pacific/8155084.stm (Accessed September 25, 2009).

185 CNN.com, "Police say Jakarta hotel bombers were guests," July 18, 2009 available at http://edition.cnn.com/2009/WORLD/asiapcf/07/17/indonesia.hotels.explosions/ (Accessed September 25, 2009).

186 Ibid.

187 Council on Foreign Relations, "Backgrounder: Jemaah Islamiya," June 19, 2009, available at http://www.cfr.org/indonesia/jemaah-islamiyah-k-jemaah-islamiah/p8948 (Accessed April 18, 2011).

188 British Broadcasting Corporation, "Hambali: 'Asia's bin Laden,'" September 6, 2006 available at http://news.bbc.co.uk/2/hi/asia-pacific/2346225.stm (Accessed September 25, 2009).

189 British Broadcasting Corporation (BBC), "Bush admits to secret CIA prisons," September 7, 2006 available at http://news.bbc.co.uk/2/hi/americas/5321606.stm (Accessed September 25, 2009).

190 World News Australia, "Factfile: 2003 Jakarta Marriott Blast," July 17, 2009 available at http://www.sbs.com.au/news/article/1052587/Factfile—2003-Jakarta-Marriott-blast (Accessed September 25, 2009).

191 Supra note 185.

192 Department of Homeland Security Office of Intelligence and Analysis, "International Terrorists Remain Focused on Targeting Luxury Hotels," September 21, 2009, 1, available at http://cnnac360.files.wordpress.com/2009/09/cip-fouo-notice-62-09-international-terrorists-remain-focused-on-targeting-luxury-hotels.pdf (Accessed September 25, 2009).

193 Ibid.

194 Imran Rosyid and Anthony Deutsch, "Terror mastermind Noordin Top killed in Indonesia," The Herald-Sun, September 17, 2009 available at http://www.heraldsun.com/view/full_story/3629108/article-Terror-mastermind-killed-in-Indonesia (Accessed September 25, 2009).

195 Scott Shane, "Rethinking Our Terrorist Fears,"The New York Times, September 26, 2009 available at http://www.nytimes.com/2009/09/27/weekinreview/27shane.html?_r=1 (Accessed September 29, 2009)

196 Ibid.

197 Ibid.

198 Supra note 195.

199 Pew Research Center: Pew Global Attitudes Project, "Key Indicators Database" available at http://pewglobal.org/database/?indicator=19&mode=table (Accessed September 29, 2009).

200 Supra note 195.

201 Ibid.

202 Ibid.

203 Dinesh, D'Souza, "Muslims Who Renounce Violence," A Common World, February 20, 2008 available at http://www.acommonword.com/index.php?page=media&item=338 (Accessed April 18, 2011).

Chapter 6: Bombs Over Baghdad

1 Transcript of President Bush's Address to a Joint Session of Congress, CNN.com, September 20, 2001, available at http://archives.cnn.com/2001/US/09/20/gen.bush.transcript/ (Accessed October 7, 2009).

2 Ibid.

3 CIA The World Factbook, "Afghanistan," available at https://www.cia.gov/library/publications/the-world-factbook/geos/af.html (Accessed October 7, 2009).

4 Supra note 1.

5 CNN.com, "U.S. and Coalition Casualties: Afghanistan," October 6, 2009, available at http://www.cnn.com/SPECIALS/2004/oef.casualties/ (Accessed October 7, 2009) .

6 Supra note 1.

7 Ted Galen Carpenter and Malou Innocent, "Escaping the 'Graveyard of Empires': A Strategy to Exit Afghanistan," CATO Institute, September 14, 2009, available at http://www.cato.org/pub_display.php?pub_id=10533 (Accessed October 7, 2009).

8 Henry Kissinger, "Deployments and Diplomacy," Newsweek magazine, October 12, 2009 at 38-40 available at http://www.newsweek.com/id/216704 (Accessed October 7, 2009).

9 Supra note 7.

10 Scott Rosenberg, "Infinite justice?" Salon.com, September 20, 2001, available at http://archive.salon.com/news/feature/2001/09/20/infinite_justice/ (Accessed October 7, 2009).

11 Ibid.

12 British Broadcasting Corporation (BBC), "Infinite Justice, out - Enduring Freedom, in" September 25, 2001 available at http://news.bbc.co.uk/2/hi/americas/1563722.stm (Accessed October 7, 2009).

13 Ibid.

14 National Geographic News, "U.S.-led Coalition Continues Bombing in Afghanistan," October 9, 2001 available at http://news.nationalgeographic.com/news/2001/10/1009_endfree2.html (Accessed October 7, 2009).

15 British Broadcasting Corporation (BBC), "US strikes continue in daylight," October 10, 2001 available at http://news.bbc.co.uk/2/hi/south_asia/1589334.stm (Accessed October 7, 2009).

16 British Broadcasting Corporation (BBC), "Summary of targets so far," October 10, 2001 available at http://news.bbc.co.uk/2/hi/south_asia/1589291.stm (Accessed October 7, 2009).

17 Carolyn Lauer, "The Daisy Cutter Bomb: Largest Conventional Bomb in Existence," University of Notre Dame Technical Review Engineering Magazine, Spring 2002 available at http://www.nd.edu/~techrev/Archive/Spring2002/a8.html (Accessed October 7, 2009).

18 Ibid.

19 Jo Thomas, McVeigh Defense Team Suggests Real Bomber was Killed in Blast, New York Times, May 23, 1997 available at http://www.nytimes.com/1997/05/23/

us/mcveigh-defense-team-suggests-real-bomber-was-killed-in-blast.html?sec=&spon=&pagewanted=all (Accessed October 28, 2009).

20 Supra note 19.

21 Donna Leinwand, Toni Locy and Vivienne Walt, "U.S. expected to target Afghanistan's opium," USA TODAY, October 16, 2001 available at http://www.usatoday.com/news/sept11/2001/10/16/opium-usatcov.htm (Accessed October 8, 2009).

22 Ibid.

23 James Risen, "Reports link Karzai's Brother to Afghanistan Heroin Trade,"The New York Times, October 4, 2008 available at http://www.nytimes.com/2008/10/05/world/asia/05afghan.html?pagewanted=all (Accessed October 8, 2009)

24 Ibid.

25 Ibid.

26 Ibid.

27 Supra note 23.

28 Ibid.

29 Ibid.

30 Mary Anne Weaver, "Lost at Tora Bora,"The New York Times Magazine, September 11, 2005 available at http://www.nytimes.com/2005/09/11/magazine/11TORABORA.html (Accessed October 8, 2009).

31 Philip Smucker, "How bin Laden got away," The Christian Science Monitor, March 4, 2002 available at http://www.csmonitor.com/2002/0304/p01s03-wosc.htm (Accessed October 8, 2009).

32 Ibid.

33 See http://www.faz.net/s/Rub594835B672714A1DB1A121534F010EE1/Doc~E87B146CDF6B04C2C9619AF3025BA6A8C~ATpl~Ecommon~Scontent.html (Accessed October 8, 2009)

34 Supra note 31.

35 Supra note 30.

36 Ibid.

37 Internet Movie Data Base (IMDB), "Memorable quotes from 'The Usual Suspects'" available at http://www.imdb.com/title/tt0114814/quotes (Accessed October 28, 2009),

38 Tommy Franks, "War of Words," The New York Times, October 19, 2004 available at http://www.nytimes.com/2004/10/19/opinion/19franks.html (Accessed October 8, 2009).

39 Supra note 30.

40 Sean Naylor, "Operation Anaconda," Massachusetts Institute of Technology Security Studies Program Seminar, March 22, 2006 available at http://web.mit.edu/ssp/seminars/wed_archives06spring/naylor.htm (Accessed May 1, 2011).

41 TIME Magazine, "Operation Anaconda," March 10, 2002 available at http://www.time.com/time/covers/1101020318/popup/1.html (Accessed May 1, 2011).

42 Ibid.

43 Ibid.

44 Ibid.

45 Ibid.

46 CNN.com "Operation Anaconda costs 8 U.S. lives," March 4, 2002 available at http://archives.cnn.com/2002/WORLD/asiapcf/central/03/04/ret.afghan.fighting/ (Accessed October 8, 2009).

47 Kenneth Katzman, "Afghanistan: Post-Taliban Governance, Security, and U.S. Policy," Congressional Research Service (CRS), July 20, 2009 available at http://fpc.state.gov/documents/organization/126512.pdf (Accessed May 1, 2011).

48 S.C. Res. 1378, (November 14 2001), available at http://www.un.org/News/Press/docs/2001/sc7212.doc.htm (Accessed May 1, 2011).

49 Agreement on Provisional Arrangements in Afghanistan Pending the Re-Establishment of Permanent Government Institutions ("Bonn Agreement"), S/2001/1154, (December 5, 2001), available at http://www.un.org/News/dh/latest/afghan/afghan-agree.htm (Accessed May 1, 2011). See also supra note 47.

50 S.C. Res. 1383 (December 6, 2001), available at http://daccess-dds-ny.un.org/doc/UNDOC/GEN/N01/681/09/PDF/N0168109.pdf?OpenElement (Accessed May 1, 2011).

51 Supra note 47.

52 Ibid.

53 Ibid.

54 The White House, "White Paper of the Interagency Policy Group's Report on U.S. Policy toward Afghanistan and Pakistan," March 2009 available at http://www.whitehouse.gov/assets/documents/Afghanistan-Pakistan_White_Paper.pdf (Accessed October 10, 2009).

55 Ibid.

56 Ibid at 2-6.

57 Ibid at 6.

58 Supra note 47.

59 The Times (UK) of London, "PROFILE: Stanley McChrystal," October 4, 2009 available at http://www.timesonline.co.uk/tol/news/world/afghanistan/article6860114.ece (Accessed May 1, 2011)

60 Ibid.

61 Ibid.

62 Bob Woodward, "McChrystal: More Forces or 'Mission Failure'," Washington Post, September 21, 2009 available at http://www.washingtonpost.com/wp-dyn/content/article/2009/09/20/AR2009092002920.html (Accessed October 10, 2009).

63 Ibid.

64 Ibid.

65 Supra note 62.

66 Ibid.

67 John Milburn, "Obama picks Army general to lead Afghan training," The Seattle Times (Associated Press), October 9, 2009 available at http://seattletimes.nwsource.com/html/nationworld/2010034328_apusafghanistancommander.html (Accessed May 1, 2011).

68 Ibid.

69 Supra note 62.

70 Supra note 62.

71 Alex Spillius, "White House angry at General Stanley McChrystal speech on Afghanistan," The Telegraph (UK) Newspaper, October 5, 2009 available at http://www.telegraph.co.uk/news/worldnews/northamerica/usa/barackobama/6259582/White-House-angry-at-General-Stanley-McChrystal-speech-on-Afghanistan.html (Accessed October 10, 2009). See also Speech, General Stanley McChrystal, London, UK, October 2009, full video available at http://www.iiss.org/recent-key-addresses/general-stanley-mcchrystal-address/watch-the-address/ (Accessed October 10, 2009).

72 Ibid.

73 Ibid.

74 Ibid.

75 Supra note 71.

76 Robert Mackey, "It's a Thin Line" The New York Times, March 2, 2007 available at http://thelede.blogs.nytimes.com/2007/03/02/its-a-thin-line/ (Accessed October 12, 2009)

77 Robert Mackey, "It's a Thin Line" The New York Times, March 2, 2007 available at http://thelede.blogs.nytimes.com/2007/03/02/its-a-thin-line/ (Accessed October 12, 2009)

78 Durand Line Agreement, November 12, 1893, available at http://www.khyber.org/pashtohistory/treaties/durandagreement.shtml (Accessed October 12, 2009).

79 Ibid.

80 Ibid.

81 Robert Mackey, "How Many Troops to Secure Afghanistan?" The New York Times, September 21, 2009 available at http://thelede.blogs.nytimes.com/tag/the-durand-line/ (Accessed October 12, 2009).

82 Robert Mackey, Pakistan's British-Drawn Borders, The New York Times, May 5, 2009 available at http://thelede.blogs.nytimes.com/2009/05/05/pakistans-british-drawn-borders/ (Accessed May 1, 2011).

83 Vartan Gregorian, "The Yearnings of the Pashtuns," The New York Times, November 15, 2001 available at http://www.nytimes.com/2001/11/15/opinion/the-yearnings-of-the-pashtuns.html (Accessed October 12, 2009).

84 Barnett Rubin, "Saving Afghanistan," Foreign Affairs, January/February 2007 available at http://www.nytimes.com/cfr/world/20070101faessay_v86n1_rubin.html?pagewanted=1 (Accessed October 12, 2009).

85 Hafizullah Gardesh and Wahidullah Amani, "Bad Fences Make Bad Neighbors," Institute for War and Peace Reporting, October 28, 2005 available at http://iwpr.net/report-news/bad-fences-make-bad-neighbours (Accessed October 12, 2009).

86 Ibid.

87 Turki al-Faisal, "A To-Do List for Afghanistan," The Washington Post, October 9, 2009 available at http://www.washingtonpost.com/wp-dyn/content/article/2009/10/08/AR2009100803805.html (Accessed October 12, 2009)

88 United States Committee on Refugees and Immigrants (USCRI), www.refugees.org (Accessed October 12, 2009).

89 See Lavinia Limon, "A Race to the Bottom," U.S. Committee for Refugees and Immigrants (USCRI), 2008 World Refugee Survey, Annual Report available at http://www.uscrirefugees.org/2010Website/5_Resources/5_5_Refugee_Warehousing/5_5_4_Archived_World_Refugee_Surveys/5_5_4_6_World_Refugee_Survey_2008/5_5_4_6_2_Articles/The_Race_to_the_Bottom.pdf (Accessed May 1, 2011).

90 CNN.com, "Angelina Jolie brings attention to plight of refugees," June 18, 2009 available at http://www.cnn.com/2009/US/06/18/world.refugee.day/index.html (Accessed October 12, 2009).

91 Ibid.

92 See official website ofThe United Nations High Commissioner for Refugees (UNHCR) at http://www.unhcr.org/pages/49c3646c8.html (Accessed October 12, 2009)

93 Supra note 90.

94 Ibid.

95 Supra note 89.

96 S.C. Res. 687 (April 3, 1991), availabl eat available at http://www.fas.org/news/un/iraq/sres/sres0687.htm (Accessed October 13, 2009).

97 Ibid.

98 Bryan Long, "Bush: 'No outcome except victory,'" CNN.com, March 20, 2003 available at http://www.cnn.com/2003/WORLD/meast/03/19/sprj.irq.war.bush/ (Accessed October 13, 2009).

99 CNN.com, "U.S. launches cruise missiles at Saddam," March 20, 2003 available at http://www.cnn.com/2003/WORLD/meast/03/19/sprj.irq.main/ (Accessed October 13, 2009).

100 Mario Cuomo, "What the Constitution says about Iraq," Los Angeles Times, September 3, 2007 available at http://www.latimes.com/news/opinion/la-oe-cuomo3sep03,0,5712011.story (Accessed October 13, 2009).

101 U.N. Charter, Chapter VII: Action With Respect to Threats to the Peace, Breaches of the Peace, and Acts of Aggression, available at http://www.un.org/en/documents/charter/chapter7.shtml (Accessed October 13, 2009)

102 Hugo Grotius, The Law of War and Peace at 1625.

103 Supra at note 101.

104 David Ackerman, "International Law and the Preemptive Use of Force in Iraq," Congressional Research Service (CRS), 6, March 17, 2003, available at http://www.au.af.mil/au/awc/awcgate/crs/rs21314.pdf.

105 CNN.com, "White House Pressed on 'mission accomplished' sign," October 29, 2003 available at http://articles.cnn.com/2003-10-28/politics/mission.accomplished_1_aircraft-carrier-conrad-chun-banner?_s=PM:ALLPOLITICS (Accessed October 16, 2009)

106 CNN.com, "Bush makes historic speech aboard warship," May 1, 2003 available at http://www.cnn.com/2003/US/05/01/bush.transcript/ (Accessed October 16, 2009)

107 Ibid.

108 CBS News, "Mission Accomplished: 5 Years Later," May 1, 2008 available at http://www.cbsnews.com/stories/2008/05/01/iraq/main4060963.shtml (Accessed October 16, 2009)

109 Ibid.

110 Brian Montopoli, "Bartlett: 'Mission Accomplished' Banner Was My Fault," CBS News, January 13, 2009 available at http://www.cbsnews.com/8301-503544_162-4718462-503544.html (Accessed May 2, 2011).

111 Ibid.

112 Ibid.

113 Associated Press, "Saddam Hussein captured," December 14, 2003 available at http://www.guardian.co.uk/world/2003/dec/14/iraq.iraq1 (Accessed October 16, 2009).

114 Ibid.

115 Ibid.

116 Arsalan Iftikhar, "His Capture Changes Nothing: I'm Anti-Saddam and Anti-war," The Providence Journal, December 17, 2003 available at http://www.commondreams.org/views03/1218-15.htm (Accessed October 16, 2009).

117 Ibid.

118 James Belgrade, William Mader, "Slobodan Milosevic: The Butcher of the Balkans," TIME Magazine, June 8, 1992, http://www.time.com/time/magazine/article/0,9171,975723,00.html (Accessed October 16, 2009).

119 Chris Stephen, "Milosevic jail under scrutiny,"TIME Magazine, March 13, 2006 http://news.bbc.co.uk/2/hi/europe/4801626.stm (Accessed October 16, 2009).

120 CNN.com, "Hussein executed with 'fear in his face,'" December 30, 2006 available at http://www.cnn.com/2006/WORLD/meast/12/29/hussein/index.html (Accessed October 16, 2009)

121 Ibid.

122 Ibid.

123 Agence France Presse, "US releases scores from Baghdad prison," February 12, 2009, http://www.google.com/hostednews/afp/article/ALeqM5jz-FyNZ_N2Sznz4Fe1LQ8YqK3zeQ (Accessed October 21, 2009).

124 British Broadcasting Corporation, "Q&A: Iraq's prison abuse scandal," January 11, 2008 available at http://news.bbc.co.uk/2/hi/americas/3701941.stm (Accessed October 21, 2009).

125 Ibid.

126 Ibid.

127 Ibid.

128 Douglas Jehl and Eric Schmitt, "The Reach of War: Abu Ghraib Scandal; Army's Report Faults General In Prison Abuse," The New York Times, August 27, 2004 available at http://www.nytimes.com/2004/08/27/world/the-reach-of-war-abu-ghraib-scandal-army-s-report-faults-general-in-prison-abuse.html (Accessed October 21, 2009).

129 Ibid.

130 Andrew Buncombe et al. "Abu Ghraib: inmates raped, ridden like animals, and forced to eat pork," The Independent (UK), May 22, 2004 available at http://www.independent.co.uk/news/world/middle-east/abu-ghraib-inmates-raped-ridden-like-animals-and-forced-to-eat-pork-564296.html (Accessed October 21, 2009).

131 Dan Glaister and Julian Borger, "1,800 new pictures add to US disgust," The Guardian (UK), May 13, 2004 available at http://www.guardian.co.uk/world/2004/may/13/iraq.usa (Accessed October 21, 2009).

132 Ibid.

133 "U.S. Army Report on Iraqi prisoner abuse: Executive summary of Article 15-6 investigation of the 800th Military Police Brigade by Maj. Gen. Antonio M. Taguba," May 2004, available at http://www.msnbc.msn.com/id/4894001/ (Accessed October 21, 2009).

134 Ibid. at 16-17.

135 Supra note 124.

136 Ibid.

137 British Broadcasting Corporation, "Quick Guide: Sunnis and Shias," December 11, 2006 available at http://news.bbc.co.uk/2/hi/middle_east/6213248.stm (Accessed October 24, 2009).

138 Ibid.

139 British Broadcasting Corporation, "Iraq clerics urge end to violence," October 20, 2006 available at http://news.bbc.co.uk/2/hi/middle_east/6066578.stm (Accessed October 24, 2009).

140 Ibid.

141 British Broadcasting Corporation, "Iraqi blast damages Shia shrine," February 22, 2006 available at http://news.bbc.co.uk/2/hi/middle_east/4738472.stm (Accessed October 24, 2009).

142 The Guardian (UK), "'1,300 dead' in Iraq sectarian violence," February 28, 2006 available at http://www.guardian.co.uk/world/2006/feb/28/iraq1 (Accessed October 24, 2009).

143 Ibid.

144 British Broadcasting Corporation, "Reprisals hit Iraq Sunni mosques," June 14, 2007 available at http://news.bbc.co.uk/2/hi/middle_east/6751909.stm (Accessed October 24, 2009).

145 Amnesty International USA, "Iraq: Carnage and despair in Iraq," March 17, 2008 available at http://www.amnestyusa.org/document.php?id=ENGUSA20080729001&lang=e (Accessed October 24, 2009).

146 Amnesty International, "2008 Annual Report for Iraq," available at http://www.amnestyusa.org/annualreport.php?id=ar&yr=2008&c=IRQ (Accessed May 2, 2011).

147 Human Rights Watch, "Iraq: Events of 2008," http://www.hrw.org/en/node/79254 (Accessed October 24, 2009).

148 Press Release, "Young editor of fledgling newspaper murdered in Baghdad," Committee to Protect Journalists (CPJ), October 29, 2007 available at http://www.ifex.org/iraq/2007/10/29/young_editor_of_fledgling_newspaper/ (Accessed October 24, 2009).

149 Ibid.

150 Rod Nordland, "Iraq's Shiites Show Restraint After Attacks," The New York Times, August 11, 2009 available at http://www.nytimes.com/2009/08/12/world/middleeast/12shiite.html?_r=2 (Accessed October 24, 2009).

151 Arsalan Iftikhar, "Commentary: Throwing shoes doesn't help Iraq," CNN.com, December 16, 2008 available at http://www.cnn.com/2008/POLITICS/12/16/iftikhar.shoe/index.html (Accessed October 25, 2009).

152 Ibid.

Chapter 7: War and/or Peace

1 See http://www.entertonement.com/clips/fxrfvgpbnw--Repay-him-in-kind-for-all-that-he%27s-done (Accessed October 3, 2009)

2 See http://www.u2.com/discography/lyrics/lyric/song/20 (Accessed October 3, 2009)

3 Samuel Huntington, "The Clash of Civilizations?" Foreign Affairs, Summer 1993 available at http://www.foreignaffairs.com/articles/48950/samuel-p-huntington/the-clash-of-civilizations (Accessed November 2, 2009)

4 See http://www.google.com/search?hl=&q=%22clash+of+civilizations%22&sourceid=navclient-ff&rlz=1B3GGGL_enUS323US323&ie=UTF-8&aq=0&oq=%22clas (Accessed April 3, 2011)

5 Harvard Gazette Online, "Obituary: Samuel Huntington, 81, political scientist, scholar", February 5, 2009 available at http://news.harvard.edu/gazette/story/2009/02/samuel-huntington-81-political-scientist-scholar/ (Accessed November 2, 2009)

6 Amina Chaudary, "Samuel Huntington, Misunderstood" PostGlobal (The Washington Post/Newsweek), March 9, 2009 available at http://newsweek.washingtonpost.com/

postglobal/needtoknow/2009/03/samuel_huntington_misunderstoo.html (Accessed November 2, 2009)

7 Ibid.

8 Amina Chaudary, "Samuel Huntington" Islamica Magazine, Issue Number 17 (2006) at pp. 28-35.

9 Supra note 5.

10 Supra note 8 at 33.

11 Ibid at 35.

12 Jane Lampman, "After 9/11, some lives recast for greater good" The Christian Science Monitor, September 12, 2008 available at http://www.csmonitor.com/2008/0912/p01s01-usgn.html?page=2 (Accessed November 2, 2009)

13 See https://www.cia.gov/library/publications/the-world-factbook/print/xx.html (Accessed November 2, 2009)

14 TIME Magazine, "The 2004 TIME 100" available at http://www.time.com/time/subscriber/2004/time100/heroes/100ebadi.html (April 3, 2011)

15 See also http://nobelprize.org/nobel_prizes/peace/laureates/2003/press.html (Accessed November 3, 2009)

16 Daily Times Newspaper (Pakistan), "Rafat Appointed Ambassador" November 14, 2008 available at http://www.dailytimes.com.pk/default.asp?page=2008%5C11%5C14%5Cstory_14-11-2008_pg7_42 (Accessed November 3, 2009)

17 Arsalan Iftikhar, "An Evening with Nobel Peace Prize Winner Dr. Shirin Ebadi" True/Slant, October 15, 2009 available at http://trueslant.com/arsalaniftikhar/2009/10/15/an-evening-with-nobel-peace-prize-winner-dr-shirin-ebadi/ (Accessed November 3, 2009)

18 Richard Allen Greene, "Nearly 1 in 4 people worldwide is Muslim" CNN.com, October 12, 2009 available at http://www.cnn.com/2009/WORLD/asiapcf/10/07/muslim.world.population/index.html (Accessed November 3, 2009)

19 Iftikhar, "An Evening with Shirin Ebadi", October 15, 2009.

20 Amal Al Malki, "Islamic feminism: Change from within"The Peninsula Newspaper (Qatar) available at http://www.thepeninsulaqatar.com/commentary/commentaryother.asp?file=maycommentary122009.xml (Accessed August 17, 2009)

21 Riffat Hassan, "On Human Rights and the Qur'anic Perspective." Journal of Ecumenical Studies, 19, 3. Summer 1982. See also report in Muslims in Dialogue: The Evolution of A Dialogue. Leonard Swidler, Ed. Lewiston, NY: The Edwin Mellen Press, 1992 at 459-63.

22 Anne Sofie Roald, "Feminist Reinterpretation of Islamic Sources: Muslim Feminist Theology in the Light of the Christian Tradition of Feminist Thought." Women and Islamization: Contemporary Dimensions of Discourse on Gender Relations Ask, Karin and Marit Tjomsland, Eds. New York: Berg, 1998 at 17-42.

23 Barbara Stowasser, Women in the Qur'an: Traditions and Interpretation. New York: Oxford Press, 1994 at 5-9.

24 Ibid at 6.

25 Roald, "Feminist Reinterpration of Islamic Sources", 1998.

26 Ibid.

27 Stowasser, Women in the Qur'an, 7.

28 See Ruth Roded, Women in Islamic Biographical Collections. Boulder: Lynne Rienner Publishers, 1994 at 58.

29 See https://www.cia.gov/library/publications/the-world-factbook/geos/pk.html (Accessed September 6, 2009)

30 Emily Friedman, “Bhutto’s Assassination Risks Security, Democracy” ABC News, December 27, 2007 available at http://abcnews.go.com/International/story?id=4056749&page=1 (Accessed September 6, 2009)

31 Video available at http://www.youtube.com/watch?v=PBUVmumbTvE (Accessed August 12, 2009)

32 Forbes.com, “Forbes’ 100 Most Powerful Women in the World” available at http://www.forbes.com/finance/lists/11/2004/LIR.jhtml?passListId=11&passYear=2004&passListType=Person&uniqueId=MVC8&datatype=Person (Accessed August 12, 2009)

33 United Nations, Ecosoc, Official Records 58th Sess. (1971), Suppl. 1, p. 36. See also http://www.aclu.org/capital/general/10441pub19971231.html#68 (Accessed August 4, 2009)

34 Ibid.

35 See http://www.uscirf.gov/index.php?option=com_content&task=view&id=1672&Itemid=1 (Accessed August 17, 2009)

36 Transcript of April 29, 2008 broadcast of The Doha Debates on BBC World News Television available at http://www.thedohadebates.com/debates/debate.asp?d=2&s=4&mode=transcript (Accessed August 30, 2009)

37 See ibid.

38 Ibid.

39 Imam Hassan Qazwini, American Crescent: A Muslim Cleric on the Power of his Faith, the Struggle against Prejudice, and the future of Islam in America, (Random House: New York, 2007), 235.

40 Ibid at 236.

41 "Charitable Giving Under Greater Scrutiny After Sept. 11" National Public Radio (NPR) Tell Me More with Michel Martin, September 19, 2008 available at http://www.npr.org/templates/story/story.php?storyId=94799530 (Accessed August 5, 2009)

42 See Volume 8, Book 73, Number 187.

43 Arsalan Iftikhar, "Islamic Pacifism Defined" TheMuslimGuy.com, September 2008 available at http://www.themuslimguy.com/islamic-pacifism-defined.html (Accessed November 19, 2009)

Made in the USA
Lexington, KY
09 September 2017